Essential Readings in
Logical Positivism

By the same author

Logical Positivism
Fundamental Problems in Philosophy (editor)

ESSENTIAL READINGS IN
LOGICAL POSITIVISM

Edited by
Oswald Hanfling

Basil Blackwell · Oxford

First published in 1981 by
Basil Blackwell Publisher Limited
108 Cowley Road
Oxford OX4 1JF
England

British Library Cataloguing in Publication Data

Essential readings in logical positivism.
    1. Logical positivism — History
    I. Hanfling, Oswald
    146'.4   B824.6

    ISBN 0-631-12566-3

Typesetting by Freeman Graphic, Tonbridge
Printed in Great Britain by Billing and Sons Ltd.,
Guildford, London, Oxford, Worcester

CONTENTS

ACKNOWLEDGEMENTS

The editor and the publishers wish to acknowledge with gratitude permission given by the following to reprint the articles that appear in this volume. The full details of each source are given on the first page of the item.

George Allen & Unwin (Publishers) Ltd., and Macmillan Publishing Co., Inc., for item D3
American Philosophical Association and Professor David Rynin for item B3
Analysis for items D6, D7
Basil Blackwell Publisher and Barnes and Noble for item A1
Dover Publications, Inc., for item E2
Macmillan, London and Basingstoke for item D4, and Macmillan, London and Basingstoke and St. Martin's Press for item B1
Mind for items B2, C2
Orthological Institute for items D2, E1
D. Reidel Publishing Company for items C1, D5
Albert M. Schlick and Barbara F. van de Velde-Schlick for items A2, C1, D1, D5
University of California Press for item E3
University of Chicago for item C3

INTRODUCTION

In the history of philosophy, as in other cultural developments, it happens from time to time that a certain view, or a certain way of doing things, establishes itself as a focus of attention. Sometimes this is encouraged by a conscious effort of promotion on the part of those belonging to the new movement. This was so in the case of the 'Vienna Circle', a group of philosophers, scientists and mathematicians which flourished, under the leadership of Moritz Schlick, in the twenties and early thirties of this century, at the University of Vienna.

Schlick and his colleagues thought that certain new ideas about language, logic and science had led them to a new, enlightened conception of philosophy; and they believed that this conception should be communicated to thinkers throughout the world as quickly and as forcefully as possible. In their writings they used such titles as 'The Turning-Point in Philosophy', 'The Elimination of Metaphysics' and 'The Rise of Scientific Philosophy'. A number of international conferences were organized to promote and discuss the new ideas; and a journal, taken over and renamed *Erkenntnis*, was used for the same purpose. In this journal many of the fruits of the new philosophy were first published. One of the main promoters, Otto Neurath, launched a twenty-six volume 'International Encyclopedia of Unified Science', which was to be comparable in importance to the great Encyclopédie begun by Diderot in the eighteenth century.[1]

The members of the Circle, and their sympathizers in other countries, thought that a radical change was about to take place in philosophy — a replacement of what had been done under that name hitherto, by science on the hand and formal logic on the other; with many of the traditional questions being rejected altogether. The new philosophy, known as Logical Empiricism or Logical Positivism,[2] was to become,

---

[1] Only two volumes of the work, containing nineteen monographs, have appeared. They are published under the title *Foundations of the Unity of Science*, University of Chicago Press.

[2] My preference is for 'Logical Empiricism', because of the connection with older forms of empiricism, as explained below. But on the whole 'Logical Positivism' has become the more usual expression.

not merely one important movement among others, but one that would absorb the whole of philosophy, or at any rate anything worthy of that name.

Today it is clear that it did not and is not likely to do this. The problems discussed by Plato, Descartes and Kant have not been rendered obsolete by this or any other new philosophy. But if the Logical Empiricists were wrong about the revolutionary power of their ideas, it would be no less wrong to think that these ideas have altogether lost their interest. It is true that serious objections were levelled against them soon after their first appearance; and few, if any, philosophers would nowadays describe themselves as Logical Empiricists. Philosophers in any case do not like attaching labels to themselves. Nevertheless the influence of the Vienna Circle's ideas is widely evident in philosophical thought today — if not in the conclusions reached, then at least in the kinds of problems discussed and the general attitudes to them. But secondly, and more relevantly from the point of view of this volume, there has been a continuing interest in the original ideas of the Circle, even if few would accept them as they stand. (A similar point may be made about most of the important philosophers of the past.) Logical Empiricism, as expounded in the writings of the Vienna Circle, remains one of the standard points of reference for anyone interested in philosophical questions about meaning and meaningfulness, about the scope of science and the nature of philosophy.

The writings in this volume are, with a few exceptions, by members of the Vienna Circle, written in the time before its dispersal in the mid-1930s. Its members of course continued to develop and publish their views in the following decades, mainly from new homes in the United States and Britain. (An exception was Moritz Schlick, who lost his life in tragic circumstances in 1936.) The same is true of those who may be described as sympathizers or disciples of the Circle. But these developments do not have the original cohesion and it would be difficult to encompass them in a single volume. (Some of them also lack the freshness and enthusiasm which may be found in the original writings.)

This collection is not intended, however, to be representative of all the members, or all the important members, of the Vienna Circle. There is, for example, nothing by Hans Hahn, Herbert Feigl, Kurt Gödel or Karl Menger. My aim has been to select writings which would give the clearest exposition of the main tenets of Logical Empiricism as I see them; and this has led me (like others) to look mainly to the works of Schlick and Carnap. I have, however, included one or two writings by non-members. Hempel and Reichenbach were early regarded as sympathizers of the Circle, and this will be evident from their writings. The item by Rynin is included because it seems to me to give a particularly good defence of one of the main ideas of Logical Empiricism. As for A. J. Ayer, he attended the meetings of the Circle in 1933 and, following the publication of his *Language, Truth and Logic* in 1936, was probably the leading representative of the new philosophy in the English-speaking world. (There has indeed been some danger of identifying it too much with Ayer's version.)

The items from Wittgenstein and Waismann require special explanation. Wittgenstein was never a member of the Circle, though he was in Vienna during much of the time. Yet his influence on the Circle's thought was at least as important as that of any of its members. For some years, from 1927 onwards, he had regular conversations with Schlick and Waismann, and a record of some of these is published, under the latter's name, in the volume *Wittgenstein and the Vienna Circle*. In the writings of Schlick and others there are frequent acknowledgements to Wittgenstein, and Carnap has described the importance of his influence in his own autobiography.[3] It was Wittgenstein, apparently, who first put forward the dictum with which the new philosophy was particularly identified — the Verification Principle, according to which 'the meaning of a statement is the method of its verification'. Nevertheless there were some aspects of the Vienna Circle's outlook with which Wittgenstein was never happy; and in his 'later' philosophy, as expounded in the *Philosophical Investigations*, we find a very different approach. The short item C2, appearing here under Wittgenstein's name, and dating from 1930-33, gives some indication of his move in this direction.

The items appearing under Waismann's name are also, however, to a greater or lesser extent the work of Wittgenstein. They came about under a remarkable arrangement, made between the two men with the encouragement of Schlick.[4] Under this arrangement Waismann was to record Wittgenstein's ideas with a view to putting them into systematic order for ultimate publication in a book. In the meantime he was also to communicate these ideas to the members of the Circle. After various

---

[3] In *The Philosophy of Rudolf Carnap*, ed. P. A. Schilpp.

[4] For details see Gordon Baker's 'Verehrung und Verkehrung: Waismann and Wittgenstein', in C. G. Luckhardt, ed., *Wittgenstein: Sources and Perspectives*, Cornell University Press, 1979.

difficulties and tensions Wittgenstein withdrew from the project in 1935. Waismann continued to revise the manuscript, and the much revised version was published in English in 1965, after Waismann's death, under the title *Principles of Linguistic Philosophy*. An extract from it appears below as item B1. An earlier and more direct product of the collaboration had been the short 'Theses', written down by Waismann about 1930; and item A1 is an extract from this work.

The name 'Logical Empiricism' indicates an affinity with the 'classic' empiricism expounded by such writers as Locke and Hume in the seventeenth and eighteenth centuries. The new empiricists maintained, as did their forebears, that knowledge is composed entirely of items of sense-experience, which they called 'sense-data'. What was new about their approach was that they saw the problems of philosophy as being primarily about language rather than about knowledge or ontology. The primary questions were to be: 'What is meaning?' and 'What kinds of statements have meaning?', rather than 'What can we know?' and 'What is there in the world?'. It was thought that the meaning of a statement could somehow be identified with the method of verifying it (the Verification Principle); and that any statement for which there was *no* method of verification must be, *ipso facto*, without meaning. Most of the claims and counter-claims that had been made by philosophers and religious thinkers through the ages were thought, by this criterion, to be without meaning. The belief in a transcendent God, for example, must be rejected, not because it is false or likely to be false, but because the statement is unverifiable and therefore meaningless. It is not, properly speaking, a statement at all, but should be described, rather, as a 'pseudo-statement'; the problems connected with it being 'pseudo-problems'. Another typical example was the problem of 'other minds'. How can I know that other people have thoughts and feelings, as distinct from their behaviour and their words, given that I can observe only the latter? The verificationist answers that this question is meaningless. To assert — or, for that matter, to deny — the existence of something that could under no circumstances be observed is to make a statement for which there is no method of verification and therefore no meaning.

Like their forebears of the seventeenth and eighteenth centuries, the new empiricists thought of verification and knowledge in empirical terms; but unlike them, they saw the matter in terms of logic rather than psychology. Whereas Locke and Hume described mental processes in which the raw materials ('ideas') of sense-experience were arranged and re-arranged, the Logical Empiricists spoke of the logical analysis of statements. They believed that statements of all kinds could be analysed by a logical procedure into 'elementary' (or 'protocol') statements, the latter corresponding as closely as possible to occurrences of sense-experience. These points will be amplified in the remarks that follow.

A. MEANING AND VERIFICATION

In reading the first two sections of this anthology, it is important to be clear about a distinction which is sometimes overlooked (perhaps because of misleading terminology). The Verification Principle ('The meaning of a statement is the method of its verification') is a claim about what meaning is, what the meaning of a statement consists in; and this is how it appears in the extracts from Waismann and Schlick (items A1 and A2). By contrast, the criterion of verifiability (as I shall call it) is a criterion for distinguishing meaningful from meaningless statements ('pseudo-statements'). The questions of meaning and meaningfulness are clearly distinguished by Rynin in item B3 (see pp. 66-7) and he proceeds to discuss only the latter. It is true that advocates of the Verification Principle have usually gone on to deduce the criterion of verifiability from it, in order to show, in particular, that this criterion is not satisfied by statements of metaphysics. (This is so in item A2, for example.) But others have advocated the criterion of verifiability without the Verification Principle. This is true of Rynin and also of A. J. Ayer, both in his *Language, Truth and Logic* and in the paper appearing here as item B2. (He speaks of the criterion as 'the principle of verifiability'.)

But the view represented in section A — the Verification Principle — is not merely a criterion for separating off the discourse of metaphysics; it is a statement of what meaning consists in. In this respect, as in others, item A1 from the 'Theses' invites comparison with Wittgenstein's *Tractatus Logico-Philosophicus*, first published in 1921. Anyone acquainted with that work will be struck by the resemblance between it and the 'Theses', both in style and in content. In both works we are given a statement of what meaning consists in. According to the *Tractatus*, words and propositions have meaning by being in a certain relation with objects and facts in the world; whereas, according to the 'Theses', it is the 'method of verification' that constitutes the meaning of a proposition; the meaning of 'signs' occurring in the proposition being explained accordingly (pp. 29-30).[5]

The *Tractatus* itself was regarded by the Vienna Circle as one of 'their' classic works and discussed section by section at their regular meetings. But if there were affinities between the *Tractatus* and the new philosophy, there were also important differences, which were sometimes overlooked. A careless reading of the 'Theses' might encourage such misunderstanding. This is true, for example, of the first part of our extract. 'To understand a proposition means to know how things stand if the proposition is true. One can understand it without knowing *whether* it is true.' This is almost identical with a passage in the *Tractatus* (section 4.024). But whereas in the 'Theses' this remark is expounded in a verificationist sense, it is not so in the *Tractatus*.

The idea of analysis into 'elementary propositions' was prominent both in the *Tractatus* and in the thought of the Vienna Circle (including the 'Theses'). These propositions were thought of as standing in a peculiarly direct relation to elements of reality: according to the 'Theses', it is by means of them, that 'language *touches* reality' (page 32). But again, while in the 'Theses' elementary propositions are defined by reference to a certain directness of verification (see end of extract), this is not so in the *Tractatus*. In this work elementary propositions were defined by their logical independence of one another (4.211, 5.134), and there is no mention of verification. Similarly, the reference to 'phenomena (experiences)' (page 32) represents an empiricist view that was not present in the *Tractatus*.

The idea that language is based on phenomena or experiences ('phenomenalism') was, indeed, one of the major themes of the new philosophy. But there is an important difference between the view represented in the 'Theses' and that of later Logical Empiricist writings. In the 'Theses' we are told (page 28) that it must be possible for a statement to be 'verified definitively', that without this it is 'not verifiable at all'. By contrast, in the writings of later analysts (for example Schlick and Carnap in itens C1 and C3 below) it was usually stressed that the analysis of ordinary statements could *not* be completed.

---

[5] I have here spoken of 'propositions', since this term (rather than 'statements') is used in these works — or rather, in their English translations. There are problems about the choice of terminology, which I have discussed in section 2.1 of my *Logical Positivism*, and will not pursue here. In what follows I shall use these terms as convenient for the text under discussion.

This made them, in a certain sense, unverifiable; but not in a sense that would render them, like the statements of metaphysics, meaningless. The looser notion of 'reduction', which came to take the place of strict analysis, is expounded by Carnap in C3.

A contrast of importance in the thought of both Wittgenstein and Schlick was that between what is called 'ostension' and 'definition' in the 'Theses' (page 29). (Schlick speaks of it in terms of 'showing' and 'verbal description' in item A2 (pages 33, 42) and again, in similar terms, in item C1 – page 88.) Here we are concerned with *giving* the meaning of a sign or statement. Schlick insisted again and again that if language is to be about the real world, then there must be parts of it which are definable, not by means of other language ('verbal description' or 'verbal definition'), but by confrontation with a corresponding item of the world outside language ('ostension' or 'ostensive definition'). This, he thought, must be the source of all definition; otherwise language would not be about the world at all.

Some of the difficulties of this view were pointed out by Wittgenstein in the opening page of the *Blue Book*, one of the first fruits of his 'later' philosophy. Here he considered the case of teaching someone the meaning of a word by pointing to a suitable object and saying 'This is X'. Wittgenstein argued that this would work only if the learner already had a certain understanding – an understanding that could not have been taught to him by such a method. He must understand, for example, which aspect of the object is meant (e.g. whether 'X' is to mean 'pencil', 'round', 'wood', 'one' or 'hard'); he must understand the word 'this'; and he must interpret the pointing gesture as intended.[6] Hence ostensive definition cannot have the primary place attributed to it by Schlick and in the 'Theses'.

The Verification Principle, as I have said, is a statement of what meaning consists in. But what exactly does the Principle mean? If one were asked 'What is the meaning of a statement?', one would hardly know how to make sense of the question. The sentence-frame 'The meaning of a statement is . . .' is not one that normally occurs in language. A careful reading of the texts surrounding the Verification Principle in A1 and A2 (pages 27 and 34; also item C1, pp. 88–9) will

---

[6] There are several discussions of ostensive definition in the *Blue and Brown Books*, *Philosophical Grammar*, *Philosophical Investigations* and other of the 'later' writings.

suggest a number of ways of understanding it.[7] It would seem, however, that Schlick was sometimes inclined to conflate the Verification Principle with his claim, mentioned above, about ostensive definition. But these claims should be kept distinct. To explain (or learn) the meaning of a statement is not the same as to verify it.

Another passage of special interest in item A2 from Schlick is that in which he considers what kind of truth can be claimed for the Verification Principle. A natural approach to this question, at least among philosophers, is to ask whether it is intended as an empirical or an analytic truth. The Logical Empiricists themselves frequently applied this dichotomy in their critique of language. They maintained that any statement whose truth could be known *a priori* must be analytic — such that its truth was entailed by the meanings of the words in it. Any other statement, they claimed, must be verifiable by empirical observation — failing which it would be meaningless. Do the Verification Principle and the criterion of verifiability fall into either of these classes? If in the former, then their truth must follow from the very meaning of 'meaning of a statement'. If in the latter, then they will be subject to empirical verification. If neither, then, it seems, they must be doomed to self-elimination. Schlick speaks of the Verification Principle as 'a mere truism' (page 34). He denies that it is a 'theory', because that would mean that it is to be 'tested by experience'. Nevertheless he regards it as a statement of what 'everybody always' actually does. Perhaps he means that it is an empirical truth, but one that may be described as 'a mere truism' because its truth is obvious to all. Similarly in the second reading from Waismann (item B1) we read, in reference to the criterion put forward there: 'It seems obvious that it is no new discovery, but only a formulation of a method used by everyone' (page 47). On the other hand, the claim that the criterion 'must already be contained in the normal use of language' (page 47) may suggest that we are to take it as an analytic truth, analytic to the concept of a normal use of language.

But perhaps, after all, it is a mistake to distinguish analytic from empirical truth in this case. For what would be the relevant empirical data here? They could only be facts of usage — of how people actually use the words in question. But analytic truths are also dependent on facts of usage. Thus if 'Horses are animals' and 'Unverifiable statements are

---

[7]I have discussed the matter in chapter 2 of my *Logical Positivism*.

meaningless' are analytic truths, then they will be so because of facts of usage of the words in question. Whether, or in what sense, these are empirical facts is a question I shall not pursue.[8] Another question, however, is whether it is indeed a fact that words are used in accordance with the verificationist criterion or principle. Waismann tries to show (page 47) that his version of the criterion does represent ordinary usage.

Another approach, often favoured by Logical Empiricists, is also to be found in item B1 from Waismann (page 51). This was to treat the criterion as a 'recommendation'. Of a recommendation we cannot ask whether it is analytic or verifiable; these description are not applicable to such speech-acts as recommendations and therefore the problem we have discussed could not even arise. On the other hand, some reason will obviously have to be given for accepting the recommendation. This question is discussed especially in item B3 by David Rynin, who claims that his own version of the criterion of verifiability can be regarded as 'a kind of well-justified proposal' (page 64). A. J. Ayer, as will be seen in item B2, regarded his criterion as a 'definition', claiming that to speak of an unverifiable statement would be 'a contradiction in terms' (page 59). But in his introduction to the second edition of *Language, Truth and Logic*, he betrayed some uncertainty on this point. Here again he spoke of it as a definition but went on, in the same paragraph, to advocate it as 'a methodological principle' (p. 21).

B. VERIFIABILITY AND THE ELIMINATION OF METAPHYSICS

There is an obvious continuity of thought between the 'Theses' and the *Principles of Linguistic Philosophy*, from which item B1 is taken. One difference is that the Verification Principle is now regarded as appropriate for elucidating the meaning, and questioning the meaningfulness, of certain kinds of statements only. Waismann gives a number of interesting examples of statements of a metaphysical character and tries to show how the Verification Principle can be useful in their case. He does not, however, recommend it for such an ordinary statement as 'It rained yesterday'. In this extract there is an insistence on the diversity

---

[8]Some discussions of it will be found in Colin Lyas, ed., *Philosophy and Linguistics*, Macmillan, 1971.

of language which is to be contrasted with what we find in the *Tractatus* and in the 'Theses', and with the general belief of the Vienna Circle in a basic uniformity of language and knowledge. (This is the subject of section C below.)

Waismann also makes the point that the logical relation between statement and method of verification may be of more than one kind. In some cases it is 'a rule of inference', in others 'an empirical connection' (page 53). Among the latter are methods of verification which may be known only after scientific discoveries and cannot therefore be part of the meaning of the statement (page 52). A similar point is made in item C2 by Wittgenstein, who uses the terms 'grammar' and 'symptom' for this purpose. In his later writings Wittgenstein spoke in this connection of 'criteria' and 'symptoms'.[9]

On page 51 Waismann draws attention to a difficulty which has troubled many verificationists. This concerns statements about the past, including such examples as 'It rained yesterday' and 'Caesar crossed the Alps'. A. J. Ayer, in item B2, argues that if some statement about a present experience can be deduced from the truth of such a statement, this is enough to render it meaningful. He shows that his example (a statement about what he had for breakfast) easily passes this test. But, as Waismann makes clear, such statements about present experience cannot be *equated* with a statement about the past, as would be required by the Verification Principle (though not the criterion of verifiability). Now Ayer had also been concerned, in *Language, Truth and Logic*, to show that statements of all kinds could be analysed in terms of present or future experiences, so that the whole of their meaning would be accounted for in that way. But in his introduction to the second edition, he rejected attempts to analyse statements about the past 'into propositions about present or future experiences'. This did not mean, however, that they 'cannot be analysed in phenomenal terms; for they can be taken as implying that certain observations would have occurred if certain conditions had been fulfilled' (pp. 24-5). In thus resorting to what might have happened, but can no longer happen, Ayer may seem to be admitting that statements about the past are unverifiable, though he could hardly regard them as meaningless. In a further attempt at the problem, Ayer claimed that the tense of a statement was not really part

---

[9]See especially *Philosophical Investigations* 354, *Zettel* 438 and *Blue and Brown Books* pp. 24-5.

of its meaning or 'factual content', so that there was no special problem concerning statements about the past.[10]

The paper by Ayer that is reprinted here provides a useful summary of some of the main tenets of *Language, Truth and Logic*. Here we find a typical verificationist approach to statements about the past, the problem of other minds, mystical experiences and ethics. Also typical is the concern about whether statements or words should be regarded as the primary bearers of meaning. In his preference for statements, Ayer is in agreement with Waismann's view, as expressed at the start of item B1.

But perhaps the main interest of Ayer's paper, and of the following item from Rynin, lies in the criterion of verifiability. The same might be said, indeed, of Ayer's book. Perhaps its most distinctive contribution to the new philosophy was Ayer's attempt to formulate a criterion of verifiability as distinct from the Verification Principle. His original formula was that quoted by him in item B2 below (see page 56). Like other Logical Empiricists, Ayer held that ordinary statements about tables and chairs are not verifiable, or not 'conclusively' so, because an indefinite number of observation-statements can be deduced from such a statement. But this, he maintained, did not make it impossible to use verifiability as a criterion of meaningfulness. To render such a statement meaningful, it would be enough 'if some experiential propositions can be deduced from it in conjunction with certain other premises . . .' (below, page 56). Thus the statement 'It is raining on Dartmoor', in conjunction with a premise about someone being there at the time, should enable us to deduce certain 'experiential propositions'; and this would be enough to validate the statement as meaningful, although of course it would not amount to a full analysis of its meaning. (Ayer spoke in this connection of 'weak' verification.)

It was soon pointed out, however, that the formula as it stood could easily be made to yield undesired results. 'Thus the statements "the Absolute is lazy" and "if the Absolute is lazy, this is white" jointly entail the observation-statement "this is white" '; and this would prove

---

[10] *Philosophical Essays*, p. 186. The matter was further discussed by Ayer and Bernard Williams in *Perception and Identity*, ed. G. F. Macdonald Macmillan, 1979. Also see Michael Dummett's 'The Reality of the Past', *Proceedings of the Aristotelian Society*, 1968/9.

that both of the premises were meaningful by Ayer's criterion.[11] Ayer now put forward an amended version of his criterion, the main purport of which was to stipulate that each of the premises must itself pass the test of verifiability. One of those who objected to the new criterion was Carl Hempel, in the paper mentioned by Rynin in item B3. Hempel maintained that no criterion of the kind proposed by Ayer would be proof against the admission of nonsensical 'pseudo-statements'. His argument is summarized and rejected by Rynin on pages 69ff.; and in subsequent postscripts Hempel conceded the point to Rynin.[12] Rynin offers his own criterion of verifiability on page 68.

But if Rynin can be seen as continuing in the verificationism of the Vienna Circle and Ayer, there is a considerable difference between his cautious tone and the confidence that is apparent in earlier verificationist writings. It was only to be expected that someone sensitive to the intervening controversies would adopt a more cautious tone than was usual in the Vienna Circle's heyday. But Rynin also takes a more modest view of the significance of the criterion of verifiability, even supposing that there is a formulation of it, such as his own, which is found acceptable. He does not think that such a criterion will provide an easy way of disposing of metaphysics in favour of science. To apply the criterion to statements about God, 'the absolute' and the like, requires careful enquiry into the ways in which these expressions are used by those who use them; and the same is true of expressions used by scientists which may seem meaningless to the layman (page 71).

Rynin's reference to the 'Oxford School' (page 79) may be puzzling to present-day readers. If there is an Oxford School today, it is hardly that described by Rynin. However, the idea that the meaning of an expression lies in its use has become prominent since the publication of the later works of Wittgenstein, where it is of central importance. But it would be a mistake, in my view, to apply Rynin's critical remarks about 'use' to Wittgenstein's account. The latter was not, in his later works, putting forward a 'system of semantics'. He did not offer his remarks about meaning and use as an *explanation* of language – of how, in general, words and sentences have meaning. Nor did he think that meaning could be accounted for by something other than language, as

---

[11] The quotation is from Ayer's own words in the second edition of *Language, Truth and Logic*, p. 15. Here he summarized the argument of Isaiah Berlin's 'Verifiability in Principle', *Proceedings of the Aristotelian Society*, vol. XXXIX.

[12] See the references to reprintings of Hempel's paper, p. 69 below.

had been the case with the Verification Principle, the 'picture theory' of the *Tractatus,* and other theories, in which meaning was thought to be due to a mental process. The latter point is worth making especially with regard to Schlick, who (as we have seen) insisted that the meaning of language must be derived from something outside language; and who (no doubt under the influence of talks with Wittgenstein) conflated the Verification Principle with a claim about 'use' — namely, that in order to 'give meaning to a sentence', we must 'indicate the rules for how it shall be used' (item A2, page 34).[13] The latter claim, about rules of use, is not the same thing as the Verification Principle. (On the other hand, it would also be unsatisfactory as an expression of Wittgenstein's later views about meaning and use.)[14]

C. REDUCTIONISM AND THE UNITY OF SCIENCE

The verificationist approach had a negative and a positive aspect. On the one hand, there was to be an exposure of certain statements as pseudo-statements; on the other hand, the meanings of *bona fide* statements, both of science and of ordinary discourse, were to be clarified. (The word 'science' was sometimes used so as to embrace all meaningful statements.) It was generally thought that this clarification would require the *analysis* or *reduction* of statements into suitable empirical components. This activity, indeed, was thought to be the legitimate task that remained to philosophers after the sweeping away of metaphysical rubbish by the new broom. It was also held that the final elements of the analysis would all be, in some sense, of the same type; so that, underlying all the apparent diversity of statements and of knowledge, there was a fundamental 'unity of science'.

The belief in analysis is not obviously the same thing as the Verification Principle. But how, after all, are we to understand 'method of verification' as it occurs in that principle? If I want to verify that there is a castle outside the city (cf. item C1, page 102), I might enquire at the information office or I might make a trip to the outskirts of the city.

---

[13] There is a more explicit conflation of these matters, together with an acknowledgement to Wittgenstein, in Schlick's 'Meaning and Verification', *Philosophical Review* 1936; reprinted in *Philosophical Papers*, vol. II; also in H. Feigl and W. Sellars, eds., *Readings in Philosophical Analysis.*

[14] I have discussed this matter more fully in section 7.6 of my *Logical Positivism.*

But it is not clear how the meaning of the statement could be identified with such acts of verification. We have already noticed (page 8) Schlick's tendency to conflate verification with ostensive definition. There was also another way in which he and other verificationists thought of verification. They thought of it as consisting in the occurrence of what were variously called 'sensations', 'sense-impressions', 'sense-data', 'perceptions' and 'experiences'. (Most of these terms occur in item C1 from Schlick.) The idea that perception and knowledge are to be analysed in terms of such entities or occurrences was taken over by the Logical Empiricists from their empiricist forebears from John Locke onwards. If this view is correct, then verification too must consist of the having of suitable sensations, experiences and the like; and this is how the matter was seen by Schlick and others. Thus, in a typical passage in item C1, 'verification always remains *thinkable*' is glossed as 'we are always able to say what sort of data we should have to experience . . .' (page 90).

In this paper, 'Positivism and Realism', Schlick is concerned to show that the meaning of statements about physical objects can be fully accounted for by the relevant method of verification — that is, by the occurrence of suitable experiences. 'If we say of some object . . . that it is real, this means . . . that under given circumstances certain data are presented' (page 98). The 'realist', as described by Schlick, is someone who thinks that there is more than that to the reality of a physical object. Schlick argues that this idea is meaningless; but he tries hard to do justice to the feeling of the realist (and, no doubt, the ordinary reader) that something has been left out of account. To some extent he does this by emphasizing that the method of verification is not exhausted by a finite set of experiences, but extends to experiences that would occur in 'indefinitely many circumstances' (page 93).

But Schlick is no less critical of the 'positivist' than of the realist. The former (as Schlick describes him) is someone who denies, in contradiction to the realist, than anything exists other than data. But this, according to Schlick, 'is metaphysical in the same sense, and to the same degree, as the seemingly opposite contention', the realist's claim (page 86). Schlick is right in regarding this point as essential to a correct understanding of the view for which he stands. The verificationist's concern is primarily about meaning rather than truth; his characteristic method in philosophy is not to take sides in disputes, but to show them to be meaningless. According to Schlick, the very meaning of what we say (about physical objects or anything else) is tied to experience; hence it is equally nonsensical to affirm or to deny the existence of anything beyond experience.

On page 101 Schlick makes an important point about verification and the possibility of doubt. Where doubt is logically impossible, there can be no place for the idea of verification (or falsification). For this reason Schlick describes Descartes' statement about his own existence as meaningless. But what happens, on this criterion, about such statements as 'I have a pain'? Is it possible to be in doubt about this and is it, accordingly, subject to verification? If not, is it meaningless? Schlick claims (page 101) that it *is* possible for me to ask whether I 'now actually feel a pain or not'. But Wittgenstein, as appears from item C2, took a different view.

In this item, from notes taken by G. E. Moore of lectures given by Wittgenstein at Cambridge in 1930-33, we find some of the latter's first doubts about the Verification Principle. Here he draws attention to the difficulty, from the verificationist viewpoint, of 'I have a pain'. He claims (page 111) that first and third person statements about having a pain 'are on a different grammatical level'.

By contrast, defenders of the 'unity of science', notably Carnap, tried repeatedly to play down the difference between the first and third person cases; to show that they are basically of the same kind and equally subject to verification. According to Carnap in 'Testability and Meaning', a person N_1 'can confirm more directly than N_2 a sentence concerning N_1's feelings, thoughts etc.'; but, he went on, 'we now believe, on the basis of physicalism, that the difference, although very great and very important for practical life, is only a matter of degree'.[15]

In the works of Carnap, Neurath, Feigl and others, the reduction of statements about feelings, thoughts etc. to terms of a common basic type was seen as a major objective in the unification of science. Neurath insisted that psychology and sociology must be treated as part of physical science and that all meaningful statements must be reducible to physical terms.[16] Carnap, on the other hand, maintained that the choice of a physical basis was not essential, and that a reduction terminating in 'phenomenal' terms (like that of Schlick in C1) could also

---

[15] H. Feigl and M. Brodbeck, eds., *Readings in the Philosophy of Science*, p. 79. Also see Carnap's account in *Minnesota Studies in the Philosophy of Science*, ed. H. Feigl, vol. I, pp. 70-1.

[16] See, for example, his 'Unity of Science and Psychology', *Einheitswissenschaft*, vol. I, 1933, and 'Sociology and Physicalism', *Erkenntnis* vol. II, 1931.

be satisfactory. The essential point was that there must be *some* 'common reduction basis (item C3, page 128).[17]

The essay appearing here as item C3 formed part of the introduction to the projected 'International Encyclopedia of Unified Science'. In it Carnap argues for the reducibility, not only of psychological terms, but also of terms used in physical science (such as 'electric charge') to what he called the 'physical thing-language' – consisting of 'those terms which we use on a prescientific level in our everyday language' in describing ordinary physical things. This language would include such words as 'hot', 'cold', 'heavy', 'light', 'large', 'small', 'red' and 'blue' (page 121). Carnap thought he had here produced a 'basis consisting of a very narrow and homogeneous class of terms' (page 128); and that a reduction of all other language to such terms would demonstrate the basic unity of language and knowledge. A difficulty about this view is that there are various logical and epistemological differences among the examples given, so that it is not clear what their homogeneity amounts to. Moreover, unless some suitable criterion were provided, it would seem that a great variety of other tems, far beyond the examples given, might be thought to qualify for inclusion in the physical thing-language as Carnap describes it.[18]

D. VERIFICATION AND EXPERIENCE

Carnap's reduction, as I have indicated, was a matter of rendering all language into terms of the thing-language. How does this leave the connection of language with the world outside language, the importance of which (as I pointed out on page 7) was so much stressed by Schlick? This brings us to a major difference of opinion among members of the Circle. The items in section D will show that Carnap and others regarded language as a self-contained system; the truth and meaning of a statement depending, not on anything outside language, but on its relations with other statements. Schlick, on the other hand, held to the view that

---

[17]In his *Logischer Aufbau der Welt* (1928), Carnap had attempted a phenomenal analysis; after that he usually preferred a physicalist alternative; but in the Schilpp volume of 1963 (p. 882) he again expressed a preference for a 'subjective' basis.

[18]Such a criterion had been attempted in Carnap's 'Testability and Meaning' (p. 63), but I do not think it meets the difficulty. See the discussion in section 6.1 of my *Logical Positivism*.

truth and meaning must depend on something outside language. Items D1 and D3 are two different attempts by Schlick to give an account of this relation.

One might think, on the face of it, that the view represented by Carnap is bound to be paradoxical, and Schlick's position closer to common sense. But a reading of the items from Schlick may not confirm this expectation. In the first of these, Schlick introduces the terms 'structure' and 'content'. A sentence, he says, can be used to express a fact in virtue of its structure − a structure that it shares with the corresponding fact. It is important to note, however, that Schlick does not mean 'structure' in the ordinary grammatical sense. He writes: 'One and the same fact may be expressed in a thousand different languages, and the thousand different propositions will all have the same structure, and the fact which they express will have the same structure too' (page 131). The first two parts of this may lead us to think of 'same structure' as meaning 'same meaning'; but this would not do in speaking, as Schlick does in the final part, of the 'structure' of a fact, since facts do not have meaning (not, at least, in the way that statements do). It was Schlick's view, however, that truth consists in an identity of structure between statement and fact. (He also speaks of this, following Wittgenstein's *Tractatus,* as the relation of a picture to what is depicted − page 142.)

It is, again, this 'structure' that is communicated, according to Schlick, when one speaker communicates a fact to another by means of a statement. But besides this there is also the experience had by the speaker, which Schlick refers to as 'content'; and this, he says, cannot be communicated; it is beyond the reach of language. According to Schlick, questions about content, for example whether the experiences of two people are the same or different, are typical of the pseudo-questions of metaphysics.

But if this is so, how can Schlick himself engage in a discussion about content? This sort of problem is not peculiar to Schlick's discussion. It is a problem that is likely to arise for any philosopher of language who tries to take up a position, so to speak, outside language, in order to give an account of the nature of language as a whole. Schlick was well aware of this problem. At the end of our passage he speaks of his discussion of content as 'a forbidden road', which he and the reader will ultimately need to renounce. This passage invites comparison with the closing sentences of Wittgenstein's *Tractatus* (6.53ff) − though here the point is not about 'content'.

In item D2, Carnap offers an account which would avoid this and similar difficulties. Here he considers the problem of first and third person statements to which I drew attention above (page 15). On page 158 he takes his stand on a version of the Verification Principle: 'a statement', he says, 'asserts no more than can be verified'. Hence, he argues, the meaning of such a statement as 'S_1 is thirsty' must be confined to what we can observe of S_1's bodily state. But could this be what S_1 himself would mean in saying that he is thirsty? Carnap considers the view that he might mean, not a bodily state, but 'something non-material' – namely 'his sensations of thirst'. This is not denied by Carnap; but he argues that if it is so, then the meaning will be private to S_1. It would follow that 'a statement about S_1's thirst would then be fundamentally unverifiable by S_2, it would be for him in principle impossible to understand, void of sense' (page 158). There will also be problems about the logical relations between the subjective and inter-subjective meanings. Is there any way of avoiding these difficulties? 'These pseudo-questions', writes Carnap, 'are automatically eliminated by using the formal mode' of speech (page 159).

Carnap's celebrated distinction between the 'formal' and 'material' modes of speech is explained in the opening pages of this extract. He claims that the philosopher can, and should, confine himself to speaking about words and statements as distinct from objects or experiences ('content'). If this is done, then the problem about S_1's thirst cannot arise, since there will be mention only of the *words* in question, and not of their relation to something outside language, an experience had by S_1. Carnap tries to show, by means of parallel columns, how what philosophers have said in the material mode may be rendered in the formal mode, thus bringing about release from intractable problems.

In reading this extract one should bear in mind (as is often the case with Carnap) that what is said may be meant as a proposal to reform language rather than as an observation about language; in this case, a *proposal* to use the formal mode, rather than a claim that it is, actually, equivalent to the material mode. On page 153, for example, Carnap seems to be claiming that when it is said of certain statements that they 'describe directly given experience . . . i.e. the simplest states of which knowledge can be had', this can be rendered in the formal mode, without mention of experience, by saying that these statements 'need no justification' and can serve 'as foundation for all the remaining statements of science'. Now an obvious question about the latter description is: *why* do these statements 'need no justification'?; and it would seem that this could only be answered by drawing on the mention of experience which occurs in the first (material) formulation. But in any case, it could hardly be claimed that the two formulations are simply equivalent.

In this reading there is much use of the notion of 'protocol statements' (these being the ones that 'describe directly given experience' etc.). It was generally held by Logical Empiricists that there is a distinct class of statements (also known as 'observation statements' or 'experiential statements'), which are peculiarly close to experience and on which all other statements ('all the remaining statements of science') are founded. But it was soon pointed out, notably by Neurath in item D3, that once the resort to experience is taken away, no class of statements can be regarded as having this privileged position. 'There is no way of taking conclusively established pure protocol statements as the starting point of the Sciences' (page 162). We are to think of science, according to Neurath, as a system of statements for which the only criterion of acceptance is internal consistency.

Neurath thought of himself as fundamentally in agreement with Carnap, taking the latter's position to its logical conclusion.[19] But Ayer, who rejected the Carnap-Neurath view, argued that, given his premises, Neurath had not gone far enough. In item D4 he points out that once the connection with experience is cut, there is no longer any point in using such terms as 'protocol statement' and 'observation statement' at all. They merely give a misleading impression that the tenets of empiricism are still being adhered to.[20]

Another important point on which Ayer takes issue with Carnap is one that had been quickly disposed of by the latter. On page 151 Carnap tries to show that there is no need for a special class of 'ostensive definitions', since these can easily be replaced by definitions of the 'verbal' sort ('translations of words'). Thus there is no need for any reference outside language. But Ayer argues (pp. 170-1) that Carnap's 'verbal' treatment of the example he gives is unsatisfactory. It is, indeed, doubtful whether a system of words from which ostensive definition is excluded could properly be regarded as a language at all. In such a

---

[19] In a rejoinder, Carnap tried to show how he would accommodate Neurath's view. See 'Über Protokollsätze', *Erkenntnis* 1932/3.

[20] Also see Ayer's 'Verification and Experience', *Proceedings of Aristotelian Society*, 1936/7.

language one would not be able to ask 'What is this called?' with reference to a presented object.

Some of the more paradoxical aspects of the Carnap-Neurath view of truth are pointed out by Schlick in item D5, 'On the Foundation of Knowledge'. Schlick argues that if this view were accepted, then there would be no ground for preferring the statements of empirical science to those of 'any fabricated tale', assuming only that the latter is internally consistent (page 184). But Schlick's positive account is again fraught with difficulties. In this paper he maintains that there is a class of statements — observation-statements — whose truth depends wholly and solely on a corresponding experience. This being so, their truth, unlike that of any other statements, can be known with 'absolute certainty'. In section VII of the paper Schlick tries to show how this certainty comes about and how it is proof even against verbal error. It may be doubted, however, whether the statements in question are statements at all, for it turns out that their very meaning is confined to the moment of making them, at which moment 'the attention is directed to something observed' (page 194). It would seem that Schlick thought of this act as being both one of verification and one of *giving meaning* to the statement. If so, he has conflated two things which should be kept distinct.[21] It is in any case doubtful whether meaning can be given by a mental act such as that which Schlick describes. It may be that Wittgenstein had Schlick in mind when, in his *Philosophical Investigations*, he came to criticize the idea of a 'private ostensive definition' (see, e.g. sections 380 and 241ff).

So close is the relation that Schlick sees between his observation-statements and the corresponding experiences or acts, that one sometimes wonders whether they are distinct at all. In this connection Schlick's use of the term *Konstatierungen* ('confirmations' or 'affirmations') should be regarded with caution. He uses it sometimes to mean observation-statements (e.g. most of the time in section VII), and sometimes the corresponding experiences (e.g. item D6, page 201, where he speaks of 'those simple experiences').

A defence of the Carnap-Neurath view was attempted by Carl Hempel in his paper 'On the Logical Positivists' Theory of Truth'.[22] Against Schlick's objection, that on their view one might believe 'any fabricated

---

[21] For a fuller discussion of this matter, see section 5.5 of my *Logical Positivism*.
[22] *Analysis*, January, 1935.

tale' no less than the statements of science, Hempel maintained that 'science may only be characterized by the historical fact, that it is the system which is actually adopted by mankind, and especially by the scientists of our culture circle' (page 57). An appropriate comment on this sort of reply is made by Ayer, who points out (below, page 173) that 'each of several incompatible systems might contain the proposition that it alone was the accepted one'.

Hempel's paper (not reprinted here) is summarized and discussed by Schlick in item D6. In this paper, and the further one by Hempel which appears as item D7, one of the main issues is that of whether, and in what sense, one can be said to 'compare' statements with facts. Schlick regards it as obvious that verification consists in a comparison of statement with fact; but Hempel draws attention to the difficulty of giving a meaning to the word 'compare' in this context. It will not do to say, as Schlick does on page 197, that 'we can compare anything to anything if we choose'; for this does not tell us in what respect we are to compare statements with facts, nor in what sense the comparison would amount to *verification* of the statement.

The arguments and counter-arguments of this section reflect an underlying difficulty about the empiricist view of language and knowledge. According to this view, the meanings of our words and statements must be wholly accounted for by experience as distinct from language; and this means that there must be, at some stage, a perfect and unambiguous match between experience and the corresponding language. The same point may be made in terms of *facts* and language, for on the empiricist view our talk about facts can only be talk about experiences. In item D1, as we have seen, Schlick speaks of an identity of 'structure' between fact and statement. In a later writing (D5) he uses the word 'confirmations' for something that can, apparently, be regarded at one time as an experience and at another as a statement. In item D6 he thinks that the correspondence between fact and statement (if true) will be found by 'comparing' them. And elsewhere, as we saw in section B, he thought that the meaning of a word can be given solely by the 'showing' (ostension) of a corresponding object. Schlick also tried hard to reconcile the subjectivity of experience ('content') with the inter-subjectivity of meaning which is necessary for communication. But Carnap and his colleagues believed that the attempts to describe these relations and correspondences could lead only to 'pseudo-problems' and metaphysics. (In this respect their views were, after all, in keeping with Schlick's warning about his own discussion of 'content'.) But if these matters were not to be described in the way required by Schlick's empiricism, what alternative was there? The conclusion drawn by Carnap and others was that there is no verification, and no source of meaning, outside the circle of language. A third alternative would be to admit that statements are (sometimes) verified by observation, but to deny that this entails a correspondence of the kind that empiricists have tried to describe.

E. ETHICS

After the application of the criterion of verifiability, what becomes of moral statements? Are they verifiable in the approved way, the way of empirical observation? If not, must we regard them as meaningless? Such a conclusion would hardly be acceptable in the case of moral statements, even if it is in the case of metaphysics. The most usual answer to this problem was to deny that moral statements are really statements. It was held that in describing something as morally right or wrong, good or bad, one is really giving a directive or something of that sort; so that the concepts of knowledge, fact, truth and verification have no application here. This kind of view was generally accepted, even taken for granted, by supporters of the new philosophy. And since that philosophy was centred on statements and verification, it is not surprising that ethics was left largely out of consideration. Some thought that the most satisfactory treatment of the subject was that provided by the moral philosopher C. L. Stevenson.[23] But although Stevenson's treatment fits in very well with the Logical Empiricists' views, he was not one of their members or supporters. The writings appearing here are, however, by Logical Empiricists.

The brief extract from Carnap is intended mainly as an introduction to the more substantial items from Schlick and Reichenbach.[24] In this extract Carnap uses the criterion of verifiability (page 206) and concludes that 'the value statements themselves' must be relegated 'to the realm of metaphysics'. (There is a comparable discussion by Ayer in item B2.)

---

[23] See his *Ethics and language*, and the anthology of his papers, *Facts and Values*.

[24] Reichenbach was a member of the Berlin group associated with the Vienna Circle, and co-editor (with Carnap) of its journal *Erkenntnis*.

Turning to the extracts from Schlick and Reichenbach, one may be struck by what seems like a flat contradiction in their opening sentences. 'Ethics seeks nothing but knowledge', declares Schlick; but according to Reichenbach, 'if ethics were a form of knowledge it would not be what moral philosophers want it to be'. Schlick goes on to argue that ethics is indeed a branch of science; whereas Reichenbach claims that 'the modern analysis of knowledge makes a cognitive ethics impossible' (page 225). This conflict is not, however, as great as it may appear. For one of Schlick's main contentions is that moral statements are expressions of people's desires — those of the speaker or those of society. He is concerned to deny that it makes sense to speak of moral values as distinct from such desires. 'If . . . I assert that a thing is desirable simply in itself, I cannot say what I mean by this statement; it is not verifiable and is therefore meaningless' (page 217). With these views Reichenbach would not disagree. But whereas he (like many others) sees the purport, or the main purport, of moral statements as being that of imperatives rather than statements, this is not so in the case of Schlick. According to him, moral statements, no less than others, are objects of knowledge and verification. Being about human desires, they are, he maintains, part of the subject matter of psychology. The main task of ethics is to examine the causes of these desires and ethics is thus a branch of psychology; the latter, in turn, being part of a single, unified science (pages 223-4).

But before embarking on the main scientific task, it is necessary to clarify the meaning of moral terms, such as 'good'; and to this task Schlick turns his attention near the start of our extract (taken from the start of his book). The word 'good' is used, he maintains, on the basis of existing desires and considerations about happiness. A careless reader may take Schlick to be a utilitarian in the tradition of Bentham and Mill. But Schlick is careful to distinguish his position from what he calls 'the classical systems of Utilitarianism'. According to the latter, he says, 'The good *is* what *brings* the greatest possible happiness to society'; his claim, by contrast, is that 'in human society, that is *called* good which is *believed* to bring the greatest happiness' (IV/3; not reprinted in this volume). Schlick's claim is about how a word – the word 'good' – is actually used. He does not think that there can be any distinct question about what *is* good, if this means going beyond the actual usage of that word. The philosopher can tell us 'what "good" *actually* means; he can never tell us what "good" *must* or *should* mean' (page 217). Schlick argues that this does not exclude the possibility of a moral reformer.

Such a person, he says, 'does not form a new concept of morality'; his achievement is, rather, to show that the existing concept 'has a different range from that supposed' (page 211).

But does Schlick give a correct account of 'what "good" actually means'? Some would claim, contrary to Schlick, that the concept of moral goodness is *not* exhausted by the facts of desire and happiness; that the question 'what ought I to do?' is distinct from questions about what I and others desire, and that it is capable, at least in some cases, of generating a different answer. Thus it sometimes happens that one says 'I desire to do X, but I know I ought not to'. It is also possible to criticize the desires of one's society from an independent moral standpoint. If these claims are correct, then it would seem that moral questions cannot be merely a matter of psychology and part of science.

Reichenbach too speaks of facts of desire ('wishes') in connection with moral utterances; but according to him they are merely 'correlated' with the latter (page 228). Moral utterances, he claims, are not expressions of 'truths of any kind. Truth is a predicate of statements; but the linguistic expressions of ethics are not statements. They are directives. A directive cannot be classified as true or false . . .' (page 227). The idea that moral statements cannot be regarded as true or false, or as possible expressions of knowledge, is widely accepted nowadays. A difficulty about it is that we do speak of truth and knowledge in regard to them (for example, in saying 'I know I ought not to').

According to Reichenbach, however, the statement-like form of moral utterances is deceptive. This form is also, he thinks, liable to conceal their essentially subjective character. Thus ' "He should not lie", or "lying is morally bad", represents a pseudo-objective mode of speech; what is expressed is actually an attitude of the speaker. The phrase "he should" is comparable to terms such as "I" and "now", which refer to the speaker or the act of speech . . .' (page 233). What Reichenbach says here in logical terminology may be compared with Hume's claim, expressed in a typically psychological way, about vice and virtue. 'The vice entirely escapes you, as long as you consider the object. You never can find it, till you turn your reflection into your own breast, and find a sentiment of disapprobation . . .'.[25]

Reichenbach is eloquent in rejecting the idea that the philosopher's task is to hand down moral principles to others. He tells us to 'stand on

---

[25] *A Treatise of Human Nature*, ed. Selby-Bigge, p. 469.

our own feet and trust our volitions'. 'Only a distorted morality can argue that our will is bad if it is not the response to a command from another source' (page 235). This remark is closer to Kant than the dismissal of that philosopher, at the start of this reading, might lead us to expect. Kant too was emphatic in his rejection of attempts to base morality on 'another source' than the person himself. But whereas Reichenbach tries to explain the moral will as a product of social influences, Kant rejected such explanations.

Another resemblance with Kant is in what is perhaps the most distinctive part of this reading – the 'democratic principle' which is put forward on page 237; 'Everyone is entitled to set up his own moral imperatives and to demand that everyone follow these imperatives.' Under this principle, as Reichenbach explains, I may 'demand that you act in a certain way, but I do not demand that you renounce your demand to the contrary' (page 238). It is true that Reichenbach hastens to add that his principle is not derived from 'pure reason' and is not 'the result of a philosophy', but that he happens to advocate it merely because he is the product of a certain society. But he also points out the special logical status of his principle: acceptance of it, he says, is a condition of the discussion of moral issues between one person and another. And this point (like the claims made by Kant in this and other contexts) is not relative to a particular society.

The moral philosophy of the Logical Empiricists has been conditioned to a large extent by their special concern about verification. But must a verificationist deny that there are moral facts? Must he maintain that moral statements can only be imperatives or expressions of desire? Those who claim that there are moral facts would also point out that *reasons* can be given for our moral statements – reasons which have a logical and not merely emotive force.[26] But if there are reasons, then it should also be appropriate to speak of verification. And indeed this seems to be so in ordinary language. Thus one may claim to have verified, by reference to certain facts, that A is under a moral obligation to B. It is true that verification may mean something rather different here from what it means in science; and no doubt the meaning of moral statements is different from that which belongs to statements of other kinds. But perhaps this is a difficulty for the 'unity of science' rather than for verificationism.

---

[26] The 'emotive' view was defended by Stevenson. I have discussed this in my *Logical Positivism*, section 8.3.

A. MEANING AND VERIFICATION

1 Verification and Definition

Friedrich Waismann

VERIFICATION

A person who utters a proposition must know under what conditions the proposition is to be called true or false; if he is not able to specify that, he also does not know what he has said.

To understand a proposition means to know how things stand if the proposition is true.

One can understand it without knowing *whether* it is true.

In order to get an idea of the sense of a proposition, it is necessary to become clear about the procedure leading to the determination of its truth. If one does not know that procedure, one cannot understand the proposition either.

A proposition cannot say more than is established by means of the method of its verification. If I say 'My friend is angry' and establish this in virtue of his displaying a certain preceptible behaviour, I only *mean* that he displays that behaviour. And if I mean more by it, I cannot specify what that extra consists in. A proposition says only what it does say and nothing that goes beyond that.

The sense of a proposition is the way it is verified.

Sense itself is a method of verification; that method is not a means, not a vehicle.

I can, to be sure, say 'I shall drive to *A*' or 'I shall walk to *A*'; in that case we have two vehicles for doing the same thing, that is, with respect to spatial distance. I cannot, however, say, 'I shall verify this proposition in this way *or* that way.' A method of verification, after all, is not something that is added to a sense. A proposition already *contains* the method of its verification. You cannot *look for* a method of verification.

Source: Friedrich Waismann, *Wittgenstein and the Vienna Circle,* edited by B. McGuinness, translated by J. Schulte and B. McGuinness, Blackwell and Barnes and Noble, 1979, pp. 243-9.

To say that a statement has sense means that it can be verified.

It can never be a question of experience whether a statement has sense. For experience only teaches whether a proposition is true or false. In order to establish whether a proposition is true or false, however, I must have given it a sense.

Whether a proposition has sense can for that reason never depend on whether it is true.

If two propositions are true or false under the same conditions, they have the same sense (even if they seem different to us.)

If I lay down under what conditions a proposition is to be counted as true or false, I thereby lay down the *sense* of that proposition. (That is the basis of the truth-functions.)

Is it *always* possible for me to doubt whether a proposition is verified? Could it not be the case that verifications only make it probable? But if I cannot specify under what conditions the proposition is to count as verified, I have not given the proposition a sense. A statement that cannot be verified definitively is not verifiable at all.

Absolute doubt is unjustifiable.

A proposition that cannot be verified in any way has no sense.

There are no unanswerable questions.

What is a question? It is a request to look for something. A question introduces a movement of thought, as it were, at the end of which the answer is to be found. The direction of that movement is determined by the logical place of the answer. If no answer exists, then there is no direction in which you can look for anything; hence there is no movement of thought, and that means that *there is no question.*

You can only ask where you can look for something. And you can only look for something where there is a method of looking for it. To look for something means to look systematically.

A statement has sense, not because it is constructed in a legitimate way,[1] but because it can be verified. Hence every verifiable statement is constructed in a legitimate way. If I specify a method of verification, I thereby lay down the form of the proposition in question, the meaning of its words, the rules of syntax, etc.

In order to learn what a sign means, you have to ask, 'How is a proposition in which that word occurs to be verified?'

---

[1]Probably an allusion to R. Carnap, cf. e.g. his 'Überwindung der Metaphysik etc.' in *Erkenntnis* 2 (1931), p. 227 (translated as 'The Elimination of Metaphysics etc.' in *Logical Positivism* (ed. A. J. Ayer), Glencoe, Ill., 1959).

The same word can have different meanings in propositions that are verified in different ways. In that case we are simply dealing with different symbols that happen to have the same sign in common.

Thus in everyday life the word 'yellow' means something completely different from what it means in physics. For in the one case a proposition about yellow is verified by looking, in the other case by measuring its wave-length. (If that difference is disregarded, it will seem as though the colours as we see them were something incomplete, as though infrared, for instance, were their complement.)

because it is verified in a different way.

DEFINITION

A *symbol* is an applied, rule-governed sign.

A sign is what can be perceived of a symbol. (So one and the same sign can be common to two symbols. The sign will then symbolize differently in those two cases.)

The way a sign is used is its *meaning*.

A meaning is what all symbols that can represent one another have in common.

Thus negation, for example, is the common rule according to which the proposition $\sim p, p/p, p \supset \sim p$, etc, are constructed.

To give a meaning to a sign means to lay down a rule for its use.

There are two ways of giving a sign meaning: 1. By means of *ostension*. In this case we explain the use of a word in statement by construction various propositions by means of that word and each time pointing to the fact in question. In that way we become aware of the meaning of the word. (Ostension really consists in two acts — in an external action, pointing to various facts, and a thought-operation, namely learning what they have in common.) 2. By means of *definition*. In this case the meaning of a sign is explained by means of signs that already have a meaning.

A definition remains within language. Ostension steps outside language and connects signs with reality. A definition can be expressed in language, and ostension cannot.

What ostension and definition have in common is that both specify rules for the use of signs.

You know the meaning of a sign if you understand the sense of the propositions in which it occurs.

propositions are verified, and have their meanings thus.

Signs have meaning through their use.

To define a sign thus means to explain the sense of propositions in which it occurs.

A definition thus consists in the specification of a rule which tells how to express by means of other signs the sense of a proposition in which the sign in question occurs.

A definition is a translation rule — it translates a proposition into other signs.

Translation preserves the sense of a proposition.

A definition is a rule dealing with signs — it is neither true nor false.

A definition must be *complete*.

Once we have introduced a sign by means of definition, it must have been introduced for all combinations. We must not define a sign piece-meal by first explaining its meaning for one class of cases and then for a different class. (Thus Russell, for example, regards negation in front of an elementary proposition as an indefinable primitive sign and then explains it again when it occurs in front of a general statement.)

A definition explains the meaning of a sign by means of other signs. In this way one sign points to another, that sign in turn points to yet another, etc., and in this way signs are arranged in an order.

A sign signifies via all the signs by means of which it has been defined.

If we analyse the signs in a statement, replacing them by other signs in accordance with their definitions and replacing those others by yet other signs, etc., the verification-path becomes visible step by step.

Definitions are signposts. They show the path leading to verification.

We used to say that a proposition contained the method of its verification. That is true in the sense that a proposition contains the definitions of the signs out of which it is constructed and that those definitions guide us in verifying it.

A verification-path cannot lead to infinity. (An 'infinite verification' would no longer be a verification.)

To be sure, a proposition can lead back to other propositions, and those back to yet other ones, etc., but ultimately we must reach pro-positions that do not indicate further propositions, but point to reality. Or rather, a proposition with sense talks about reality via the whole chain of definitions.

If it were otherwise, no proposition could be verified. There would then be no connection between language and the world.

The propositions that deal with reality immediately are called elementary propositions.

It is not an hypothesis that there are elementary propositions. The requirement that elementary propositions should exist is the requirement that our statements have sense. The fact that we understand the propositions of our ordinary language already guarantees that there are elementary propositions.

The elementary propositions are what give all other propositions sense.

We can understand the propositions of our ordinary language without knowing what the elementary propositions look like. Just as we understand most expressions without knowing their definitions, or just as we move without knowing how every particular movement is brought about.

One could ask, How is it possible that we understand the propositions of our ordinary language if we do not know the elementary propositions? The answer is that to *apply a rule* does not mean to *know about the rule.* We can, for example, introduce new signs and analyse the familiar signs by means of definitions. In the latter case definitions only *elucidate* the sense of propositions. The propositions themselves, however, can be understood without our knowing how the definitions are to be formulated.

In the same way logical analysis elucidates the sense of propositions by analysing their signs; it is, however, not through analysis that they first acquire sense. Once we have completely analysed a proposition, we must in the end have the feeling that that was the very thing we had always meant when uttering the proposition. (An analysis must never surprise us.)

If the sense of our statements was not already fixed − how would we then know *which* analysis was the right one?

What a strange view to think that only logical analysis *explains* what we mean by the propositions of ordinary language! Do I, accordingly, not know what I mean when I say 'Today it is colder than it was yesterday'? Do I have to wait for the result of logical analysis? But it is just the other way about, isn't it? Our statements already have sense, and it is that sense that determines their logical analysis.

But can we not be wrong? Is it not possible that we imagine we mean something by a proposition which turns out to be senseless on a closer look? No, for a statement has sense if there is a method of verifying it. And vice cersa, if we know how to verify a proposition, then the proposition does have sense. We can only be in the dark about that as long as we go by the external linguistic structure of a proposition.

To analyse a proposition means to consider how the proposition is to be verified.

It is by means of elementary propositions that language *touches* reality.

To specify the elementary propositions means to specify the states of affairs in the world.

It is clear that statements about bodies (tables, chairs) are not elementary propositions. Nor will anybody believe that in talking about bodies we have reached the ultimate elements of descriptions.

Phenomena (experiences) are what elementary propositions describe.

I can say, to be sure, 'This conductor is charged with electricity, *since* the electroscope displays a deflection.' But I cannot say 'This patch in my visual field is yellow, *since* . . .' If, in order to verify a proposition, I can no longer appeal to other propositions, this indicates that the proposition is elementary. . . .

2 Meaning and Verification

Moritz Schlick

. . . In the preceding arguments we have often made use of the principle that the meaning of a statement can be given only by indicating the way in which the truth of the statement is *tested*. What is the justification of this principle? There has been a great deal of dispute about this question in modern philosophy, and certainly it deserves our full attention, for if I am not mistaken it is *the* fundamental principle of philosophizing, and neglect of it is the cause of all serious troubles in metaphysics.

The object of every proposition is to express a fact. It seems, then, that in order to state the meaning of the proposition we have to indicate

Source: Moritz Schlick, *Philosophical Papers*, volume II (1925-1936), edited by H. L. Mulder and B. van de Velde-Schlick, D. Reidel, 1979, pp. 309-12, 361-9. The lectures entitled 'Form and Content. An Introduction to Philosophical Thinking', of which this is an extract, were first published in Moritz Schlick, *Gesammelte Aufsätze 1926-1936*, Gerold & Co., Vienna, 1938.

the fact which it expresses. But how strange! Is not the fact in question already indicated by the proposition itself? In fact, we have convinced ourselves long ago ... that a proposition expresses its own meaning, it does not stand in need of an explanation. An explanation which said *more* than the proposition itself would not be a correct explanation of it, and if it said the same thing as the proposition it would be superfluous. As a matter of fact, when we hear somebody make a statement and ask him 'What do you mean by it?' we usually get and expect as an answer a mere repetition of the first statement, only in different words, and very often we are actually satisfied by this procedure which is nothing but a translation from one language into another one. Why are we satisfied? Evidently because we did not *understand* the first expression, but do understand the second one.

This last remark gives us the clue to solve the paradox. We can ask for a meaning only as long as we have not understood a statement. And as long as we have not understood a sentence it is actually nothing but a series of words; it would be misleading to call it a proposition at all. A series of words (or other signs) should be regarded as a proposition only when it is understood, when its meaning is comprehended. If we agree to use our terms in this way there will be no sense in asking for the meaning of a proposition, but we may very well inquire (and that was our actual problem) after the meaning of a *sentence* or any complex of signs which we suppose to express something.

Now there is not the slightest mystery about the process by which a sentence is given meaning or turned into a proposition: it consists in defining the use of the symbols which occur in the sentence. And this is always done by indicating the exact circumstances in which the words, according to the rules of the particular language, should be used. These rules must be taught by actually applying them in definite situations, that is to say, the circumstances to which they fit must actually be *shown*. It is of course possible to give a verbal description of any situation, but it is impossible to *understand* the description unless some kind of connection between the words and the rest of the world has been established beforehand. And this can be done only by certain *acts*, as for instance gestures, by which our words and expressions are correlated to certain experiences.

Thus, if I utter a sentence, and you ask me what I mean by it (perhaps by shrugging your shoulders or by looking at me with a vacant stare), I shall have to answer you by translating the sentence into a language you understand, or, if you do not understand any language yet, I shall have to teach you one; and this involves certain acts on our part, I have to make you undergo certain experiences. All your future understanding will be by virtue of these experiences. In this way all meaning is essentially referred to experience.

It must be clear by this time that there is only one way of giving meaning to a sentence, of making it a proposition: we must indicate the rules for how it shall be used, in other words: we must describe the facts which will make the proposition 'true', and we must be able to distinguish them from the facts which will make it 'false'. In still other words: The Meaning of a Proposition is the Method of its Verification. The question: 'What does this sentence mean?' is identical with (has the same answer as) the question: 'How is this proposition verified?'

It is one of the most serious errors in philosophy to think of a proposition as possessing meaning independently of the possible ways of its verification. People have fallen into hopeless confusion because they believed they knew the meaning of a phrase, and yet had to declare themselves unable *in principle* to define any circumstances in which it would be true. As long as it is logically impossible for me to indicate a method of ascertaining the truth or falsity of a proposition, I must confess I do not know what is actually asserted by the proposition.

After you have once seen this clearly you will no longer understand even the possibility of a different opinion: you will recognize that no opinion can even be formulated without admitting the truth of the preceding remarks. The view contained in these remarks has, it is true, found many opponents, but the very name by which it is usually called shows that it has not been properly understood. It is known as the 'experimental theory of meaning'. But it is not a theory; there can be no 'theory' of meaning. A theory is a set of hypotheses which may be either true or false and have to be tested by experience. It is not necessary to make hypotheses about meaning, and they would come too late, because we must presuppose meaning in order to formulate any hypothesis. We have not made any assumptions, we have done nothing but formulate the rules which everybody always follows whenever he tries to explain his own meaning and whenever he wants to understand other people's meaning, and which he never actually violates — except when he begins to philosophize.

In establishing the identity of meaning and manner of verification we are not making any wonderful discovery, but are pointing to a mere truism. We are simply maintaining that a proposition has meaning for us only if it makes *some* kind of difference to us whether it is true or false, and that its meaning lies entirely in this difference. Nobody has ever explained the meaning of a sentence in any other way than by explaining what would be different in the world if the proposition were false instead of true (or vice versa).

This, I am sure, cannot be denied. But the great objection usually raised against the view I have been defending consists in maintaining that the 'difference in the world' expressed by the proposition may not be observable or in any way discoverable. In other words: if a sentence is to have meaning for us we must, of course, know which fact it expresses, but it may be absolutely impossible for us to find out whether the fact actually exists. In this case the proposition could never be verified, but it would not be meaningless. Therefore, our adversaries conclude, meaning is distinct from verifiability, and not dependent upon it.

This argument is faulty on account of an ambiguity of the word 'verifiability'. In the first place, one might call a proposition verifiable, if the actual facts are such as to permit our finding out its truth or falsity whenever we feel like it. In this sense it would be impossible for me to verify the statement: 'There is gold to be found in the earth 300 feet below my house', for there are many empirical circumstances which absolutely prevent me from discovering its truth; and yet the assertion was certainly not nonsensical. Or take the statement: 'On the back side of the moon there are mountains 10,000 feet high'. It is not improbable that no human being will ever be able to verify or falsify it, but which philosopher would be bold enough to declare the sentence to be devoid of meaning! I think it must be clear that we have nothing to do with this use of the term 'verifiability', and that we must have had something else in mind when we said that the Meaning of a Proposition was its Method of Verification.

As a matter of fact, we call a proposition verifiable if we are able to *describe* a way of verifying it, no matter whether the verification can actually be carried out or not. It suffices if we are able to *say* what must be done, even if nobody will ever be in a position to do it. . . .

Every proposition is essentially verifiable. This is the most fundamental principle of philosophizing; we shall do well to devote the rest of our time to its elucidation.

Whenever we assert anything we must, at least in principle, be able to say how the truth of our assertion can be tested; otherwise we do not know what we are talking about; our words do not form a real proposition at all, they are mere noises without meaning, This must be admitted by everyone who asks himself sincerely and carefully how he becomes aware of the *meaning* of a proposition. What criterion have we to find out whether the meaning of a sentence has been grasped? How can I assure myself, for instance, that a pupil has properly understood the sense of a proposition which I try to explain to him?

There is only one answer, and it is this: a person knows the meaning of a proposition if he is able to indicate exactly the circumstances under which it would be true (and distinguish them from the circumstances which would make it false). This is the way in which Truth and Meaning are connected (it is clear that they must be connected in some way). To indicate the meaning of a proposition and to indicate the way in which it is verified *are identical procedures.*

Every proposition may be regarded as an answer to a question, or (if the question is difficult) as the solution of a problem. A sentence which has the grammatical form of a question (with an interrogation mark at the end) will have meaning only if we can indicate a method of answering it. It may be technically impossible for us to do what the method prescribes, but we must be able to point out some way in which the answer could be found. If we are, in principle, unable to do this, then our sentence is no genuine question at all. And where there is no question, there can be no answer; we are confronted with an 'insoluble problem'. This is the only case of an 'absolutely unanswerable question': it is unanswerable, because it is no question. It may look like one, because outwardly it has the grammatical form of a question, but in reality it is a meaningless series of words, followed by a question mark.

Now we understand the nature of the so-called insoluble problems about which philosophers have worried so much: they are insoluble not because their solution lies in a region forever inaccessible to the knowing mind, not because they pass the power of our understanding, but simply because they are no problems. Unfortunately — no, fortunately — all genuine 'metaphysical questions' turn out to be of this kind. Metaphysics, as we stated before, consists essentially in the attempt to express content,* i.e., in a self-contradictory enterprise, but it is by no means easy to see that a question inquiring into the nature of content is nothing but a meaningless arrangement of words. The difficulty of perceiving this is the real cause of all the troubles from which philosophical speculation has been suffering for about twenty-five centuries. If the nonsense in the typical metaphysical issues had been as easy to

---

*An extract from Schlick's discussion of 'content' appears as item D1 below.—*Ed.*

(MUSEO LATER. - SEC. II)

BONUS PASTOR

Dominus regit me et nihil mihi deerit
(Psal. XXII - 1)

CIETÀ AMICI CATACOMBE - ROMA

...ay) in the question, 'is time more logical
...e discussions of our great thinkers would

...s is so important that I may perhaps be
...tration of the way in which it disappears

..., maintained the view that only human
...consciousness' and that we must look
...a behaving exactly 'as if' they were 'con-
...being condemned to a 'soulless' existence.
...it out that Descartes' argument might be
... beings. How can I ever be sure that my
...re more than mechanical automata and
...to my own?
..., are inclined to regard this question as a
...ver it in this way: the behaviour of all
...aviour of all animals down to insects and
...tant respects, so similar to my own be-
...existence of consciousness 'within' them;
..., it is true, but based on such striking
...be regarded as valid with a degree of
...be distinguished from certainty. Never-
...it that the probability is not exactly equal
... that it is not absolute certainty, and that here we are confronted
with a case where absolute certainty can never be gained. According to
their opinion the existence of consciousness in beings other than myself
is a typical insoluble problem. There is no imaginable way of deciding it.

What are we to think of it? Our verdict is simple: if the question is
really definitely unanswerable it can be only because there is no meaning in it. And if this is so, if there is no problem at all, there can be no
probable answer either, it must be nonsense to assert that animals and
human beings 'very likely' possess consciousness. We can speak of
probability only where there is at least a theoretical possibility of
discovering the truth.

The fact is that our question is actually meaningless because it is
interpreted in a metaphysical way: the word 'consciousness' (one of the
most dangerous terms in modern philosophy) is supposed to stand for
content, and this is the reason why it was declared that we could not be
absolutely sure of its existence except in our own ego, for did not
content require intuition, and was not intuition restricted to our own

consciousness? I know that most people find it very difficult to admit that there is no sense in this reasoning, but I must insist that without admitting it we cannot even take the first step in philosophy.

Our 'problem' is meaningless, because the word 'consciousness' occurs in it in such a way that we cannot possibly express what we mean by it. It is used in such a way that it makes no discoverable difference in the world whether my fellow creatures are 'conscious' beings or not. Whether the answer is 'yes' or 'no', it cannot be verified, and this means that we did not know what we were talking about when we put the question.

It is one of the most important tasks of philosophy to analyse how the word 'consciousness' must be interpreted in order to make sense in different contexts. We know, of course, that some structure must be indicated by it. Keeping this in mind we can easily give a non-metaphysical interpretation to our question: 'Are animals conscious beings?' If it is to be a real, legitimate question it can mean nothing but: 'Does the behaviour of animals show a certain structure?' Now it has become a genuine problem and can receive a definite answer. The answer is, of course, not given by the philosopher but by the biologist. It is his business to define carefully the kind of structure which comes into question (he will probably describe it in terms of 'stimuli' and 'response'), and to state by observation in each case whether a particular animal or human being under particular circumstances exhibits this particular structure. This is an entirely empirical statement to which truth or probability may be ascribed in the same way as to another expression of a fact. It must be noted that wherever the phrase 'a person is conscious (or unconscious)' is used in everyday life it has a perfectly good meaning and is verifiable because it expresses nothing but observable facts (which a physician, for instance, may enumerate). It is only on the lips of the metaphysician that the word is employed in a different way, in a 'philosophic' way, which he believes to be a consistent interpretation, but which actually is a metaphysical abuse.

Our discussion of the 'problem' of other people's 'consciousness' or 'soul' has shown that the confusion is due not only to a careless use or lack of analysis of the terms 'consciousness' or 'self', but that a misunderstanding of 'existence' has also something to do with it. For clearly our question could have been formulated by asking: 'Does "consciousness", or "a soul", or "a mind" *exist* in other living beings?' The same misunderstanding is the cause of the nonsensical problem concerning the 'existence of an External World'. In order to get rid of such meaningless questions we need only remember, once for all, that, since *every* proposition expresses a fact by picturing its structure, this must also be true for propositions asserting the 'existence' of something or other. The only meaning such a proposition can have is that it pictures a certain structure of our experience. This was seen quite clearly even by Kant. He expressed it in his own way by saying that 'reality' was a 'category', but from his explanation of his own thought we can infer that what he had in mind practically coincides with the interpretation we have to give to the term 'existence'. According to this interpretation such questions as, 'does the inside of the sun exist?', 'did the earth exist before it was perceived by any human beings?' etc., have a perfectly good sense, and must, of course, be answered in the affirmative. There are certain ways of verifying these positive answers, certain scientific reasons for believing them to be true, and they assure us of the reality of mountains and oceans, stars, clouds, trees and fellow men by the same methods of observation or experience by which we learn the truth of any proposition. If by 'external world' we mean this empirical reality, its existence is no problem, and if a philosopher means something else, if he is not satisfied with empirical reality, he must tell us what he does mean. He says he is concerned with 'transcendent' reality. We do not understand this word and ask him for an explanation, which he may give by saying that 'transcendent' refers to genuine metaphysical Being, not to merely empirical reality. If we ask him what is meant by this distinction and how a proposition asserting transcendent existence of anything can be verified, he must answer that there is no way of ever testing the truth of such a proposition definitely. We must inform him that, if this is the case, there is no meaning in his propositions about a metaphysical external world, and that we must continue to use this phrase in the good old innocent sense in which it stands for stars, mountains, trees as contrasted with dreams, feelings and wishes which form the 'internal' world. We must inform the philosopher that it is not his business to tell us what is real and what is unreal — this must be left to experience and science, but it is his business to tell us what we *mean* when we judge of a certain thing or event that is 'real'. And in every case he can answer the question concerning the sense of such a judgement only by pointing to the operations by which we should actually verify its truth. If I know exactly what I have to do in order to find out whether the shilling in my pocket is real or imagined, then I know also what I mean by declaring that the shilling is a real part of the external world, and there is no other meaning of the words 'real' or 'external world'.

For, let us repeat it once more: the complete and only way of giving the meaning of a proposition consists in indicating what would have to be done in order to find our whether the proposition is true or false (no matter whether we are actually able to do it). This insight is often called 'the experimental (or operational) theory of meaning', but I should like to point out that it would be unjust to call it by such an imposing name. A 'theory' consists of a set of propositions which you may believe or deny, but our principle is a simple triviality about which there can be no dispute. It is not even an 'opinion', since it indicates a condition without which no opinion can be formulated. It is not a theory, for its acknowledgement must precede the building of any theory. A proposition has no meaning unless it makes a discoverable difference whether it is true or false; a proposition whose truth or falsity would leave the world unchanged does not say anything about the world, it is an empty sentence without meaning. 'Understanding' a proposition means: being able to indicate the circumstances which would make it true. But we could not describe these circumstances if we were not able to recognize them, and if they are recognizable it means that the proposition is, in principle, verifiable. Thus, understanding a statement and knowing the way of its verification is one and the same thing.

This principle is nothing surprising or new or wonderful: on the contrary, it has always been followed and used by scientists as a matter of course, at least unconsciously, and in the same way it has always been acknowledged by common sense in everyday life; the only place where it has been neglected is in philosophical discussions. Science could not possibly act otherwise, because its whole business consists in testing the truth of propositions, and they cannot be tested except on the strength of our principle.

Now and then it happens in the development of science that a concept is used in a vague manner so that there is no absolute clarity about the verification of the propositions in which the concept occurs. Within certain limits of accuracy the ordinary tests of their truth may suffice for years or centuries, and then suddenly some contradiction will show up and force the scientists to inquire carefully into the signification of his symbols. He will have to stop and think. He will pause in his scientific investigations and turn to philosophic meditation until the meaning of his propositions has become perfectly clear to him.

The most famous instance of this kind, and one which will forever be memorable, is Einstein's analysis of the concept of Time. His great achievement, which is the basis of the Restricted Theory of Relativity, consisted simply in stating the *meaning* of assertions that physicists used to make about the simultaneity of events in different places. He showed that physics had never been quite clear about the signification of the term 'simultaneity', and that the only way of becoming clear was to answer the question: 'How is the proposition "two distant events happen at the same time" actually verified?' If we show how this verification is done, we have shown the *complete* sense of the proposition and of the term, and it has no meaning besides. All those philosophers who have condemned Einstein's ideas and theory (and some are condemning it even to this day) do it on the ground that there is a simultaneity the significance of which is understood without verification. They call it 'absolute simultaneity'. This sounds very well, but unfortunately those philosophers have failed to tell us how their simultaneity can actually be distinguished from that of Einstein; they have not been able to give us the slightest hint how anyone can ever find out whether two distant events occur 'absolutely simultaneously' or not. Considering this, I think we must take the liberty of regarding their assertion as meaningless.

I have just alluded to the difference between the scientific attitude and the philosophical attitude. We can formulate it by saying: Science is the pursuit of Truth, and Philosophy is the pursuit of Meaning.

Of course the two cannot actually be separated. It is impossible to discover the truth of a proposition without being acquainted with its meaning. No one can essentially contribute to the progress of science without having before his mind the genuine and final sense of the truths he is investigating. That is why all great scientists have also been philosophers. They have been inspired by the philosophic spirit. Nevertheless the distinction must be made, and it has the advantage of giving a satisfactory answer to the endless questions concerning the nature and task of philosophy. Our definition of philosophy gives a clear and full account of its relationship to science and makes it easy to understand the historical development of this relationship.

Philosophy is most certainly not a science, not even the Science of the sciences, and it has been one of its greatest misfortunes that it has been mistaken for one and that philosophers have, in outward appearance, adopted scientific methods and language. It often makes them a little ridiculous, and there is a good deal of truth in the way in which Schopenhauer describes the contrast between the genuine philosopher and the academic scholar who regards philosophy as a sort of scientific pursuit.

A science is a connected system of propositions which form the result of patient observation and clever combination. But philosophy, as Wittgenstein has put it,[1] 'is not a theory, but an activity. The result of philosophy is not a number of "philosophical propositions", but to make propositions clear.' As a matter of fact, the results of the pursuit of meaning cannot be formulated in ordinary propositions, for if we ask for an explanation of a meaning, and the answer is given in a sentence, we should have to ask again, 'but what is the meaning of this sentence?' and so on. If we are to arrive at any sense at all, this series of questions and definitions cannot go on forever, and the only way in which it can end is by some prescription that will tell us what to *do* in order to get the final meaning. You want to know what this particular note here signifies? Well, strike this particular key of the piano! That puts an end to your questions.

Thus a teacher of philosophy cannot provide us with certain true propositions which will represent the solution of the 'philosophical problems': he can only teach us the activity or art of thinking which will enable us for ourselves to analyse or discover the meaning of all questions. And then we shall see that the so-called philosophical problems are either meaningless combinations of symbols, or can be interpreted as perfectly sound questions. But in the latter case they have ceased to be philosophical and must be handed over to the scientists, who will try to answer them by his methods of observation and experiment.

Kant, who in spite of his complicated philosophy had many bright moments of profound insight, has said that he could teach philosophizing, but not philosophy. That was a very wise statement, and it implies that philosophy is nothing but an art or activity, that there are no philosophical propositions, and consequently no system of philosophy. Another great thinker who seems to have been well aware of the nature and place of philosophy was Leibniz. When he founded the Prussian Academy of Science in Berlin and sketched out the plans for its constitution, he assigned a place in it to all the sciences, but philosophy was not one of them. He must have felt somehow that it could not be regarded as the pursuit of a particular kind of truth, but that the determination of meaning must pervade *every* search for truth.

When we look for the most typical example of a philosophic mind we must direct our eyes towards Socrates. All the efforts of his acute mind and his fervent heart were devoted to the pursuit of meaning. He

---

[1] *Tractatus Logico-Philosophicus*, London 1922, 4.112.

tried all his life to discover what it really was that men had in their minds when they discussed about Virtue and the Good, about Justice and Piety; and his famous irony consisted in showing his disciples that even in their strongest assertions they did not know what they were talking about and that in their most ardent beliefs they hardly knew what they were believing.

As long as people speak and write so much more than they think, using their words in a mechanical, conventional manner, disagreeing about the Good (in Ethics), the Beautiful (in Aesthetics) and the Useful (in Economics and Politics), we shall stand in great need of men with Socratic minds in all our human pursuits. And since also in science the great discoveries are made only by those superior minds who in the routine of their experimental and theoretical research keep wondering what it is all about and therefore remain engaged in the pursuit of meaning, the philosophical attitude will be recognized more than ever as the most powerful force and the best part of the scientific attitude.

B. VERIFIABILITY AND THE ELIMINATION OF METAPHYSICS

1 Meaning and Verification

Friedrich Waismann

I LANGUAGE AND SYMBOLS

It has been pointed out in the last chapter that what is necessary in order to understand the meaning of a sentence without previous explanation is only that we should know the meaning of the individual words which compose it and be familiar with the manner in which they are combined. But this formulation must be further corrected. There are certainly cases where we seem to understand the meaning of the individual words and grasp the grammatical structure, and yet the meaning of the sentence itself is by no means clear to us. If, for example, someone tells us that he owns a dog which is able to think, then we should at first not really understand what he meant by this statement. But if he described to us the behaviour of the animal in detail, then we could say 'Now we understand you, that is what you mean by thinking'.

How is it that we have not understood such a sentence? Is understanding a sentence *more* than understanding its individual words and grasping its grammatical structure? It will be easier to answer this question if we cast a glance at the understanding of mathematical expressions. How is it that we understand expressions of the form a^{b^c}, but not expressions of the form $^c a^b$? Or, that we understand a sign like 27865, but not $27\frac{8}{3}65$? The answer is obviously that we have stepped outside the bounds of the usual notation. We do not know how we should deal with such a combination of figures. We shall not say that it was absolutely meaningless; we *can* attach a meaning to it by giving new rules of the operating with such expressions. In doing this we expand the notation, or, to put it better, we construct a new notation.

These examples cast light on the situation in the case of word language. It is quite true that we understand the meaning of a sentence

Source: Friedrich Waismann, *The Principles of Linguistic Philosophy*, reprinted by permission of Macmillan, London and Basingstoke, and St Martin's Press, 1965, pp. 323-33.

if we know the meaning of the individual words and its grammatical structure; but only in so far as the words are used in their normal way. Sometimes it happens that a word is used in a quite novel way (e.g. 'a dog thinks'), and then we step beyond the bounds of ordinary language; we extend language or we construct a new symbolism. And in doing so we must give rules as to the use of the new expressions.

However, if we pursue further the analogy between language and mathematical symbolism, we become aware of an important difference. In the mathematical examples mentioned before, it is quite clear when we step beyond the notation; we cannot say precisely when this happens in the case of language. If we speak here of a notation we must say that its boundaries are blurred and that it is often impossible to lay down the limits of the normal usage of language, i.e. to define exactly the dividing-line between the use of words in the ordinary sense and their use in the new way.

If, in mathematics, we introduce novel expressions we must give rules for operating with them. What is it that we have to do in the case of language? We need only consider our example. We did not give a new definition of the words nor did we introduce any new rules for their combination. All we have done was simply to describe circumstances under which we should say that the statement was true or false, in other words to describe its verification. The explanation of the verification of a sentence is a contribution to its grammar, to its use, or, as we can equally well say, to its meaning.

This brings us to an exceedingly important question which we will discuss in the following section.

2 WHEN DO WE UNDERSTAND THE MEANING OF A SENTENCE?

In daily life this question causes us no difficulty. If a traveller reports to us that he has met dwarfs in the central regions of Africa, then we understand what is meant. There seems to be no further problem here which could disquiet us. Yet cases can arise where a thorough consideration of that which is meant in a sentence is absolutely necessary and where those who think that they are able to gather the meaning directly from the words of the sentence would go far astray. If a philosopher says to us 'Only the experience of the present moment has reality', and if another contradicts him, then it is by no means clear what the dispute is about; in fact, it is not even clear whether both the opponents mean anything with their words at all (and that is why the dispute can continue so long). In such cases it is necessary to find a criterion which indicates whether one has understood the meaning of a sentence. Such a criterion must already be contained in the normal use of language. We need only select it from ordinary language and express it in a clear sentence in order to find the answer to our question.

When are we *certain* that we understand the meaning of a sentence? Let us imagine that wave-mechanics is explained in a lecture. How can we ascertain whether a listener has understood the meaning of this theory? Is it sufficient that he can repeat it in his own words? Or that he has vivid images? Or that he can draw normal conclusions? All this would not prove to us that he has really understood the meaning. There is only one method which we must adopt in order to find the answer: we must ask him how he would set about investigating the truth of this theory. If he is unable to describe the conditions necessary to prove the truth of the theory, then we should say: 'he is mistaken, he has not really grasped what the theory states'. If, on the other hand, he can state some experiment which confirms or refutes the propositions of wave-mechanics, then he has understood the theory — even if it turns out that for practical reasons the experiment cannot be performed. It seems obvious that it is no new discovery, but only the formulation of a method used by everyone, when we say: 'the criterion of understanding a sentence is the knowledge of the method of its verification'.

In order, however, to avoid misunderstandings about what has been said two points must be added:

(i) Our criterion does not demand that we should know whether the proposition is true. It demands only that we should be able to describe theoretically a way in which the assertion could be examined. We can obviously understand a proposition without knowing whether it is true.

(ii) Our criterion is: can the sentence be theoretically verified? and *not*: can it be verified in practice? There are many propositions the truth of which at present cannot be verified — for example, the proposition whether there are mountains on the back of the moon. But we can describe now the observations which would make the proposition true.*

---

*1959—*Ed.*

3 ARE UNVERIFIABLE STATEMENTS MEANINGLESS?

The most controversial problem is this: have only those propositions meaning which are verifiable? If one answers with 'Yes', this answer has the air of an empirical statement which will arouse all sorts of opposition. For it could be objected: why should not facts exist which will always be inaccessible to us? If certain speculations of contemporary astronomy should prove true the expanding universe must finally separate into segments which are no longer causally connected. Under those circumstances we would not be able to have any knowledge of events outside our part of the universe. Another example: certain facts of quantum-mechanics could not be expressed at all in the language of classical physics, much less could they be verified – have these events because of this not occurred? Such an objection would be a complete misunderstanding. We do not say that everything which exists is accessible to our knowledge, or even to expression by ordinary language. We only say: if someone makes an assertion, then he must be able to state some possible method of verification, otherwise he is not clear about what he says. However, even this formulation still sounds dogmatic and may provoke opposition. Let us make the situation clear with the help of an example.

Let us imagine a man who says 'The universe has expanded to twice its original size this night'. How would the world appear to us on waking up in the morning? Well – just exactly as before. All things have become twice as large, consequently also the standard with which I measure, and thus I shall count with it the same number of metres. Our visual perceptions would also remain unchanged since that transformation leaves the angles unchanged. In short, this remarkable change of our world could not be verified in any way, it would remain completely unnoticed by us – at least, if we only consider spatial measurements. (It would, on the other hand, become manifest as soon as we measure the weight, the density, etc. We will for the sake of simplicity leave this possibility out of consideration.)

Now someone could say: 'we have seen that it is conceivable that the world should expand to twice its original size without our noticing it'. Perhaps it has really done so? And now it looks as if this proposition, though it could never be verified, nevertheless has a certain meaning: it states that the world has become twice as large. It might be said: 'if I want to put forward this hypothesis I can do so, and I am sure that no one can disprove it'.

Arguments of this kind could be used only because the logical situation remained obscure. The argument sounds as if an accidental combination of circumstances prevented me from getting knowledge of an event which in fact really has occurred. It lays stress upon the possibility that there could always be facts about which we can never know anything. The point in question, however, is not what we can know and what we cannot know, but only whether that sentence expresses a meaning.

Let us now investigate the meaning of the single words, in order to bring more clarity into the matter. We ask those who oppose us: You consider it possible that everything in the world has become twice as large as before. Clearly then also my hand is twice its original size. Now what does that mean? In daily life we understand the meaning of these words perfectly well. A thing has become twice as large means: if I measure it with a given standard, the number of linear units will be twice the number of units as measured before; or if I look at that thing it appears to me twice as large. We now ask: has the expression 'twice as large' the same significance in our case? Evidently not. According to the assumption it is not possible to determine the change either through applying a given standard or measuring the angles. Well, then, what does the expression mean? It has lost the old meaning; what is the new meaning? One might say ' "My hand has become twice as large" means: when measured with a standard measure which is not subject to the change, then it is twice as large as before'. We now ask the further question: 'And what does it mean to say the standard measure has remained unchanged? What is the criterion for this?' If I am to understand what is meant by a 'standard measure of unchangeable length', then the explanation of this phrase must give a criterion for ascertaining the invariability, or else I should not know when to use the expression and when not.

Let us sum up: either one explains the meaning of the words of the sentence; then the statement is verifiable, and the explanation shows the way to the verification; or, if the statement cannot be verified in any way, this is due to the fact that we have given no meaning to one of the expressions occurring in it. Though one is using words which have a clear meaning in ordinary language one is using them in a context, in which they lose this meaning. What we do here is merely to draw attention to the fact that they do lose their meaning.

Anyone who believes that he understands the meaning of the sentence 'The universe has expanded to twice it original size' is subject to a delusion. This delusion may be due to two circumstances: firstly, to the use of well-known words which are combined with each other in such a way that they sound like a familiar sentence; secondly, to the influence of images. If somebody says 'certainly I can imagine that the world has expanded to twice its size', no doubt he thinks that he can do so because he can call up an image, say an image of the solar system expanding – while he himself remains unchanged in size. But he has not imagined the situation which would verify the proposition, namely, that he as well as the universe has changed in size – but an entirely different situation.

If thus we deny meaning to such a sentence we do not do this out of prejudice or on the basis of some philosophical 'theory', but merely because we see that in forming this sentence we have not fulfilled the conditions under which words acquire their meaning. The fact that this has often not been noticed has led to a great number of violent disputes to which the history of philosophy is a witness. We will place some examples side by side here which speak for themselves.

(i) Schopenhauer believed that Kant was mistaken when he said: 'It is not time itself which passes, it is only phenomena, occurring in time, which pass'. He put his argument in the following way: that this view is utterly false is proved by the fact that we all know with certainty that, even if everything in heaven and on earth came to a sudden standstill, time would pass on undisturbed; in such a way that, if subsequently nature started to work again, the question as to the length of the interval could be given an exact answer. If this were not the case, then time would have to stop with the stopping of the clock and move with the clock's movement.

(ii) Paul Mongré (Felix Hausdorff): 'If the movement of events in the Universe were suddenly to be a hundred times faster or slower than at present – this transcendental change in pace would remain completely unnoticed by us, since the standard of measurement would be subject to the same change as the periods of time which are measured by it. Or even past and future could be reversed if only our experiences and our memory remain unaltered.

'All this is transcendentally conceivable, because it is empirically unnoticeable; objectively admissible, because subjectively inaccessible'.

(iii) Otto v. Guericke considered air to be the scent of a substance which we do not perceive only because we have been used to it from our childhood.

(iv) Pierre d'Ailly, a late scholastic, believed it to be conceivable that our perceptions of reality should continue, even if reality itself had ceased to exist. How then, he asked, could we possible know that physical objects exist?

4 'THE MEANING OF A STATEMENT IS THE METHOD OF ITS VERIFICATION.'

In such cases it is useful to say: 'the meaning of a statement is the method of its verification'. To say this is not to hold a theory which can be true or false – but it is rather a recommendation as to the way in which we should deal with certain sentences when they have no conventional meaning. We could also formulate it in this way: 'if you are not clear what the meaning of a statement is, or whether it has any meaning at all, then consider how it can be verified'. Once you realize how this can be done, then you will understand what the sentence means.

But if we were tempted to take the dictum 'The meaning of a statement is the method of its verification' as a *definition* of 'meaning', then it would not be difficult to raise various objections against it. I am not going to consider the meaning of imaginary sentences or of rules where it is quite obvious that this equation does not hold. The examples which I have in mind are, for instance: 'It rained yesterday', 'This man died five hours ago', 'Julius Caesar crossed the Alps'. Let us consider the first example. Surely this sentence seems to have a clear meaning straight away. However, if I were asked how it could be verified, I should perhaps in the first moment be at a loss and then make various suggestions: I could ask other persons, or look up the meteorological report of the previous day, I could examine the traces of moisture on the ground, or resort to my own memory. There is a vast number of possibilities which can hardly be exhausted. It is even possible that some discovery might be made by which the time of the last rain could be exactly ascertained. But do I *mean* by the statement the existence of any one of these facts? What I mean is surely that yesterday a definite occurrence took place of which the traces of moisture, etc., are only 'indications'. Now it seems that the meaning of a sentence has nothing whatsoever to do with its verification. One is inclined to say: 'I just do understand the sentence, I understand it because I know the English language'.

It looks now as if it were right to say: 'I can only suggest a method of verification *after* I have understood the meaning'. Usually, when considering such statements of daily life, I do not think of the verification, but could, if necessary, propose this or that procedure. By doing this, however, the meaning is, of course, not changed nor does it become *clearer* to me what I originally meant by the statement. On the contrary: the method of verification is irregular, loose, fluctuating, while the sentence always means the same.

Obviously I know what it means that it is now raining; I also know what the word 'yesterday' means; and now I understand the sentence 'It rained yesterday', and I understand it only because I understand the single words and know the usage of English syntax. This, however, does not mean that I know how the proposition is to be verified. If, subsequently, I learn to know one or the other method of verification, nothing is added to the meaning. What is it that leads me to suggest a particular method of verification? Well, I have learned from experience that rain leaves traces of moisture on the earth, or that the appearance of the plants is changed, etc. I remember such experiences and say that in this manner it can be determined whether it has rained yesterday. In such cases, therefore, to explain the method of verification is *not* to explain the meaning.

Let us take the second example: 'This man died five hours ago'. If I were asked whether I understood this sentence, I would truly answer: Of course I do; otherwise one could object that I do not know English. But if I were asked how I should verify it, I should not know what to say. Suppose it had been discovered how the moment of the death of the man can be precisely found out, say by examining the condition of the blood, I would not say, 'Ah, now at last I understand what the sentence means'. The meaning of the sentence had already been established before that discovery.

If a child does not understand a sentence, then what we explain to him is the meaning of the words, but not the method of its verification. In the normal use of language the questions 'What does this sentence mean?' and 'How do I find out whether this sentence is true?' are two entirely different questions, and everyone will refuse to regard them as alike.

Strange how irregular language is. Sometimes the meaning of a sentence is entirely clear to us while we do not know anything suitable to say about its verification or at least we hesitate between different possibilities. In other cases the meaning of a sentence is obscure to us, and only when the verification is given do we understand what the sentence expresses.

This shows that there are two ways of explaining the meaning of a sentence. One way is to give the meaning of the various words in the sentence and explain the way in which they are combined. The other consists in the description of the verification.

5 THE DESCRIPTION OF VERIFICATION

Let us now consider carefully the expression 'method of verification'. What are we doing when we describe the method of verification? In other words, what sort of an answer can we expect if we ask: how is a statement verified? Let us take an example: supposing that a metal ball is lying in front of me and someone says that it is charged with electricity — how can I verify this statement? I should connect the ball with an electroscope and observe whether the gold leaves diverge. The statement 'The gold leaves of the instrument diverge' describes the verification of the statement 'The ball is charged'. What, then, is it that I do when I describe the verification of the proposition p? I give a second proposition q, and determine that the second is to follow from the first. This is giving a rule of inference which connects these two propositions with each other. This rule is a part of the grammar of the expression p; and it must be determined *before* we can significantly apply the proposition p.

In ordinary language these two cases are not clearly distinguished. The question 'How do you tell whether his statement is true?' is answered now by giving a rule of inference, now by stating an empirical connection. And from this spring most of the confusions that disturb us in the question 'Is the meaning of a sentence the method of its verification?' Length can be measured in this way, or in that way, and we call the result of both measurements the 'length of the line'. Sometimes, however, we use the expression 'The length of a line' in such a way that it corresponds only to the result of one measurement. Then it is necessary for us to call to mind this convention. To make such a convention is, of course, nothing more than a grammatical procedure, and to give the method of verification is to give this rule.

Another example would be the question: under what conditions do we say that a human being is dead? Supposing we give the following explanation: a person is dead when his heart has stopped beating. Scarcely anyone would protest against such a definition. But if it were discovered that, given certain circumstances, human beings move, behave and act exactly as they do normally while their hearts have stopped beating, then the question would arise: shall we still say to them that they are dead?; or should we not rather speak of different meanings of the word 'dead' and distinguish between, say, 'heart-dead' and 'dead' in some other way? If now someone were to say that a person is dead, then we should ask him: 'What do you mean by "dead"? Heart-dead or dead in the other sense?' This question is a question as to the verification of the sentence, and the answer is a contribution to its grammar.

But there are cases where the situation is entirely different. Remember the example 'It rained yesterday', where the meaning is clear to start with and where there is a vast number of methods of verification. We are now in a position to explain the problem which has been troubling us in this chapter: how is it that sometimes the meaning of a sentence is absolutely certain while the method of verification is loose and variable — while in other cases the blurred meaning becomes clear and definite only when the method of verification is given. We must be aware of the fact that until now we have used the expression 'method of verification' in two entirely different senses. One could formulate the difference thus: when I say 'If it rained yesterday, the earth is moist today', then this is not a rule of inference, but an empirical statement. Empirical statements of this kind help us to find out the truth of the assertion, but they do not determine its meaning. The meaning was already established before a method of checking was even mentioned. Therefore the method of testing conforms to the meaning. On the other hand, when I say 'If the ball is charged, the leaves of the electroscope diverge' I am giving a rule of inference which explains the meaning of the first sentence. The meaning of the sentence is now dependent upon the method of verification. If I specify other rules for the expression, then I thereby change its meaning.

To give the method of verification is therefore only *one* aspect of the explanation of the meaning of the sentence. Another is, for example, the explanation of a word through demonstrative definition; another, to produce a drawing. The statement which expresses the method of verification of a proposition in the one sense is certainly a grammatical explanation and can explain the meaning of the sentence to us. We would not, however, call every explanation of the meaning an explanation of the verification, and thus the dictum: 'The meaning of a sentence is the method of its verification' is decidedly misleading.

It is always an exceedingly useful way in learning to understand the meaning of a sentence to transform the question as to the meaning into the question as to the verification. This is analogous to the way in which, in order to find out the subject of a sentence, a child asks: 'What is doing this?' The question as to the verification has a similar function. Therefore we could say: 'the answer to the question as to the verification of a proposition is given in a certain grammatical transformation of this proposition − a transformation determined by this question'.

Nothing else is to be expected. For if the answer to the question about the verification consists in an explanation of the meaning, then the question as to the meaning can have no other answer than the statement itself, even if in a different form. If we write down the entire explanation of the meaning of a statement, this must yield the proposition and no more; this implies again that a rule added to a proposition yields the proposition. For − what purpose does the sentence serve? Strictly speaking, it is an abbreviation: it stands for all that is, as it were, spread out before us in the explanation of its verification. As long as we merely consider sentences of daily life we understand their meaning without considering their verification. We understand it, because we are familiar with the language in which these sentences function. In science and philosophy, on the other hand, we are using words of daily life in a new context. Remember the questions: 'Is all memory fallible?', 'Have two people the same experience when they look at a green surface?' In these cases we are extending the normal use of language and we must try to become clear about the meaning of the familiar words in these new contexts, and this can be done by describing the method of verification.

2 The Principle of Verifiability

A. J. Ayer

In an article entitled 'Metaphysics and Meaning', which appeared in *Mind* in October, 1935, Prof. W. T. Stace attacked the verificational theory of meaning which I, in common with other logical positivists, had made a ground for the rejection of metaphysics. He argued that the principle of verifiability proved too much; that its use as a criterion of meaning led not merely to the elimination of metaphysics, but also

Source: Mind, 1936, pp. 199-203.

to the elimination of all statements about the past, and that this was a fatal objection to it. He objected to it also on the ground that it ruled out significant questions concerning the experiences of other minds, and that it condemned as meaningless any objective theory of value. He himself put forward a criterion of meaning which he held to be free from these defects, and also to be less destructive to metaphysics than the principle of verifiability. For, while it led him to dismiss Kant's doctrine of the 'thing-in-itself' as meaningless, it allowed him to find meaning in Bradley's theory of the Absolute. I shall discuss Prof. Stace's theory briefly at the end of this paper. My main purpose is to defend my own criterion of meaning against his criticisms.

The first point that I must make clear is that I do not hold that a sentence can be factually significant only if it expresses what is conclusively verifiable; for I maintain that no empirical propositions are conclusively verifiable. All that I require of a putative statement of fact is that it should be verifiable in what I have called the 'weak' sense of the term; that some possible observations should be relevant to the determination of its truth or falsehood. As I have shown elsewhere,[1] this principle can be given a more formal expression. 'Let us call a proposition which records an actual or possible observation an experiential proposition. Then we may say that it is the mark of a genuine factual proposition, not that it should be equivalent to an experiential proposition, but simply that some experiential propositions can be deduced from it in conjunction with certain other premises without being deducible from those other premises alone.'

It can be seen that this criterion denies meaning to metaphysical statements such as those which deny the reality of the sensible world or assert the existence of things-in-themselves. Does it also deny meaning to all propositions about the past? Surely not. Let us consider Prof. Stace's own example, 'I ate bacon and eggs for breakfast this morning'. This would be a meaningless statement, according to my criterion, only if there were no experiences I could conceivably have which would have any bearing on its truth or falsehood. Surely Prof. Stace would not maintain this. Surely he would not say that the evidence of my own memory, my wife's memory, the words written in my diary, the diminution of the household store of eggs, was altogether irrelevant. The experiential proposition 'I am now hearing the words "bacon and eggs" ' does not follow from the proposition 'I am now hearing my wife

---

[1] *Language, Truth and Logic*, p. 26. (Penguin ed., p. 52.)

utter the words which most English people would use to describe what I had for breakfast this morning; and "bacon and eggs" are the words which most English people would use to describe bacon and eggs' by itself, but it does not follow from that proposition in conjunction with the proposition 'I ate bacon and eggs for breakfast this morning'. Accordingly, it appears that the proposition 'I ate bacon and eggs for breakfast this morning' is not unverifiable, in the sense in which I am using the term, and that I am not committed to the absurd view, attributed to me by Prof. Stace, that all propositions about the past are meaningless.

Prof. Stace may reply that I have avoided this absurdity only by resorting to the error of equating the proposition 'I ate bacon and eggs for breakfast this morning' with the proposition 'My wife tells me that I ate bacon and eggs for breakfast this morning', just as he accuses Prof. Lewis of equating the proposition 'Brutus killed Caesar' with the proposition 'It is stated in a book that Brutus killed Caesar', and points out quite correctly that these two propositions cannot be equivalent, since the latter could be true even though the former was false. But this objection would hold good against me only if I were maintaining that my wife's telling me that I ate bacon and eggs for breakfast this morning was both a conclusive, and the only possible, verification of the proposition that I ate bacon and eggs for breakfast this morning. And I do not maintain this. I do not say that I can ever verify such a proposition conclusively, or even that the number of experiences which would go to verify it is finite. All I am saying is that I can have experiences, such as that furnished by my wife's information, which have some bearing on its validity, either as substantiating or as discrediting it. And this is all that the principle of verifiability, as I interpret it, requires.

In discussing the experiences of other minds, Prof. Stace does not do justice to the logical positivists. He is wrong in thinking that we should deny all meaning to the statement that one man's sensations were qualitatively the same as another's. We should, in fact, analyse it in terms of the observable behaviour of the people in question. 'We define the qualitative identity and difference of two people's sense-experiences in terms of the similarity and dissimilarity of their reactions to empirical tests. To determine, for instance, whether two people have the same colour sense we observe whether they classify all the colour expanses with which they are confronted in the same way; and when we say that a man is colourblind, what we are asserting is that he classifies certain colour expanses in a different way from that in which they would be classified by the majority of people.'[2] Prof. Stace himself appears to favour an analysis of this kind. At least, this is the conclusion which I drew from the passage in his article where he argues that 'concepts *are* structure'.[3]

I think it is misleading to say, as Prof. Stace does, that the principle of verifiability rules out all objective theories of value. For I think that utilitarian theories, with which the principle is plainly compatible, may reasonably be called objective. But I admit that it does rule out the intrinsic theory which he mentions; that is, the theory that goodness is a non-natural quality. I do not admit, however, that he has succeeded in showing that this is an error. He says that logical positivists, in condemning this theory of value as nonsensical, are assuming that the only possible kind of experience is sensuous, and that this is a dogmatic and uncritical assumption, for which we have failed to provide any evidence. But we do not make this assumption. A logical positivist would not say that it was inconceivable that anyone should have an experience which Prof. Stace might reasonably describe as non-sensuous. He would not deny even that people might conceivably have experiences which Prof. Stace would describe as non-sensuous experiences of value. But he would ask Prof. Stace whether the occurrence of such experiences constituted the only possible verification of the statement that goodness was a non-natural quality. If the answer was that it did, he would conclude that the statement that goodness was a non-natural quality, as Prof. Stace interpreted it, meant no more than that people did have what might be described as non-sensuous value experiences; and he would allow that, thus interpreted, the statement was significant. But this is not the interpretation which those who hold the view in question normally put upon it. They would say that the proposition that people had value experiences was not even part of what they meant to assert when they said that goodness was a non-natural objective quality. But if they do not mean this, and cannot indicate to us how we could verify what they do mean, we are surely justified in holding that they have not provided us with any significant information at all.

The same considerations govern our treatment of mysticism. We do not, as Prof. Stace supposes, hold that 'the claim to mystical experience is as such meaningless'. We do not even deny that an experience, which would reasonably be described as mystical, may be genuinely cognitive.

---

[2] *Language, Truth and Logic*, p. 206. (Penguin ed. pp. 173-4.)

[3] *Mind*, October, 1935, pp. 433-435.

We do however insist that we can have no ground for supposing that the mystic's experience is cognitive, unless we have reason to believe that its 'object' could be described in propositions for which we could conceivably obtain some empirical evidence. The statement that my friend is experiencing the Absolute is significant to me if I am allowed to understand it as a description of his state of mind. If, as the result of having this mystical experience, my friend assures me that only the Absolute is wholly real, I am unable either to agree or to disagree, because I do not understand him. Accordingly, I try to elucidate his utterance. I ask him whether he means it to be a definition or a statement of fact, that is to say, whether the proposition his sentence is intended to express is analytic or synthetic. If he says that he is making a statement of fact I ask him how its truth or falsehood may be empirically determined. For until I know this I cannot understand him. If he replies that my question is unanswerable, inasmuch as his statement is not of the kind which is subject to the test of experience, then and then only do I conclude that he has been employing signs to which, even in his own usage, no meaning is attached.

Prof. Stace argues that 'metaphysical propositions are not necessarily, and as such, meaningless' on the ground that 'the assertion of a reality which lies behind our experience, and which can never be experienced *by us*, may be meaningful provided it is conceived as the possible experience of some other mind which shares structure with our own'.[4] I allow that it is significant to say that there may be people who have experiences which we do not have. But this does not imply, as Prof. Stace thinks, that metaphysical utterances may be significant. For it does not follow from the fact that it can intelligibly be said that other people have experiences which we do not have that anything which purports to be a description of these experiences will be intelligible to us. It will be so only if it is susceptible of verification in our experience. And this metaphysical utterances are not.

I hope I have said enough to show that the acceptance of the principle of verifiability, in the 'weakened' form which I have given it, does not inevitably land the logical positivist in a 'quagmire of absurdities'. I now hold the principle, not as an empirical hypothesis, but as a definition. I should say that to speak of a completely unverifiable statement of fact was to be guilty of a contradiction in terms. The way to refute me is to produce an example of an unverifiable statement which I

---

[4] *Mind*, October, 1935, p. 436.

cannot without obvious dishonesty deny to be a genuine statement of fact. This is the course which Prof. Stace has actually pursued; but I have endeavoured to show that his instances are not sufficient to overthrow my principle.

With regard to Prof. Stace's own criterion of meaning, I agree with Mr. Sidgwick[5] that it is defective because it is stated only in terms of concepts. Prof. Stace suggests that a statement can be said to have meaning if and only if every concept employed in it has empirical application.[6] It is not difficult to find an instance to show that this will not do. The concepts of 'density', 'death' and 'fatherhood' all have empirical application, but I hope Prof. Stace will agree that the sentence 'density death fatherhood' does not express a significant proposition. For a sentence to have a meaning it is not sufficient, as Prof. Stace appears to hold, that each of the words comprising it should have a meaning. It is necessary also that they should be combined in a significant way.

Finally, I think it should be said that Prof. Stace has over-emphasized the destructive element in logical positivism. We do not maintain that philosophy should 'entirely shut up shop'. For, when metaphysics is eliminated, analysis remains. And we claim that our conception of philosophizing as an activity of analysis accords at any rate with the general practice of the majority of the great philosophers of the past.

---

[5] Writing on "Verifiability and Meaning" in *Mind*, January, 1936, *vide* pp. 65-66.
[6] *Mind*, October, 1935, p. 426.

3 Vindication of L*G*C*L P*S*T*V*SM

David Rynin

... It has been alleged that he who defends himself accuses himself, and I am a little troubled lest it be also thought that one who seeks to vindicate a doctrine thereby condemns it. Since I do not wish to bring any doctrine into unjustified disrepute, I refrain from naming the position I wish to defend and leave my title in obscurity. However, it is

---

Source: Proceedings and Addresses of the American Philosophical Association, 1957, pp. 46-66 (with revisions by the author).

not from this motive alone that I offer it to you in its present form. The porosity reveals the gaps, alas!, that will be found in my vindication. But more than this, it indicates that I am not altogether certain that the position I wish to defend corresponds at all closely to any existing named viewpoint. Hence I refrain from identifying it under a familiar label also because it will probably turn out that it is in many respects in radical opposition to views that careful students of my title might justifiably assume to be more or less identical with it.

For I must confess that it does have some superficial resemblance to certain other doctrines which, like it, take as central a notion of meaning associated with the concept of truth and (dare I admit it?) verifiability. There! subterfuge will serve no longer and the truth is out! I intend to offer a defence of a kind of verifiability principle of meaning and a vindication of the philosophical position that is based upon it. Whether this will make me a logical positivist I really wouldn't know, and must admit that I care even less. That it will make me a knave or something very close to one will be the opinion of those who suppose that it commits me to the view that the most important questions, the questions of value, are pseudo-questions, and that anything called 'metaphysics' is by that very fact nonsensical; and that it will make me out a fool will be the opinion of those very able thinkers who deem the verifiability principle to be, in the language of a distinguished logician, 'nonsense and the root of much nonsense', or of those who somewhat more politely hold that it simply will not do, in view of the many demonstrable shortcomings it has been shown to possess.

That it may indeed have certain shortcomings is very likely, and if true this will be regrettable; but in this life we often have to make do with doctrines which fall somewhat short of being perfect; — many a man goes to his grave never having reached perfection in deed or doctrine. One does not, however, abandon a position because it is not without flaw, but only because one knows of a better one. I shall be content, then, if I can show good reasons for holding to this view of meaning; and if I can show that most of the 'sins' of the way of philosophizing which rests upon it are largely the products of a certain obtuseness which, surprisingly enough, characterizes some of our sharpest wits. It is certainly unlikely that I shall succeed in this enterprise, but with your forbearance I should like to try. Who knows?, I may find I have a leg to stand on, or possibly even two.

Like practically every other philosophic doctrine, the verifiability principle comes in a variety of formulations; at least this is a legitimate inference from the rather different kinds of statements, analyses and criticisms of it occurring in the literature. And it would be surprising if some of them at least were not vulnerable to legitimate and serious objections. I shall not assume, therefore, that even an exhaustive analysis of the various versions would reveal some common core immune to even most attacks, although this is certainly possible. I shall rather content myself with formulating, more or less briefly, a version which seems to me to be fully consistent with the spirit of the principle and relatively free of most of the allegedly objectionable features made prominent in familiar animadversions against the position.

First: As I understand and wish to defend the principle, it is not a theory, despite the fact that most of its critics call it one, even in the face of repeated insistence by many of its chief defenders that they do not think of it as such. Of course, this may be a verbal difference; those who insist on calling it a theory, meaning by 'theory' perhaps precisely what others may mean when they call it a proposal, a heuristic principle, a definition, or stipulation. It is not a theory because it is not offered as either true or false, and *a fortiori* not as a *hypothesis* about either usage or certain properties of certain linguistic expressions. I am confident that an examination of most relevant texts would support this view of how the principle has been understood by its proponents, but even if I should be mistaken in this opinion, the version *I* propose to defend is not a theory in the sense mentioned. What some have considered a devastating criticism of the principle, that its application to itself shows it to be meaningless, because unverifiable, seems to me therefore to be an obvious confusion. One may quarrel over the utility of definitions, but it hardly makes sense to discuss their truth or falsity, or to classify as meaningless a sentence[1] that is not intended as a statement at all, and is explicitly denied this status by those who utter it. It makes no sense to discuss the truth or falsity of a definition, that is, if it be intended not as what may be called a 'real definition', one that presupposes assigned meanings and then asserts an empirically ascertained synonymity relationship between two or more expressions, but as a kind of explication, one that reflects a reasoned decision regarding proposed usage, but is not an assertion about existing usage. I hope I may be excused for flogging this dead horse; but what is one to do

---

[1] Here and elsewhere in the text 'sentence' represents 'declarative sentence', while 'statement' represents 'sentence governed by truth rules, specifying ascertainable truth conditions'. Thus not all sentences are statements, but all statements are sentences.

when men who should know better insist on treating it as if it were alive and in good health?

By 'explication' I understand the same as what I believe is intended by Carl Hempel when, in his *Fundamentals of Concept Formation in Empirical Science*, he says (pp. 11 ff.):

'Explication is concerned with expressions whose meaning in conversational language or even in scientific discourse is more or less vague ... and aims at giving those expressions a new and precisely determined meaning, so as to render them more suitable for clear and rigorous discourse on the subject matter at hand.' 'An explication sentence does not simply exhibit the commonly accepted meaning of the expression under study but rather proposes a specified new and precise meaning.' 'Explications, having the nature of proposals, cannot be qualified as being either true or false. Yet they are by no means a matter of arbitrary convention, for they have to satisfy two major requirements: First, the explicative reinterpretation of a term, or – as is often the case – of a set of related terms, must permit us to reformulate, in sentences of a syntactically precise form, at least a large part of what is customarily expressed by means of the terms under consideration. Second, it should be possible to develop, in terms of the reconstructed concepts, a comprehensive, rigorous, and sound theoretical system.' 'Taking its departure from the customary meanings of the terms, explication aims at reducing the limitations, ambiguities, and inconsistencies of their ordinary usage by propounding a reinterpretation intended to enhance the clarity and precision of their meanings as well as their ability to function in hypotheses and theories with explanatory predictive force. Thus understood, an explication cannot be qualified simply as true or false; but it may be adjudged more or less adequate according to the extent to which it attains its objectives.'

I claim that the verifiability principle, as I shall formulate and defend it, satisfies to a high degree both of Hempel's requirements; for it permits us to reformulate in sentences of syntactically precise form a large part of what is customarily expressed by the several concepts of cognitive meaning, and makes possible the development of a comprehensive, rigorous and, I think sound, theoretical system of semantics. I cannot deny that it is a slight source of embarrassment to me at this point to have to acknowledge that Hempel himself has given up as hopeless the task of saving the verifiability principle; but I shall attempt later in this paper to show why I think that he is mistaken in at least most of his criticisms of the view.

Since I do not view the principle as a hypothesis about meaning, but rather as a kind of well-justified proposal, I do not, of course, wish to argue that other conceptions of meaning different from it are mistaken. Especially I do not wish to argue that the verifiability principle taken by itself suffices to give an adequate account of all the dimensions of meaning that custom or ingenuity can conjure up. I take for granted, that is, (what all its defenders have stated more than sufficiently) that it is meant to apply only to what is sometimes called 'cognitive meaning'. A sensible defender of the verifiability principle may, and indeed must, therefore recognize that there is a great deal more to a general account of meaning, even when this is restricted to linguistic expressions, than can be directly accounted for by means of the verifiability principle. I say 'directly accounted for', because I consider it as one of the merits of the verifiability principle that it can give us invaluable assistance in constructing such a system of interrelated concepts enabling us to talk intelligently about meaning in its several forms and categories.

I hope it will be understood, therefore, that in defending the verifiability principle, I do not wish to be thought of as necessarily disparaging other ways of talking about even cognitive meaning. It is a source of genuine pleasure to me to know that there are other ways to talk about it, and I do not in the least rule out the possibility that some other way may prove at least as useful as the one I wish to defend. I shall be content to show, if I can, that it is not beneath serious consideration, at least when limited to its proper domain.

This phrase, 'cognitive meaning', which is often used in this connection is perhaps not altogether clear, but it is clear that when one speaks of cognitive meaning one has in mind a sense of 'meaning' peculiarly concerned with knowledge, and hence with statements. For some writers seem to identify knowledge with true statements, or at least speak as if knowledge or cognition is to be understood as expressed only in terms of them, while others define 'knowledge' or 'to know' in such a manner that at least a necessary condition for someone to know something, is that some certain statement be true.

Now I take it as evident that if some statement P is to be true, this will be because and only because certain conditions exist that are sufficient to establish it as true, and that if it is false this is because and only because certain conditions necessary for its truth happen not to exist. The *existence* of what may be called 'a sufficient truth condition' for a statement thus necessitates the truth of the statement, and the non-existence of what may be called 'a necessary truth condition' of the statement necessitates its falsity. If we do not know what would qualify as at least one sufficient truth condition for a statement, we could never ascertain that the statement in question is true, and if we did not know what would constitute at least one necessary truth condition for a statement we should be unable to ascertain that it is false. In short, in the sense intended here, for a statement to be true there must be conditions under which it would be true, and for a statement to be false there must be conditions under which it would be false.

I believe it to be the general insight motivating the proponents of the verifiability principle that the concepts of cognitive meaning are intimately connected with these facts. From the point of view of cognition or knowledge, our interest in the meaning or meaningfulness of statements derives from our need to determine what their conditions of truth and/or falsity are; for only if this be known to us can we possibly hope to determine the truth of statements, the truth which if not identical with cognition is at least an essential element in it. There may be those who believe, or think they believe, or who tell us they believe that knowledge is impossible and truth unascertainable. I do not wish to enter into any debates with them at the present time, if only because I am in very great doubt as to whether I understand them; I address myself to those others who are able to go along with what I have said as more or less intelligible and germane to the problem of cognitive meaning.[2]

It is common enough in answer to the question 'What do you mean by sentence P,' to say 'I mean by P that Q and R,'[3] where Q and R are statements purporting to assert some matter of fact. Thus in answer to the question, 'What do you mean by "a is a nephew of b"?' one would not be in error or misusing common speech to answer, 'By "a is a nephew of b" I mean that a is a male and that b is a brother or sister of one of a's parents.' This fact would seem to show that a specification of what we mean by a statement is not wholly unconnected with its truth conditions. In fact in this example we explain *what* we mean, what may be called *the meaning* of the statement, precisely by specifying the condition that is both necessary and sufficient for its truth.

---

[2] Henceforth the terms 'meaning', 'meaningful' and 'meaningless' are to be understood as preceded by 'cognitive' or 'cognitively' as the case may require, unless otherwise indicated.

[3] In this formula, slanted capital letters are to be understood as sentence-name variables; and upright capitals as sentence variables.

Similarly, it would not be a far-fetched departure from common usage to argue that it is a sufficient condition for a sentence to be meaningful, that it be true, and likewise sufficient provided it be false. Indeed this might constitute a kind of axiom of semantics, or at any rate some sort of adequacy requirement for a definition of 'meaningful sentence'; I at least should consider it as self-evident that for a sentence to be cognitively meaningful it must be possible for it to be true or false, that it have conditions of truth or falsity, hence necessary or sufficient truth conditions. And I take it as obvious that those who put forward their several versions of the principle were in fact attempting to formulate a concept that was meant to express this fact. Most of the difficulties, indeed, that have been found in the several versions seem to me to stem from the fact that their authors were at one and the same time attempting, probably without being fully aware of it, to express two different but closely related concepts: (1) the concept of cognitive meaningfulness and (2) the concept of cognitive meaning.

These two concepts are similar enough to lead one to think them identical and to attempt in one formula to express what requires in fact two separate and distinct formulas. In terms of the axiom mentioned above, a declarative sentence to be meaningful must have either a necessary or a sufficient truth condition, otherwise it would not have the property of being possibly true or false; but it need not have necessary *and* sufficient truth conditions for it to have at least one of either. On the other hand, when we attempt to explain *what* we mean by a statement, i.e. *the meaning* of the statement, we find that we cannot do so to our satisfaction unless we are able to specify a condition that is at once *both* necessary *and* sufficient for its truth, which is something else again.

According to this way of looking at the matter, while it is necessary in order to specify the meaning of a statement to specify a sufficient truth condition for it, it is certainly not sufficient; and likewise, while it is necessary in order to specify the meaning of a statement that at least a necessary truth condition for it be specified, it is also certainly not sufficient. But it is sufficient for a sentence to be meaningful if either a necessary or a sufficient truth condition is specified for it (in terms at least of the above mentioned axiom). Hence it does not follow from the fact that we have shown that a sentence is meaningful that we have specified its meaning, i.e. what it means. And we cannot deduce from the fact that we know *that* a sentence is meaningful that we know *what* it means. Indeed, that it is meaningful does not entail that there is something which is its meaning. But it should not be inferred from this that we can not ever specify the meaning: normally we have little difficulty in making clear to ourselves and others the condition both necessary and sufficient for the truth of a sentence, as we understand it.

The importance of this distinction between the meaningfulness of a sentence and its meaning, which I believe is generally and unfortunately ignored in discussions of meaning, can perhaps be brought out by examining some of the versions of the verifiability principle to be found in the literature. Moritz Schlick for example in one of his better known passages on this topic says: 'Stating the meaning of a sentence amounts to stating the rules according to which the sentence is to be used, and this is the same as stating the way in which it can be verified (or falsified)—.'[4] Now it seems to me that the confusion I mentioned earlier may be exhibited in this passage. I understand 'verified' and 'falsified' here in such a way that a sentence can be verified by and only by ascertaining the occurrence of a sufficient truth condition for it, and can be falsified by and only by ascertaining the non-occurrence of a necessary truth condition for it. In order to establish that it can be verified or falsified and hence is meaningful, it is sufficient to show that one of these can be done, but this is not enough to establish its meaning. For example, it is sufficient to verify 'This object has one of the rainbow colours' to ascertain that it is green, but no one supposes that the meaning is given in the truth rule: This object is green → 'This object has one of the rainbow colours' is true. Nor is the meaning of 'This person is a father' given in the truth rule: 'This person is a father' is true only if this person is a male, — although the truth rule tells us how to determine its falsity. It is in, fact, evident that stating the meaning of a sentence is to state the necessary *and* sufficient truth conditions for it. But it *is* sufficient to establish its meaningfulness, to state some way in which it can be verified or falsified, for if either can be done then the sentence can be true or false, and hence meaningful.

I do not wish to give the impression that I think Schlick never gave a more satisfactory formulation of the principle. For example he says elsewhere:[5]

---

[4] 'Meaning and Verification' para. 9, in Moritz Schlick, *Philosophical Papers,* vol II, ed. H. L. Mulder and B. van de Velde–Schlick; also: *The Philosophical Review,* vol. 44, 1936.

[5] 'Positivismus und Realismus', *Erkenntnis,* vol. 3, p. 6; also (in English translation) in *Philosophical Papers,* vol II. (Reprinted as item C1 below.)

'It is ... impossible to give the meaning of an assertion except by describing the state of affairs that must exist if the statement is to be true.' Assuming that he means by 'the state of affairs that must exist if the statement is to be true' that totality of necessary truth conditions which together constitute a sufficient truth condition for a statement, his formulation will be quite in order so far as I am concerned, except perhaps for the use of the term 'impossible'. — Not that this need be as dogmatic as it sounds, for of course it presupposes a sense of the terms involved according to which the assertion is analytic.

I shall now in a quite informal manner try to tie in the concept of Verifiability with that of truth conditions in such a way as to indicate the sense in which I am prepared to defend the Verifiability principle (which I capitalize in order to distinguish it from other versions):

(1) a sentence is verifiable (with a small v) $\leftrightarrow$ the sentence has at lease one ascertainable sufficient truth condition (stc);

(2) a sentence is falsifiable $\leftrightarrow$ the sentence has at least one ascertainable necessary truth condition (ntc);

(3) a sentence is Verifiable (with a large V) $\leftrightarrow$ the sentence is either verifiable or falsifiable (i.e. has either at least 1 ntc or 1 stc);

(4) a sentence is meaningful $\leftrightarrow$ the sentence is Verifiable (with a large V);

(5) the meaning of a sentence is the condition (if any) both necessary and sufficient for the truth of the sentence;[6]

(6) two sentences are synonymous (have the same meaning) $\leftrightarrow$ they have the same necessary and sufficient truth condition.

It is to be understood that, in the above, ascertainable truth conditions are facts or states of affairs, not linguistic entities. Without attempting at this time to formulate in anything like a precise and adequate formal manner the concept of necessary or of sufficient truth condition, I shall simply lay it down that a sufficient truth condition for a sentence is a state of affairs that entails the truth of that sentence, and that a necessary truth condition for a sentence is a state of affairs whose non-existence entails the falsity of that sentence. Hence it

---

[6] This formulation does not commit one to any reification of meanings. Rather, it is to be understood as asserting that to *specify* the meaning (if any) of a sentence is to *specify* the condition (if any) whose existence would be both necessary and sufficient for its truth. This can sometimes be done, without any commitment as to the ontological status of meanings, possible facts, platonic entities and the like. Not does it commit one to holding that 'What is meaning?' is an intelligible interrogative.

should be noted that I understand by 'entailment' a relation stronger than that of necessary or strict implication, at least in this respect, that states of affairs that stand in entailment relations to sentences being true may not be necessary or impossible, if by chance these notions make any sense predicated of states of affairs, or facts.

I shall now attempt to see how this version of the Verifiability principle fares when confronted with some of the better known objections to the principle. Since Carl Hempel has marshalled the more important objections to the position in his article: 'Problems and Changes in the Empiricist Criterion of Meaning'[7] (*Revenue Internationale de Philosophie*, No. 11, Jan. 15, 1950) I shall examine the principle in the light of the objections he presents there, which for him are sufficient to require its abandonment.

Hempel is concerned only with what he calls a criterion of 'empirical meaning' and hence restricts his considerations to sentences that are not analytic. Furthermore, instead of talking of truth conditions he prefers to formulate the verifiability principle in terms of relationships holding between the sentences whose meaning is in question and what he calls "observation sentences," which I think it fair to treat as true sentences affirming the occurrence of ascertainable states of affairs. – This difference in manner of formulation seems to me to be non-essential.

He first attacks what he calls 'the requirement of complete verifiability,' which he describes as follows: 'A sentence has empirical meaning if and only if it is not analytic and follows logically from some finite and logically consistent class of observation sentences.' And he observes that it has several defects: (a) it rules out all sentences of universal form, and thus all statements purporting to express general laws; (b) it rules out such sentences as 'For any substances there exists some solvent,' which contain both existential and universal quantifiers, for no sentence of this kind can be deduced from any finite set of observation sentences; (c) it makes meaningful all sentences of the disjunctive form, S v N, one of whose disjuncts is a consequence of some finite class of observation sentences and the other any sentence whatever, say, 'The absolute is perfect', – according to Hempel the empiricist criterion of meaning is not intended to countenance sentences of this sort; (d) it has the consequence that an existential sentence of the form:

---

[7] Also available in A. J. Ayer (ed.) *Logical Positivism*. A revised version appears in Hempel's *Aspects of Scientific Explanation*, section 4.

'There exists at least one thing that has the property P' which, P being an observation predicate, is completely verifiable, has as its negation the meaningless sentence: 'Nothing has the property P', for this is not completely verifiable, not following from any finite class of observation sentences.

With respect to the Verifiability principle I am attempting to defend, according to which a sentence is meaningful if verifiable or falsifiable, we may at once eliminate Hempel's objections (a) and (d) as listed above; for universal sentences while not verifiable in the sense of having ascertainable sufficient truth conditions (i.e. are not deducible from any finite set of observation sentences in Hempel's language) are certainly falsifiable, and hence meaningful.

With respect to objection (c) that, say, 'There are some people in this room or the absolute is perfect' is, according to the principle, meaningful, a more careful analysis is called for. Hempel's position is apparently that either we must abandon the familiar truth rule for disjunction or the principle that a sentence is meaningful if completely verifiable. For if we accept the usual truth rule for disjunctions, this disjunction is completely verifiable and hence meaningful according to the principle. But he considers this absurd. Since he obviously is unwilling to abandon the truth rule, he considers it a serious flaw in the verifiability principle which, as he interprets it, has this consequence, and for this reason holds it to be unsatisfactory.

Now let us accept the truth rule for disjunctions. Accordingly, the sentence Hempel finds so unacceptable is completely verifiable in terms of his own analysis, and in fact it will be true if 'There are some people in this room' is true. But if true, then surely it must be meaningful. Hence it is Hempel's turn to make a decision: Either he denies that the questionable disjunction is true by virtue of having the obviously meaningful and true disjunct, i.e. he abandons the logical principle in question or he abandons the position that a sentence if true is *a fortiori* meaningful. I assume he is not prepared to abandon the view that a sentence if true is meaningful, hence *he* must abandon the truth rule for disjunctions or admit that the disjunction is meaningful. As he is not prepared to abandon the logical principle, I take it that he must accept the sentence as meaningful, despite his criticism.

In his discussion regarding disjunctions of the type in question he simply asserts that '. . . clearly, the empiricist criterion of meaning is not intended to countenance sentences of this sort'. Now it is by no means clear to me what the empiricist criterion of meaning is intended to countenance, or even what exactly the criterion is supposed to be that it presumes to countenance or not countenance. If the empiricist or any other criterion of meaning knows its business it would do well to countenance the meaningfulness of true sentences; if not I, and I suppose everyone interested in a criterion of meaningfulness, will willingly part company with it. But, however that may be, the Verifiability principle I am attempting to defend has no objections to such a disjunction *if it is indeed the case* that it is true, or at least that its truth does follow from that of the disjunct which is an observational sentence in good standing.

It may be worth taking a little more time to look into the question of the meaningfulness of such sentences as "The absolute is perfect." Hempel and many others who seem to speak in the name of an empiricist criterion of meaning take it for granted that "The absolute is perfect" is somehow in and of itself empirically meaningless. But surely no sentence is in and of itself meaningless or meaningful. It *becomes* meaninfgul for some one just in so far as that someone attaches to it a truth rule, laying down either necessary or sufficient truth conditions for it; and it lacks meaning for that person, but not necessarily for all others, just to the extent that he has not in some way supplied truth rules, i.e. specified truth conditions for it. Now I must confess that I for one have not done so and am not especially interested in doing so, because the term 'absolute' seems to me to be useful for purposes of communication. But I have read enough of a certain, by now rather dated, kind of literature to have come across the word, and in those contexts it often seems to stand for the universe as a whole. Some use it instead of 'God,' a term which I also do not find cropping up in my speech, except under rather irritating circumstances. But I am aware that these play a role in some kinds of discourse, and I even recognize the appropriateness of predicating perfection of what I suppose is intended to be designated by the terms. In short, if God not only can be but, in a very ancient and respectable tradition, *must* be perfect, I cannot see why the absolute should not likewise be perfect, whatever be meant by 'perfect', or 'the absolute'.

I do not wish to minimize the vagueness of these terms, but I trust that the issue is not one of vagueness or ambiguity, but of meaninglessness. It happens that I am very unclear about what, if anything, the term 'anti-matter' refers to in the language of the most recent speculation physics, but then I am not a nuclear physicist. I suppose that the physicist would be able to throw at least a little light on how he uses this term, if I were prepared to undergo the necessary training and indoctrination; and there are no *a priori* grounds for supposing that I might not likewise come to a fairly clear understanding of what, if anything, some metaphysician understands by 'The absolute is perfect', in terms of truth conditions. Of course, he might fail utterly to make his meaning clear, but it must be said that, with the kind of mind I have, so might the nuclear physicist. But why should I pretend that it is his fault? Must an empiricist be so conceited as to suppose that what he does not understand no one may? — This really has nothing to do with empiricism in any sense of the term in which it is desirable to be an empiricist.

But let us suppose, what we certainly can never establish, that no one knows what he means by 'The absolute is perfect', that the sentence is in some absolute sense meaningless for everyone and for all time, — what then? Can we agree with Hempel (and others equally dominated by certain mistaken notions of the authority of logic) that logic demands that any disjunction of which this putatively meaningless sentence is a disjunct is meaningful according to the Verifiability principle, provided that it contains at least one meaningful disjunct? I think not. No one supposes that 'There are some people in this room or please pass the spaghetti' is completely verifiable just because 'There are some people in this room' is. And the reason is clear: the components of a disjunction must all be genuine statements, i.e. sentences possessed of a truth value. If a compound is itself not possessed of a truth value, its truth cannot follow from anything; and clearly the above hybrid is not a statement at all, although it contains a statement component. Similarly, the expression 'There are some people in this room or all blaps are draps' does not become a disjunction to which the truth rule for disjunctions is applicable simply because it contains a meaningful and furthermore true component. It is simply not the case that this compound is a statement, and *a fortiori* not one that follows logically from its meaningful component. Why then may we assume that logic guarantees that 'There are some people in this room or the absolute is perfect' follows from 'There are some people in this room'? If, indeed, 'the absolute is perfect' is possessed of a truth value, the compound is a genuine disjunction and logic guarantees that it follows from its admittedly meaningful component. But then no one could argue with any plausibility that there is something wrong with the complete verifiability view on the ground that it makes the compound a statement. On the other hand, if 'The absolute is perfect' is not a statement, neither is the disjunction, and hence the truth rule for disjunctions does not apply to what is in fact, under our assumptions, not a compound statement at all. I think, therefore, that what Hempel and others consider to be a devastating argument against the Verifiability principle is demonstrably worthless.

But Hempel, after eliminating to his satisfaction the requirement of complete verifiability in principle, goes on to discuss other versions of the verifiability principle, and we must follow him. He now examines what he calls the 'Requirement of complete falsifiability in principle', which runs as follows: 'A sentence has empirical meaning if and only if its denial is not analytic and follows logically from some finite logically consistent class of observation sentences.' This requirement corresponds in my language to the requirement that to be meaningful a sentence must have associated with it a truth rule for its falsehood, i.e., there must be specifiable for it some necessary truth condition.

Hempel says: 'This criterion qualifies a sentence as empirically meaningful if its denial satisfies the requirement of complete verifiability; as is to be expected, it is therefore inadequate on similar grounds as the latter.' And he lists the difficulties: (a) it rules out purely existential hypotheses and all sentences whose formulation calls for mixed quantifications; (b) if a sentence S is completely falsifiable whereas N is a sentence that is not, then their conjunction S.N is completely falsifiable. Thus the criterion allows empirical significance to many sentences which an adequate empiricist criterion should rule out, such as, say, 'All swans are white and the absolute is perfect'; (c) if 'P' is an observation predicate, then the assertion that all things have the property P is qualified as significant, but its denial being equivalent to a purely existential hypothesis, is disqualified, hence the criterion of complete falsifiability in principle gives rise to the same problems as does the principle of complete verifiability in principle.

As nothing new occurs in these criticisms, I conclude that they are no better than those considered earlier, and the Verifiability criterion, according to which a sentence is meaningful if and only if either verifiable or falsifiable, remains intact — except in so far as it is unable to cope with the problem of mixed quantification.

Hempel next turns his attention to a proposal of Ayer, according to which in Hempel's description of it, 'a sentence S has empirical import if from S in conjunction with suitable subsidiary hypotheses it is possible to derive observation sentences which are not derivable from the subsidiary hypotheses alone.' Hempel states that this criterion is much

too liberal as it stands, which is granted by Ayer, who admits that this
criterion allows empirical import to any sentence whatever (*Language,
Truth and Logic*, 2nd edition, pp. 11-12*). The argument runs as follows:
if S is the sentence 'The absolute is perfect' it suffices to choose as a
subsidiary hypothesis the sentence 'If the absolute is perfect then this
apple is red', in order to make possible the deduction of the observation
sentence 'This apple is red', which clearly does not follow from the
subsidiary hypothesis alone.

Now it is indeed the case that if 'The absolute is perfect' has truth
values it can be conjoined with other such statements in arguments, but
then there will be no objection to 'The absolute is perfect' being meaningful; and if the empiricist criterion of meaning has any objections, so
much the worse for it. On the other hand if, as Hempel seems to take
for granted, we already know that 'The absolute is perfect' is meaningless
(in what sense one wonders?) then what right have we to treat it as a
premise in an argument and attempt to draw conclusions from it alone
or in conjunction with other sentences? It is only by virtue of its truth
values that this sentence can play a role in argument. If it qualifies as a
legitimate premise, hence as a statement, all is in order, but if not, no
one can rightfully draw any conclusions from it together with some
other sentences, since nothing follows from a 'conjunction' containing
a meaningless component.

After some further discussion of related topics, Hempel concludes
as follows:

> I think it useless to continue to search for an adequate criterion . . .
> in terms of deductive relationships to observation sentences. The
> past development of this search . . . seems to warrant the expecta-
> tion that as long as we try to set up a criterion . . . for individual
> sentences in a natural language, in terms of logical relationship to
> observation sentences, the result will be either too restrictive or too
> inclusive, or both. In particular it appears likely that such criteria
> would allow empirical import . . . either to any alternation or to any
> conjunction of two sentences of which at least one is qualified as
> empirically meaningful; and this peculiarity has undesirable con-
> sequences because the liberal grammatical rules of English as of any
> other natural language countenance as sentences certain expressions
> which even by the most liberal empiricist standards make no asser-

---

*Page 15 of Penguin edition—*Ed.* Also see p. 11 above.

tion whatever; and these would then have to be permitted as components of empirically significant statements.

I have indicated, fairly clearly I hope, why none of this impresses me and why I must insist that the Verifiability principle remains unaffected by the kind of argument summarized above.

Hempel next turns to the development of what he calls the Translatability criterion of cognitive meaning, according to which a sentence has cognitive meaning if and only if it is translatable into an empiricist language. I can only wish him well in this difficult enterprise. I shall not follow him into its details, but turn now to the problem of mixed quantification.

Whether all sentences like 'For any substance there exists some solvent' are such that we can specify neither sufficient nor necessary truth conditions for them is questionable. We might lay it down, after the manner of some well known models, that for example, every substance is soluble in itself. But this is perhaps implausible. In the case of the system of integers we might claim that it is not only meaningful but indeed analytically true that for every such number there exists a successor. But this wouldn't help us with 'For any substance there exists some solvent', if this is understood as a contingent statement. We could, of course, specify sufficient conditions for the truth of mixed quantifications if we were to give them a finitistic interpretation. Thus with respect to the statement 'For every person in this room there exists a taller person', we should have no difficulty; but, of course, we must assume that such an interpretation is not always, although sometimes, pertinent. We must grant that we cannot specify either necessary or sufficient truth conditions for every such sentence, and it would seem therefore that we should have to call some of them 'meaningless' in the sense of the Verifiability principle.

This might be slightly disturbing, but it is hopeless to seek the kind of precision we wish for without at some point coming up against rather strange consequences, − at least this appears to be the practically universal experience of all those who embark on the kind of explication we are concerned with. And if we recall that we are concerned with a notion of *cognitive* meaningfulness, it will not seem a catastrophe if we have to eliminate from the class of meaningful sentences those that are admittedly such that we could never hope to determine their truth or falsity. On the other hand, in view of the variety of conceptions of meaning we have already examined, it would seem possible, without abandoning too much, to allow for some slight reformulations, so long as we do not altogether abandon the notion of truth conditions as our basic conception. How then does the matter stand with such mixed quantifications?

Probably most people will feel that there is some kind of weak confirmation of the generalization in the fact that, say, a given substance is soluble in a certain other substance, and greater confirmation each time a solvent is found for a different substance. Just what this notion of confirmation involves is not easy to say, but if we could make it clear we might throw light on some very important and interesting matters. For it is widely held that a criterion of empirical meaningfulness based on the notion of confirmation is in some sense the right one, neither too weak nor too strong. Thus for example Reichenbach argues (*Experience and Prediction*, p. 190) that the verifiability principle must be replaced by one which makes use not of the concept of truth but that of weight, a concept closely connected with that of probability and confirmation.

There are however two senses of 'confirmation', at least, according to which sentences are confirmable if and only if they are Verifiable, and in these senses nothing is gained by resort to the notion of confirmation by way of going beyond the Verifiability principle: (1) We often speak of a hypothesis, say a law, being confirmed when we ascertain that some necessary condition for it is satisfied; and in this case the sentence confirmed is, of course, in our sense Verifiable, having a necessary truth condition. (2) We sometimes speak of a hypothesis being confirmable, when we can assign a probability number to it. In the sense of the frequency theory of probability this will be possible only when we can, at least in theory, verify the statement. If we can determine that the probability that something having the property A has the property B is m/n, this is possible only on the basis of our being able to determine that some things have the property A and some things have the property B. The determination that a certain proportion of A's and B's would be impossible in the frequency sense of probability if we could not ascertain sufficient truth conditions for something being an A and something being a B.

Likewise, the or at least *a* sense of probability according to which it is based on a logical relationship presupposes that the sentences standing in probability relationships have truth conditions, hence be Verifiable in our sense. Carnap's *probability*$_1$* is in fact of this kind,

---

*See R. Carnap, *Logical Foundation of Probability*, Chicago, 1950—*Ed.*

resting on the notion of overlapping of truth ranges, which amounts roughly to saying that certain pairs of statements standing to one another in the *probability*$_1$ relationship have some truth conditions in common, in particular sufficient truth conditions. If, therefore, we think of a sentence as meaningful if and only if confirmable, some at least of the main senses show that this is a notion equivalent to or entailing that of Verifiability. And the same holds if we adopt the criterion that a sentence is meaningful if and only if we can assign a probability number to it, at least in the two main senses of 'probability' just mentioned.

Accordingly, in the relatively clear senses of 'confirmable' we have been dealing with, if a sentence is confirmable, it is also Verifiable, and nothing is gained by way of a more liberal conception of meaningfulness by involving confirmation. However, the case of mixed quantifications is rather special. When we ascertain that a certain substance is soluble in another, this neither verifies nor falsifies the sentence and, in fact, as we have seen, there are some intended interpretations of mixed quantifications according to which they have neither sufficient nor necessary truth conditions, and one might suppose that ended the matter. But there is still a logical relationship between 'For any substance there exists some solvent', and 'Substance A is soluble in substance B'. In fact, the latter describes a sufficient condition for the satisfaction of a necessary condition for the hypothesis to be true. It is because the singular statement does not also describe a necessary condition for that necessary condition, and because no other does, that we are forced to conclude that the hypothesis is not strictly falsifiable. I am at a loss, however, for a suitable name for this kind of logical relationship, and none of my logical friends has been of much help to me here. But the name is not important.

What should we say about the meaningfulness of those sentences that have such a weak connection with matter of fact? On the one hand, one would like to include them in the class of statements in terms of the criterion of possessing truth conditions; on the other hand they seem not to qualify fully. Might one call them 'quasi-meaningful'? This doesn't seem to be very elegant, and I am at a loss how to make a decision. While I feel very strongly the necessity of tying in the concept of meaningfulness with the notion of truth, I should be willing to weaken the requirement to that of even a kind of confirmability not reducible to Verifiability if I knew of any very clear and plausible way to do this which would enable one to resolve the issue as to what degree of confirmation such a mixed quantification would come to possess by virtue of the existence of a sufficient condition for the satisfaction of a necessary condition for it.

If the degree of confirmation that the satisfaction of a necessary condition for the truth of a law lends to the law is infintesimal, it would seem that in this more complex case the degree of confirmation would be that degree squared. This is a very small quantity, and one wonders what possible use it could be in the business of cognition? I shall assume that the answer is 'none', and go the young lady one better, by pretending that such a small illegitimate baby isn't one at all, and I hope I may be forgiven. Happily, I have saved a few asterisks for the term 'vindication' as it occurs in my title.

I conclude this section of my v*nd*c*t**n by summing up: I pointed out at the beginning that to vindicate a position is not the same as to show that it is perfect, and we see the kind of imperfection that remains. It strikes me as minute enough so that one can with some justification adopt the Verifiability principle with a minimum of sacrifice of sentences that might be thought to be meaningful. To weaken it so as to include the relevant cases of mixed quantification is to introduce an extremely unclear notion of confirmation, one that seems of little if any use in the pursuit of knowledge. But, if one chooses to weaken it in the manner indicated, we are still left with a conception *resting* on the notion of truth conditions or something very much like it; and I daresay that most of those who object to the stronger version of the principle would not be very much more content with the weaker. Among these objectors I shall single out two types for brief comment.

It is well known that there are those who claim that there is no sense to raising the question of the truth, falsity, probability or even meaningfulness of a sentence taken in isolation, out of the context of the whole of science, or at least of the context of a particular system of science. As I have paid my respects to this view in a recently published article ('The Dogma of Logical Pragmatism', *Mind*, July, 1956) I shall deal with but a single aspect of the position, one which seems to me to be peculiarly germane to the issue at hand. The view is that we must judge the meaning of a scientific system as a whole, and not its component sentences taken singly. Any system of sentences that has empirically testable consequences will qualify as meaningful, but no individual sentence may be considered in relation to its own meaning or truth.

To this I answer that a sentence may enter into a system of sentences having consequences only if it itself have a truth value. But if it have a truth value then it is meaningful taken by itself. It cannot play any role in the business of formulating theories and making inferences except via its truth values. Any sentence, therefore, that can play the role of a premise in a system of science must be meaningful in our sense; must be, that is, so long as science is concerned with truth or with probability as based on truth. A concept of probability not reducible to that of truth might enable us to escape this consequence, but one would like to see it worked out and a suitable logic worked out with it. Perhaps it has been, and if so I shall be willing to reconsider what I have said when I come to understand it; but as of now, I must confess myself unconvinced by latter-day pragmatism. This is very likely a judgement on me, but if so I cannot help it. In any case, the view that no sentence taken by itself is meaningful will be of little comfort to those who wish to affirm that a sentence taken by itself can be meaningful while lacking truth conditions.

The second view I wish to touch upon briefly is that connected with the Oxford School. The abler representatives of this movement have made important contributions to our understanding of language, and no one is more appreciative than I of some of them. They have thrown light on certain neglected dimensions of meaning. Cognitive meaning as here discussed obviously comprises but a part of the subject matter of a general 'theory' of meaning, as I observed at the beginning. My only quarrel, then, is with those who may think that Verifiability has little or nothing to do with cognitive meaning, who occasionally give the impression that in the concept of *use* they possess the key to the problems of semantics.

Of course, one can conceive the term 'use' so generally that it covers everything, but then only at the risk of missing all the details that have concerned us. If one should seek a most-general criterion of over-all meaningfulness for expressions of any kind whatever, I should suppose that of *use* is as good as any, and perhaps better. Thus I should be willing to accept the following: An expression is meaningful (in the widest sense of 'meaningful') if it has a use in discourse. But I should certainly not be willing to deduce from this truism that the meaning of a sentence is its use, as some would appear to do. For one thing, I tried to indicate earlier that it is dangerous to identify meaningfulness with meaning. That we know that a sentence is meaningful does not imply that we know what the meaning of that sentence is or even that there is any such thing.

An adequate system of semantics will want not merely a criterion of meaningfulness for the several types of linguistic expressions, but a concept of *the* meaning of an expression, wherever possible; as well as a concept of identity of meaning or synonymity, in such cases as sense and common usage seem to require. If, then, we argue that the meaning of a sentence is its use, we seem committed to the view that two sentences have the same use if and only if they have the same meaning. Now there may be ways in which this could in some contexts be made out as plausible, but I have serious doubts that it will do where the meaning in question is what has been called 'cognitive meaning'.

In the first place, it is not at all clear how we are to determine what the use of a given expression in a given context is, if any. It seems fairly obvious that an expression may have at one and the same time different uses, if these correspond to such infinitives as "to amuse," "to describe," etc., etc. And it has been argued with some merit that the use to which an expression can be put is, in fact, often if not always a function of its meaning, and not contrariwise. If the use is made specific enough to fit each individual case it will follow that no two expressions can have the same meaning, since the particular use will be different in each occurrence of the expression. But the moment we clarify the general notion of use sufficiently to enable us to deal with the problem of use in particular contexts we find ourselves forced to distinguish kinds of use, and the general formula ceases to be of much relevance.

Turning to sentences and the problem of cognitive meaning, we can see that one of their main uses is to enable us to formulate and express knowledge or truths. The concept of use in this context takes on a very special character, and we need not be surprised if it turns out that one of the main senses is precisely that which we have been attempting to capture in the semantic formulas based on truth conditions. In fact, to observe how sentences are used cognitively is in a sense nothing more not less than to observe under what conditions their users understand them to be true or false; but this amounts to treating the Verifiability principle as a special criterion of meaning or meaningfulness formulated under the *use* slogan.

The point I wish to make here is simply the following: the Verifiability principle is not something superseded by the *use* formula, but constitutes an essential aspect of it. The dazzling light from the east, while illuminating areas of meaning purposely neglected by the more restricted principle of cognitive meaning, does not obliterate from the centre of attention the essential distinctions we have been concerned with. My quarrel is with those who seem to think that the conquest of new insights somehow necessarily invalidates old ones — I would be happy to learn that there are no such persons, but I have a strong suspicion that some could be found in this very audience.

At long last I come to the end of my discussion of the Verifiability principle. What of the way of philosophizing based upon it? Does it commit one to the view that questions of value and metaphysics are pseudo-questions? This *could* be so only if some clear sense were attached to these terms values and metaphysical, and it *would be* demonstrably so only if these terms were used with meanings, if one may speak in such a manner, according to which sentences concerning values and sentences of a metaphysical character were meaningless by their very nature, this is by virtue of the meanings attached to them. But what meanings expressions have depends upon what meanings, if any, men have assigned to them, or upon no one having assigned any meaning to them. But all this is of a most contingent character. No one who understands what is involved in the Verifiability principle and who has not, perhaps temporarily, abandoned thought and reason in order to make questionable propaganda, can defend the view that sentences of ethics or metaphysics *must* be without meaning — except by virtue of the question-begging procedure of settling the matter by some prior stipulation, which he can do only for himself. But one man's stipulation is probably at least as good another's, as a mere stipulation, and nothing very interesting follows from definitions of value and metaphysical according to which it is demonstrable that the sentences of ethics or metaphysics are not meaningful — although it is not forbidden, and some definitions are necessary. Any one who takes this line does so purely on his own, and can claim no sanction whatever from the Verifiability principle. It is, of course, conceivable that the generalization: 'All sentences of ethics and metaphysics are meaningless' should be a well-confirmed hypothesis, provided one had a clear notion of the class of ethical and metaphysical sentences. But this is the most that theory can grant, and there is no doubt whatever that many such sentences so classified by respectable thinkers are as meaningful as most others, — which is perhaps not to say very much.

It is worth noting that the only prominent thinker committed to the Verifiability principle who was interested enough in ethics to write a book on the subject, Moritz Schlick,* emphatically did not treat

---

*An extract from Schlick's book appears as item E2 below—*Ed.*

ethical sentences as meaningless, and on the subject of metaphysics wrote the following: 'If one wishes to characterize every view which denies the possibility of metaphysics as positivistic this is quite un-objectionable, as a mere definition; and I should in this sense call myself a strict positivist. But this holds, of course, only under the presupposi-tion of a special definition of "metaphysics" '. And concerning that special definition, he wrote '. . . it hardly agrees with the formulations usual in philosophic literature . . .'[8] It was in fact a definition according to which metaphysical sentences attempt to express what is not, in his sense, expressible, i.e. content.

If to be a logical positivist is to be one who adopts the Verifiability principle for use in dealing with the problem of the meaning and meaningfulness of statements as they function within the context of cognition, then I am prepared to call myself one; but if it be to be one characterized by the above mentioned bad logic and worse manners I wish not to be called one. In either case, it is for a philosopher of little importance what one is called but all important what one is. I shall not here stay to argue that it is better to be one who takes cognition seriously enough not to stultify himself when engaged in the cognitive activity, than one who has no concern for such matters; but I am certainly not clear that it is worse.

One final point: It is often thought that the Verifiability principle is somehow especially wedded to sense data, that according to it only statements verifiable or falsifiable, or perhaps confirmable, in terms of the data of one or more of the five senses are meaningful. But this is surely not essential. How many senses there are and what constitute the data of sense are themselves not very well formulated questions, and it would be much more illuminating, I believe, to define 'the given' in terms of 'ascertainable truth conditions' than the latter in terms of the former. — Truth is our goal. What difference does it make in what form or what materials ascertainment comes to us, so long as it comes? It is certainly in some sense correct that all ascertainment involves the confrontation of data of some kind; but let not the paucity of language blind us to the fact that there is more under heaven than is dreamt of in our vocabularies.

---

[8] 'Positivismus und Realismus', para. 4. (Reprinted as item C1 below—*Ed.*)

C. REDUCTIONISM AND THE UNITY OF SCIENCE

1 Positivism and Realism

Moritz Schlick

1 PRELIMINARY QUESTIONS

Every philosophical movement is defined by the principles that it regards as fundamental, and to which it constantly recurs in its arguments. But in the course of historical development, the principles are apt not to remain unaltered, whether it be that they acquire new formulations, and come to be extended or restricted, or that even their meaning gradually undergoes noticeable modifications. At some point the question then arises, as to whether we should still speak at all of the development of a single movement, and retain its old name, or whether a new movement has not in fact arisen.

If, alongside the evolved outlook, an 'orthodox' movement still continues to exist, which clings to the first principles in their original form and meaning, then sooner or later some terminological distinction of the old from the new will automatically come about. But where this is not clearly so, and where, on the contrary, the most diverse and perhaps contradictory formulations and interpretations of the principles are bandied about among the various adherents of a 'movement', then a hubbub arises, whose result is that supporters and opponents of the view are found talking at cross purposes; everyone seeks out from the principles what he can specifically use for the defence of his own view, and everything ends in hopeless misunderstandings and obscurities. They only disappear when the various principles are separated from each other and tested individually for meaning and truth on their own account, in which process we do best, at first, to disregard entirely the contexts in which they have historically arisen, and the names that have been given to them.

Source: Moritz Schlick, *Philosophical Papers,* volume II (1925-1936), edited by H. L. Mulder and B. van de Velde-Schlick, D. Reidel, 1979, pp. 259-84. Copyright © 1979 by Albert M. Schlick and Barbara F. B. van de Velde-Schlick. Reprinted by permission of D. Reidel Publishing Company. This paper, originally entitled 'Positivismus und Realismus', first appeared in *Erkenntnis* volume III, 1932-33.

I should like to apply these considerations to the modes of thought grouped under the name of 'positivism'. From the moment when Auguste Comte invented the term, up to the present day, they have undergone a development which provides a good example of what has just been said. I do this, however, not with the historical purpose of establishing, say, a rigorous concept of positivism in its historical manifestation, but rather in order to contribute to a real settlement of the controversy currently carried on about certain principles which rank as positivist axioms. Such a settlement is all the dearer to me, in that I subscribe to some of these principles myself. My only concern here is to make the meaning of these principles as clear as possible; whether, after such clarification, people are still minded to impute them to 'positivism' or not, is a question of wholly subordinate importance.

If every view is to be labelled positivist, which denies the possibility of metaphysics, then nothing can be said against it as a mere definition, and in *this* sense I would have to declare myself a strict positivist. But this, of course, is true only if we presuppose a particular definition of 'metaphysics'. What the definition of metaphysics is, that would have to be made basic here, does not need to interest us at present; but it scarcely accords with the formulations that are mostly current in the literature of philosophy; and closer definitions of positivism that adhere to such formulations lead straight into obscurities and difficulties.

For if, say — as has mostly been done from time immemorial — we assert that metaphysics is the doctrine of 'true being', of 'reality in itself', or of 'transcendent being', this talk of true, real being obviously presupposes that a non-true, lesser or apparent being stands opposed to it, as has indeed been assumed by all metaphysicians since the days of Plato and the Eleatics. This seeming being is said to be the realm of 'appearances', and while the true transcendent reality is held to be accessible with difficulty only to the efforts of the metaphysician, the special sciences are exclusively concerned with appearances, and the latter are also perfectly accessible to scientific knowledge. The contrast in the knowability of the two 'kinds of being' is then traced to the fact that appearances are 'given' and immediately known to us, whereas metaphysical reality has had to be inferred from them only by a circuitous route. With this we seem to have arrived at a fundamental concept of the positivists, for they, too, are always talking of the 'given', and state their basic principle mostly by saying that, like the scientist, the philosopher must abide throughout in the given, that an advance beyond it, such as the metaphysician attempts, is impossible or absurd.

It is natural, therefore, to take the given of positivism to be simply identical with the metaphysician's appearances, and to believe that positivism is at bottom a metaphysics from which the transcendent has been omitted or struck out; and such a view may often enough have inspired the arguments of positivists, no less than those of their adversaries. But with this we are already on the road to dangerous errors.

This very term 'the given' is already an occasion for grave misunderstandings. 'To give', of course, normally signifies a three-termed relation: it presupposes in the first place someone who gives, secondly someone given to, and thirdly something given. For the metaphysician this is quite in order, for the giver is transcendent reality, the receiver is the knowing consciousness, and the latter appropriates what is given to it as its 'content'. But the positivist, from the outset, will obviously have nothing to do with such notions; the given, for him, is to be merely a term for what is simplest and no longer open to question. Whatever term we may choose, indeed, it will be liable to occasion misconceptions; if we talk of 'acquaintance' [*'Erlebnis'*], we seem to presuppose the distinction between he who is acquainted and what he is acquainted with; in employing the term 'content of consciousness', we appear to burden ourselves with a similar distinction, and also with the complex concept of 'consciousness', first excogitated, at all events, by philosophical thought.

But even apart from such difficulties, it is possibly still not yet clear what is actually meant by the given. Does it merely include such 'qualities' as 'blue', 'hot' and 'pain', or also, for example, relations between them, or the order they are in? Is the similarity of two qualities 'given' in the same sense as the qualities themselves? And if the given is somehow elaborated or interpreted or judged, is this elaboration or judgement not also in turn a given in some sense?

It is not obscurities of this type, however, which give occasion to present-day controversies; it is the question of 'reality' that first tosses among the parties the apple of discord.

If positivism's rejection of metaphysics amounts to a denial of transcendent reality, it seems the most natural thing in the world to conclude that in that case it attributes reality only to non-transcendent being. The main principle of the positivist then seems to run: 'Only the given is real'. Anyone who takes pleasure in plays upon words could even make use of a peculiarity of the German language in order to lend this proposition the air of being a self-evident tautology, by formulating it as: '*Es gibt nur das Gegebene*' [Only the given exists].

What are we to say of this principle?

Many positivists may have stated and upheld it (particularly those, perhaps, who have treated physical objects as 'mere logical constructions' or as 'mere auxiliary concepts'), and others have had it imputed to them by opponents — but we are obliged to say that anyone who asserts this principle thereby attempts to advance a claim that is metaphysical in the same sense, and to the same degree, as the seemingly opposite contention, that 'there is a transcendent reality'.

The problem at issue here is obviously the so-called question as to the reality of the external world, and on this there seem to be two parties: that of 'realism', which believes in the reality of the external world, and that of 'positivism', which does not believe in this. I am convinced that in fact it is quite absurd to set two views in contrast to one another in this fashion, since (as with all metaphysical propositions) both parties, at bottom, have not the least notion of what they are trying to say. But before explaining this I should like to show how the most natural interpretations of the proposition 'only the given is real' in fact lead at once to familiar metaphysical views.

As a question about the existence of the 'external' world, the problem can make its appearance only through drawing a distinction of some kind between inner and outer, and this happens inasmuch and insofar as the given is regarded as a 'content' of consciousness, as belonging to a subject (or several) to *whom* it is given. The immediate data are thereby credited with a conscious character, the character of presentations or ideas; and the proposition in question would then assert that *all* reality possesses this character: no being outside consciousness. But this is nothing else but the basic principle of metaphysical *idealism*. If the philosopher thinks he can speak only of what is given to himself, we are confronted with a solipsistic metaphysics; but if he thinks he may assume that the given is distributed to many subjects, we then have an idealism of the Berkeleyan type.

On this interpretation, positivism would thus be simply identical with the older idealist metaphysics. But since its founders were certainly seeking something quite other than a renewal of that idealism, this view must be rejected as inconsistent with the antimetaphysical purpose of positivism. Idealism and positivism do not go together. The positivist Ernst Laas* devoted a work in several volumes to demonstrating the

---

*[E. Laas, *Idealismus und Positivismus. Eine kritische Auseinandersetzung*, Berlin 1879-1881.] *–original editors.*

irreconcilable opposition that exists between them in all areas; and if his pupil Hans Vaihinger gave his *philosophy of As If* the subtitle of an 'idealist positivism', that is just one of the contradictions that infect this work. Ernst Mach has particularly emphasized that his own positivism has evolved in a direction away from the Berkeleyan metaphysics; he and Avenarius laid much stress on not construing the given as a content of consciousness, and endeavoured to keep this notion out of their philosophy altogether.

In view of the uncertainty in the positivists' own camp, it is not surprising if the 'realist' ignores the distinctions we have mentioned and directs his arguments against the thesis that 'there are only contents of consciousness', or that 'there is only an internal world'. But this proposition belongs to the idealist metaphysics; it has no place in an anti-metaphysical positivism, and these counter-arguments do not tell against such a view.

The 'realist' can, indeed, take the line that it is utterly inevitable that the given should be regarded as a content of consciousness, as subjective, or mental — or whatever the term may be; and he would consider the attempts of Avenarius and Mach to construe the given as neutral, and to do away with the inner-outer distinction, as a failure, and would think a theory without metaphysics to be simply impossible. But this line of argument is more rarely encountered. And whatever the position there, we are dealing in any case with a quarrel about nothing, since the 'problem of the reality of the external world' is a meaningless pseudo-problem. It is now time to make this clear.

II ON THE MEANING OF STATEMENTS

It is the proper business of philosophy to seek for and clarify the *meaning* of claims and questions. The chaotic state in which philosophy has found itself throughout the greatest part of its history is traceable to the unlucky fact that firstly it has accepted certain formulations with far to much naiveté, as genuine problems, without first carefully testing whether they really possessed a sound meaning; and secondly, that it has believed the answers to certain questions to be discoverable by particular philosophical methods that differ from those of the special sciences. By philosophical analysis we are unable to decide of anything whether it is real; we can only determine what it *means* to claim that it is real; and whether this is then the case or not can only be decided by the ordinary methods of daily life and science, namely by *experience*. So here the task is to get clear whether a meaning can be attached to the question about the reality of the 'external world'.

When are we certain, in general, that the meaning of a question is clear to us? Obviously then, and only then, when we are in a position to state quite accurately the circumstances under which it can be answered in the affirmative — or those under which it would have to receive a negative answer. By these statements, and these alone, is the meaning of the question defined.

It is the first step in every kind of philosophizing, and the basis of all reflection, to realize that it is absolutely impossible to give the meaning of any claim save by describing the state-of-affairs that must obtain if the claim is to be true. If it does not obtain, then the claim is false. The meaning of a proposition obviously consists in this alone, that it expresses a particular state-of-affairs. This state-of-affairs must actually be pointed out, in order to give the meaning of the proposition. One may say, indeed, that the proposition itself already gives this state-of-affairs; but only, of course, for one who understands it. But when do I understand a proposition? When I know the meaning of the words that occur in it? This can be explained by definitions. But in the definitions new words occur, whose meaning I also have to know in turn. The business of defining cannot go on indefinitely, so eventually we come to words whose meaning cannot again be described in a proposition; it has to be pointed out directly; the meaning of the world must ultimately be *shown*, it has to be *given*. This takes place through an act of pointing or showing, and what is shown must be given, since otherwise it cannot be pointed out to me.

In order, therefore, to find the meaning of a proposition, we have to transform it by introduction of successive definitions, until finally only such words appear in it as can no longer be defined, but whose meanings can only be indicated directly. The criterion for the truth or falsity of the proposition then consists in this, that under specific conditions (stated in the definitions) certain data are, or are not, present. Once this is established, I have established everything that the proposition was talking about, and hence I know its meaning. If I am *not* capable, in principle, of verifying a proposition, that is, if I have absolutely no knowledge of how I should go about it, what I would have to do, in order to ascertain its truth or falsity, then I obviously have no idea at all of what the proposition is actually saying; for then I would be in no position to interpret the proposition, in proceeding, by means of the definitions, from its wording to possible data, since insofar as I *am* in a position to do this, I can also, by this very fact, point out the road to verification in principle (even though, for practical reasons, I may often be unable actually to tread it). To state the circumstances under which a proposition is true is *the same* as stating its meaning, and nothing else.

And these 'circumstances', as we have now seen, have ultimately to be found in the given. Different circumstances imply differences in the given. The *meaning* of every proposition is ultimately determined by the given alone, and by absolutely nothing else.

I do not know if this view should be described as positivistic; though I should like to believe that it has been in the background of all efforts that go under this name in the history of philosophy, whether, indeed, it has been clearly formulated or not. It may well be assumed to constitute the true core and driving force of many quite erroneous formulations that we find among the positivists.

Anyone who has once attained the insight, that the meaning of any statement can be determined only by the given, no longer even grasp the *possibility of another* opinion, for he sees that he has merely discerned the conditions under which opinions can be formulated at all. It would thus be quite erroneous as well to perceive in the foregoing any sort of 'theory of meaning' (in Anglo-Saxon countries the view outlined, that the meaning of a statement is wholly and solely determined by its verification in the given, is commonly called the 'experimental theory of meaning'); that which precedes all formation of theories cannot itself be a theory.

The content of our thesis is in fact entirely trivial (and that is precisely why it can give so much insight); it tells us that a statement only has a specifiable meaning if it makes some testable difference whether it is true or false. A proposition for which the world looks exactly the same when it is true as it does when it is false, in fact says nothing whatever about the world; it is empty, it conveys nothing, I can specify no meaning for it. But a *testable* difference is present only if there is a difference in the given, for to be testable certainly means nothing else but 'demonstrable in the given'.

It is self-evident that the term 'testability' is intended only *in principle*, for the meaning of a proposition does not, of course, depend on whether the circumstances under which we actually find ourselves at a given moment allow of, or prevent, actual verification. The statement that 'there are 10,000 ft mountains on the far side of the moon' is beyond doubt absolutely meaningful, although we lack the technical means for verifying it. And it would remain just as meaningful even if we knew for certain, on scientific grounds of some kind, that no man would ever reach the far side of the moon. Verification always remains *thinkable*, we are always able to say what sort of data we should have to encounter, in order to effect the decision; it is *logically* possible, whatever the situation may be as regards the actual possibility of doing it. And that is all that is at issue here.

But if someone advanced the claim, that within every electron there is a nucleus which is always present, but produces absolutely no effect outside, so that its existence in nature is discernible in no way whatever — then this would be a meaningless claim. For we should at once have to ask the fabricator of this hypothesis: What, then, do you actually *mean* by the presence of this 'nucleus'?, and he could only reply: I mean that something exists there in the electron. We would then go on to ask: What is that supposed to mean? How would it be if this something did not exist? And he would have to reply: In that case, everything else would be exactly as before. For according to his claim, no effects of any kind proceed from this something, and everything observable would remain absolutely unaltered, the ream of the given would not be touched. We would judge that he had not succeeded in conveying to us the meaning of his hypothesis, and that it is therefore vacuous. In this case the impossibility of verification is actually not a factual, but a *logical* impossibility, since the claim that this nucleus is totally without effects rules out, *in principle*, the possibility of deciding by differences in the given.

Nor can it be supposed that the distinction between essential impossibility of verification and a merely factual and empirical impossibility is not sharp, and therefore often hard to draw; for the 'essential' impossibility is simply a logical one, which differs from the empirical, not by degrees, but absolutely. What is merely empirically impossible still remains *thinkable*; but what is logically impossible is contradictory, and cannot, therefore, be thought at all. We also find, in fact, that with sure instinct, this distinction is always very clearly sensed in the practice of scientific thinking. The physicists would be the first to reject the claim in our example, concerning the eternally hidden nucleus of the electron, with the criticism that this is no hypothesis whatever, but an empty play with words. And on the question of the meaning of their statements, successful students of reality have at all times adopted the standpoint here outlined, in that they acted upon it, even though mostly unawares.

Thus our position does not represent anything strange and peculiar for science, but in a certain sense has always been a self-evident thing. It could not possibly have been otherwise, because only from this stand-point can the truth of a statement be tested at all; since all scientific activity consists in testing the truth of statements, it constantly acknow-ledges the correctness of our viewpoint by what it does.

If express confirmation be still needed, it is to be found with the utmost clarity at critical points in the development of science, where research is compelled to bring its self-evident presuppositions to con-sciousness. This situation occurs where difficulties of principle give rise to the suspicion that something may not be in order about these presuppositions. The most celebrated example of this kind, which will forever remain notable, is Einstein's analysis of the concept of time, which consists in nothing else whatever but a statement of the *meaning* of our assertions about the simultaneity of spatially separated events. Einstein told the physicists (and philosophers): you must first say what you *mean* by simultaneity, and this you can only do by showing how the statement 'two events are simultaneous' is verified. But in so doing you have then also established the meaning fully and *without remainder*. What is true of the simultaneity concept holds good of every other; every statement has a meaning only insofar as it can be verified; it only *signifies* what is verified and absolutely *nothing* beyond this. Were someone to maintain that it contains more, he would have to be able to say what this more is, and for this he must again say what in the world would be different if he was wrong; but he can say nothing of the kind, for by previous assumption all observable differences have already been utilized in the verification.

In the simultaneity example the analysis of meaning, as is right and proper for the physicist, is carried only so far that the decision about the truth or falsity of a temporal statement resides in the occurrence or non-occurrence of a certain physical event (for example, the coincidence of a pointer with a scale-mark); but it is clear that one may go on to ask: What, then, does it *mean* to claim that the pointer indicates a particular mark on the scale? And the answer to this can be nothing else whatever but a reference to the occurrence of certain data, or, as we are wont to say, of certain 'sensations'. This is also generally admitted, and especially by physicists. "For in the end, positivism will always be right in this", says Planck[1], "that there is no other source of knowledge but sensations",

---

[1] M. Planck, *Positivismus und reale Aussenwelt*, Leipzig 1931, p. 14.

and this statement obviously means that the truth of falsity of a physical assertion is quite solely dependent on the occurrence of certain sensations (which are a special class of the given).

But now there will always be many inclined to say that this grants only that the truth of a physical statement can be tested in absolutely no other way save by the occurrence of certain sensations, but that this, however, is a different thing from claiming that the very *meaning* of the statement is thereby exhaustively presented. The latter would have to be denied, for a proposition can contain *more* than allows of verification; that the pointer stands at a certain mark on the scale means *more* than the presence of certain sensations (namely, the 'presence of a certain state-of-affairs in the external world').

Of this denial of the identity of meaning and verification the following needs to be said:

1. Such a denial is to be found among physicists only where they leave the proper territory of physical statements and begin to philosophize. (In physics, obviously, we find only statements about the nature or behaviour of things and processes; an express assertion of their 'reality' is needless, since it is always presupposed.) In his own territory the physicist fully acknowledges the correctness of our point of view. We have already mentioned this earlier, and have since elucidated it by the example of the concept of simultaneity. There are, indeed, many philosophers who say: Only relative simultaneity can admittedly be established, but from this it does not follow that there is no such thing as absolute simultaneity, and we continue, as before, to believe in it! There is no way of demonstrating the falsity of this claim; but the greater majority of physicists are rightly of the opinion that it is meaningless. It must be emphatically stressed, however, that in both cases we are concerned with exactly the same situation. It makes absolutely no difference, in principle, whether I ask: Does the statement 'two events are simultaneous' mean more than can be verified? Or whether I ask: Does the statement 'the pointer indicates the fifth scale-mark' signify more than can be verified? The physicist who treats the two cases differently is guilty of an inconsistency. He will justify himself by arguing that in the second case, where the 'reality of the external world' is concerned, there is philosophically far more at stake. This argument is too vague for us to be able to assign it any weight, but we shall shortly examine whether anything lies behind it.

2. It is perfectly true that every statement about a physical object or event says *more* than is verified, say, by the once-and-for-all occurrence

of an experience. It is presupposed, rather, that this experience took place under quite specific conditions, whose fulfilment can, of course, be tested in turn only by something given; and it is further presupposed that still other and further verifications (after-tests, confirmations) are always possible, which themselves of course reduce to manifestations of some kind in the given. In this way we can and must make allowance for sense-deceptions and errors, and it is easy to see how we are to classify the cases in which we would say that the observer had merely dreamt that the pointer indicated a certain mark, or that he had not observed carefully, and so on. Blondlot's claims about the N-rays that he thought he had discovered were intended, after all, to say more than that he had had certain visual sensations under certain circumstances, and hence they could also be refuted.[2] Strictly speaking, the meaning of a proposition about physical objects is exhausted only by the provision of indefinitely many possible verifications, and the consequence of this is, that in the last resort such a proposition can never be proved absolutely true. It is generally acknowledged, indeed, that even the most assured propositions of science have always to be regarded merely as hypotheses, which remain open to further definition and improvement. This has certain consequences for the logical nature of such propositions, but they do not concern us here.

Once again: the meaning of a physical statement is never defined by a single isolated verification; it must be conceived, rather, as of the form: If circumstances x are given, data y occur, where indefinitely many circumstances can be substituted for x, and the proposition remains correct on every occasion (this also holds, even if the statement refers to a once-and-for-all occurrence – a historical event – for such an event always has innumerable consequences whose occurrence can be verified). Thus the meaning of every physical statement ultimately lies always in an endless chain of data; the individual datum as such is of no interest in this connection. So if a positivist should ever have said that the individual objects of science are simply the given experiences themselves, he would certainly have been quite wrong; what every scientist seeks, and seeks alone, are rather the rules which govern the connection of experiences, and by which they can be predicted. Nobody denies that the sole verification of natural laws consists in the fact that they provide correct predictions of this type. The oft-heard objection, that the immediately given, which at most can be the object of psychology, is

---

[2] Cf. *ibid*., p. 11.

now falsely to be made into an object of physics, is thereby robbed of its force.

3. The most important thing to say, however, is this: If anyone thinks that the meaning of a proposition is not in fact exhausted by what can be verified in the given, but extends far beyond that, then he must at least admit that this surplus of meaning is utterly indescribable, unstatable in any way, and inexpressible by any language. For let him just try to state it! So far as he succeeds in *communicating* something of the meaning, he will find that the communication consists in the very fact that he has pointed out some circumstances that can serve for verification in the given, and he thereby finds our view confirmed. Or else he may believe, indeed, that he has stated a meaning, but closer examination shows that his words only signify that there is still 'something' there, though nothing whatever is said about its nature. In that case he has really communicated nothing; his claim is meaningless, for one cannot maintain the existence of something without saying *of what* one is claiming the existence. This can be brought out by reference to our example of the essentially indemonstrable 'nucleus of the electron'; but for the sake of clarity we shall analyse yet another example of a very fundamental kind.

I am looking at two pieces of green paper, and establish that they have the same colour. The proposition asserting the likeness of colour is verified, *inter alia*, by the fact that I twice experience the same colour at the same time. The statement 'two patches of the same colour are now present' can no longer be reduced to others; it is verified by the fact that it describes the given. It has a good meaning: by virtue of the significance of the words occurring in the statement, this meaning is simply the existence of this similarity of colour; by virtue of linguistic usage, the sentence expresses precisely this experience. I now show one of the two pieces of paper to a second observer, and pose the question: Does he see the green just as I do? Is his colour-experience the *same* as mine? This case is *essentially* different from the one just examined. While there the statement was verifiable through the occurrence of an experience of similarity, a brief consideration shows that here such a verification is absolutely impossible. Of course (if he is not colour-blind), the second observer also calls the paper *green*; and if I now describe this green to him more closely, by saying that it is more yellowish than this wallpaper, more bluish than this billiard-cloth, darker than this plant, and so on, he will also find it so each time, that is, he will agree with my statements. But even though all his judgements about colours were to agree entirely with mine, I can obviously never conclude from this that he experiences 'the same quality'. It might be that on looking at the green paper he has an experience that I should call 'red'; that conversely, in the cases where I see red, he experiences green, but of course calls it 'red', and so forth. It might even be, indeed, that my colour-sensations are matched in him by experiences of sound or data of some other kind; yet it would be impossible in principle ever to discover these differences between his experience and mine. We would agree completely, and could never differ about our surroundings, so long only (and this is absolutely the only precondition that has to be made) as the inner *order* of his experiences agrees with that of mine. Their 'quality' does not come into it at all; all that is required is that they can be brought into a *system* in the same fashion.

All this is doubtless uncontested, and philosophers have pointed out this situation often enough. They have mostly added, however, that such subjective differences are indeed theoretically possible, and that this possibility is in principle very interesting, but that nevertheless it is 'in the highest degree probable' that the observer and I actually experience the *same* green. We, however, must say: The claim that different individuals experiences the *same* sensation has this verifiable meaning alone, that all their statements (and of course all their other behaviour as well) display certain agreements; hence the claim *means* nothing else whatever but this. It is merely another mode of expression if we say that it is a question of the likeness of two systems of order. The proposition that two experiences of different subjects not only occupy the same place in the order of a system, but *beyond that* are *also* qualitatively like each other, has no meaning for us. It is not false, be it noted, but meaningless: we have no idea at all what it is supposed to signify.

Experience shows that for the majority of people it is very difficult to agree with this. One has to grasp that we are really concerned here with a *logical* impossibility of verification. To speak of the likeness of two data in *the same* consciousness has an acceptable meaning; it can be verified through an immediate experience. But if we wish to talk of the likeness of two data in *different* consciousness, that is a new concept; it has to be defined anew, for propositions in which it occurs are no longer verifiable in the old fashion. The new definition is, in fact, the likeness of all reactions of the two individuals; no other can be found. The majority believe, indeed, that no definition is required here; we know straight off what 'like' means, and the meaning is in both cases the same. But in order to recognize this as an error, we have only to recall the concept of simultaneity, where the situation is precisely analogous. To the concept of 'simultaneity at the same place' there corresponds here the concept of 'likeness of experiences in the same individual'; and to 'simultaneity at different places' there corresponds here the 'likeness of experiences in different individuals'. The second is in each case something new in comparison with the first, and must be specially defined. A directly experienceable quality can no more be pointed out for the likeness of two greens in different consciousnesses than for simultaneity at different places; both must be defined by way of a system of relations.

Many philosophers have tried to overcome the difficulty that seemed to confront them here by all sorts of speculations and thought-experiments, in that they have spoken, say, of a universal consciousness (God) embracing all individuals, or have imagined that perhaps by an artificial linkage of the nerve-systems of two people the sensations of the one might be made accessible to the other and could be compared – but all this is useless, of course, since even by such fantastical methods it is in the end only contents of one and the same consciousness that are directly compared; but the question is precisely whether a comparison is possible between qualities insofar as they belong to different consciousnesses, and *not* the same one.

It must be admitted, therefore, that a proposition about the likeness of the experiences of two different persons has no other *stateable* meaning save that of a certain agreement in their reactions. Now it is open to anyone to believe that such a proposition also possesses another, more direct meaning; but it is certain that this meaning is not verifiable, and that there can be no way at all of stating or pointing out what this meaning is supposed to be. From this it follows, however, that there is absolutely no way at all in which such a meaning could be made a topic of discussion; there could be absolutely no talk about it, and it can in no way enter into any language whereby we communicate with each other.

And what has, we hope, become clear from this example, is of quite general application. All we can understand in a proposition is what it conveys; but a meaning can be communicated only if it is verifiable. Since propositions are nothing else but a vehicle of communication, we can assign to their meaning only what can be communicated. For this reason I should insist that 'meaning' can never signify anything but 'stateable meaning'.

But even if someone insisted that there was a non-verifiable meaning, this would actually be of no consequence whatever; for in everything he says and asks, and in everything that we ask him and reply to him, *such* a meaning can never in any way come to light. In other words, if such a thing were to exist, all our utterances and arguments and modes of behaviour would still remain totally untouched by it, whether it was a question of daily life, of ethical or aesthetic attitude, of science of any kind, or of philosophy. Everything would be exactly as though there were no unverifiable meaning, for insofar as anything was different, it would in fact be verifiable through this very difference.

That is a serious situation, and we must absolutely demand that it be taken seriously. One must guard above all things against confusing the present logical impossibility with an empirical incapacity, just as though some technical difficulties and human imperfection were to blame for the fact that only the verifiable can be expressed, and as though there were still some little backdoor through which an unstateable meaning could slip into the daylight and make itself noticeable in our speech and behaviour! No! The incommunicability is an absolute one; anyone who believes in a non-verifiable meaning (or more accurately, we shall have to say, imagines he believes in this) must still confess that only *one* attitude remains in regard to it: absolute silence. It would be of no use either to him or us, however often he asserted: 'but there is a non-verifiable meaning', for this statement is itself devoid of meaning, and says nothing.

III WHAT DOES 'REALITY' MEAN? WHAT DOES 'EXTERNAL WORLD' MEAN?

We are now prepared to make application of the foregoing to the so-called problem of the reality of the external world.

Let us ask: What meaning has it, if the 'realist' says 'there is an external world'? or even: What meaning attaches to the claim (which the realist attributes to the positivist) 'there is no external world'?

To answer the question, it is necessary, of course, to clarify the significance of the words 'there is' and 'external world'. Let us begin with the first. 'There is x' amounts to saying 'x is real' or 'x is actual'. So what does it mean if we attribute actuality (or reality) to an object? It is an ancient and very important insight of logic or philosophy, that the proposition 'x is actual' is totally different in kind from a proposition that attributes any sort of *property* to *x* (such as '*x* is hard'). In other words, actuality, reality or existence is not a property. The statement 'the dollar in my pocket is round' has a totally different logical form from the statement 'the dollar in my pocket is actual'. In modern logic this distinction is expressed by an altogether different symbolism, but it had already been very sharply emphasized by Kant, who, as we know, in his critique of the so-called ontological proof of God's existence had correctly found the error of this proof in the fact that existence was treated like a property there.

In daily life we very often have to speak of actuality or existence, and for that very reason it cannot be hard to discover the meaning of this talk. In a legal battle it often has to be established whether some document really exists, or whether this has merely been falsely claimed, say, by one of the parties; nor is it wholly unimportant to me, whether the dollar in my pocket is merely imaginary or actually real. Now everybody knows in what way such a reality-claim is verified, nor can there be the least doubt about it; the reality of the dollar is proved by this, and this alone, that by suitable manipulations I furnish myself certain tactual or visual sensations, on whose occurrence I am accustomed to say: this is a dollar. The same holds of the document, only there we should be content, on occasion, with certain statements by others claiming to have seen the document, that is, to have had perceptions of a quite specific kind. And the 'statements of others' again consist in certain acoustic, or — if they were written utterances — visual perceptions. There is need of no special controversy about the fact that the occurrence of certain sense-perceptions among the data *always* constitutes the sole criterion for propositions about the reality of a 'physical' object or event, in daily life no less than in the most refined assertions of science. That there are okapis in Africa can be established only by observing such animals. But it is not necessary that the object or event 'itself' should have to be perceived. We can imagine, for example, that the existence of a trans-Neptunian planet might be inferred by observation of perturbations with just as much certainty as by direct perception of a speck of light in the telescope. The reality of the atom provides another example, as does the back side of the moon.

It is of great importance to state that the occurrence of some one particular experience in verifying a reality-statement is often not recognized as such a verification, but that it is throughout a question of regularities, of law-like connections; in this way true verifications are distinguished from illusions and hallucinations. If we say of some event or object — which must be marked out by a description — that it is *real*, this means, then, that there is a quite specific connection between perceptions or other experiences, that under given circumstances certain data are presented. By this alone is it verified, and hence this is also its only stateable meaning.

This, too, was already formulated, in principle, by Kant, whom nobody will accuse of 'positivism'. Reality, for him, is a category, and if we apply it anywhere, and claim of an object that it is real, then all this asserts, in Kant's opinion, is that it belongs to a law-governed connection of perceptions.

It will be seen that for us (as for Kant; and the same must apply to any philosopher who is aware of his task) it is merely a matter of saying what is meant when we ascribe real existence to a thing in life or in science; it is in no sense a matter of correcting the claims of ordinary life or of research. I must confess that I should charge with folly and reject *a limine* every philosophical system that involved the claim that clouds and stars, mountains and the sea, were not actually real, that the 'physical world' did not exist, and that the chair against the wall ceases to be every time I turn my back on it. Nor do I seriously impute such a claim to any thinker. It would, for example, be undoubtedly a quite mistaken account of Berkeley's philosophy if his system were to be understood in this fashion. He, too, in no way denied the reality of the physical world, but merely sought to explain what we mean when we attribute reality to it. Anyone who says here that unperceived things are ideas in the mind of God is not in fact denying their existence, but is seeking, rather, to understand it. Even John Stuart Mill was not wanting to deny the reality of physical objects, but rather to explain it, when he declared them to be 'perrmanent possibilities of sensation', although I do consider his mode of expression to have been very unsuitably chosen.

So if 'positivism' is understood to mean a view that denies reality to bodies, I should simply have to declare it absurd; but I do not believe that such an interpretation of positivist opinions, at least as regards their competent exponents, would be historically just. Yet, however that may be, we are concerned only with the issue itself. And on this we have established as follows: our principle, that the question about the meaning of a proposition is identical with the question about its verification, leads us to recognize that the claim that a thing is real is a statement about lawful connections of experiences; it does *not*, however, imply this claim to be false. (There is therefore no denial of reality to physical objects in favour of sensations.)

But opponents of the view presented profess themselves by no means satisfied with this assertion. So far as I can see, they would answer as follows: 'You do, indeed, acknowledge completely the reality of the physical world, but – as we see it – only in words. You simply *call* real what we should describe as mere conceptual constructions. When *we* use the word "reality", we mean by it something quite different from you. Your definition of the real reduces it to experiences; but we mean something quite independent of all experiences. We mean something that possesses the same independence that you obviously concede only to the data, in that you reduce everything else to them, as the not-further-reducible'.

Although it would be a sufficient rebuttal to request our opponents to reflect once more upon how reality-statements are verified, and how verification is connected with *meaning*, I do in fact recognize the need to take account of the psychological attitude from which this argument springs, and therefore beg attention to the following considerations, whereby a modification of this attitude may yet, perhaps, be effected.

Let us first enquire whether, on our view, a 'content of consciousness' is credited with a reality that is denied to a physical object. We ask, therefore: does the claim that a feeling or sensation is real have a meaning different from the claim that a physical object is real? For us, this can mean only: are different types of verification involved in the two cases? The answer is: no!

To clarify this, we need to enter a little into the logical form of reality-statements. The general logical recognition that an existence-statement can be made about a datum only if it is marked out by a description, but not if it is given by an immediate indication, is also valid, of course, for the 'data of consciousness'. In the language of symbolic logic, this is expressed by the fact that an existence-claim must contain an 'operator'. In Russell's notation, for example, a reality-statement has the form $(\exists x)fx$, or in words, 'there is an x that has the property f'. The form of words 'there is a', where 'a' is supposed to be the individual name of a directly indicated object, therefore means no more than 'this here'; this form of words is meaningless, and in Russell's symbolism it cannot even be written down. We have to grasp the idea that Descartes' proposition 'I am' – or, to put it better, 'contents of consciousness exist' – is absolutely meaningless; it expresses nothing, and contains no knowledge. This is due to the fact that 'contents of consciousness' occurs in this connection as a mere *name* for the given; no characteristic is asserted, whose presence could be tested. A proposition has meaning, and is verifiable, only if I can state under what circumstances it would be true, and under what circumstances it would be false. But how am I to describe the circumstances under which the proposition 'My contents of consciousness exist' would be false? Every attempt would lead to ridiculous absurdities, to such propositions, say, as 'It is the case that nothing is the case', or the like. Hence I am self-evidently unable to describe the circumstances that make the proposition true (just try it!). Nor is there any doubt whatever that Descartes, with his proposition, had really obtained no knowledge, and was actually no wiser than before.

No, the question about the reality of an experience has meaning only where this reality can also be meaningfully *doubted*. I can ask, for example: Is it really true that I felt joy on hearing that news? This can be verified or falsified exactly as when we ask, say: Is it true that Sirius has a companion (that this companion is real)? That I felt joy on a particular occasion can be verified, for example, by examination of other people's statements about my behaviour at the time, by my finding of a letter that I then wrote, or simply by the return to me of an exact memory of the emotion I experienced. Here, therefore, there is not the slightest difference of principle: to be real always means to stand in a definite connection with the given. Nor is it otherwise, say, with an experience that is present at this very moment. I can quite meaningfully ask, for example (in the course, say, of a physiological experiment): Do I now actually feel a pain or not? (Notice that 'pain', here, does not function as an individual name for a 'this here', but represents a conceptual term for a describable class of experiences.) Here, too, the question is answered by establishing that in conjunction with certain circumstances (experimental conditions, concentration of attention, etc.) an experience with certain describable properties occurs. Such describable properties would be, for example: similarity to an experience that has occurred under certain other circumstances; tendency to evoke certain reactions; and so on.

However we may twist and turn, it is impossible to interpret a reality-statement otherwise than as fitting into a perceptual context. It is absolutely the *same* kind of reality that we have to attribute to the data of consciousness and to physical events. Scarcely anything in the history of philosophy has created more confusion than the attempt to pick out one of the two as true 'being'. Wherever the term 'real' is intelligibly used, it has one and the same meaning.

Our opponent, perhaps, will still feel his position unshaken by what we have said, having the impression, rather, that the arguments here presented presuppose a starting-point at which he cannot, from the outset, station himself. He has to concede that the decision about the reality or unreality of anything in experience takes place, in every case, in the manner outlined, but he claims that in this way we only arrive at what Kant called *empirical* reality. It designates the area governed by the observations of daily life and of science, but beyond this boundary there lies something else, *transcendent* reality, which cannot be inferred by strict logic, and is thus no postulate of the understanding, though it is a postulate of sound *reason*. It is the only true *external world*, and this alone is at issue in the philosophical problem of the existence of the external world. The discussion thereupon abandons the question about the meaning of the term 'reality', and turns to that about the meaning of the term 'external world'.

The term 'external world' is obviously used in two different ways: firstly in the usage of daily life, and secondly as a technical term in philosophy.

Where it occurs in everyday life, it has, like the majority of expressions employed in practical affairs, an intelligibly stateable meaning. In contrast to the 'internal world', which covers memories, thoughts, dreams, wishes and feelings, the 'external world' means nothing else, here, but the world of mountains and trees, houses, animals and men. What it means to maintain the existence of a certain object in this world, is known to every child; and it was necessary to point out that it really means absolutely nothing *more* than what the child knows. We all know how to verify the proposition, say, that 'There is a castle in the park before the town'. We perform certain acts, and if certain exactly specifiable states-of-affairs come about, then we say: 'Yes, there really is a castle there'; otherwise we say: 'That statement was an error or a lie.' And if somebody now asks us: 'But was the castle there in the night as well, when nobody saw it?' we answer: 'Undoubtedly! for it would have been impossible to build it in the period from early this morning till now, and besides, the state of the building shows that it was not only already *in situ* yesterday, but has been there for a hundred years, and hence since before we were born'. We are thus in possession of quite specific empirical criteria for whether houses and trees were also there when we were not seeing them, and whether they already existed before our birth, and will exist after our death. That is to say, the claim that these things 'exist independently of us' has a perfectly clear, testable meaning, and is obviously to be answered in the affirmative. We are very well able to distinguish such things in a stateable way from those that only occur 'subjectively', 'in dependence upon ourselves'. If, owing to an eye-defect, I see, for example, a dark speck when I look at the wall opposite me, I say of it that it is there only when I look, whereas I say of the wall that it is also there when I am not looking. The verification of this difference is in fact very easy, and both claims assert precisely what is contained in these verifications and nothing more.

So if the term 'external world' is taken in the everyday sense, the question about its existence simply means: Are there, in addition to memories, wishes and ideas, also stars, clouds, plants and animals, and my own body? We have just affirmed once more that it would be utterly absurd to say no to this question. There are obviously houses and clouds and animals existing independently of us, and I have already said earlier that a thinker who denied the existence of the external world in this sense would have no claim to our attention. Instead of telling us what we mean when we speak of mountains and plants, he wishes to persuade us that there are no such things at all!

But now how about science? When it speaks of the external world, does it, unlike daily life, mean something other than things such as houses and trees? It seems to me that this is by no means the case. For atoms and electric fields, or whatever else the physicist may speak of, are precisely what houses and trees consist of, according to his teaching; the one must therefore be real in the same sense as the other. The objectivity of mountains and clouds is just exactly the same as that of protons and energies; the latter stand in no greater contrast to the 'subjectivity' of feelings, say, or hallucinations, than do the former. We have long since convinced ourselves, in fact, that the existence of even the most subtle of the 'invisible' things postulated by the scientist is verified, in principle, in exactly the same way as the reality of a tree or a star.

In order to settle the dispute about realism, it is of the greatest importance to alert the physicist to the fact that his external world is nothing else but the *nature* which also surrounds us in daily life, and is not the 'transcendent world' of the metaphysicians. The difference between the two is again quite particularly evident in the philosophy of Kant. Nature, and everything of which the physicist can and must speak, belongs, in Kant's view, to empirical reality, and the meaning of this (as already mentioned) is explained by him exactly as we have also had to do. Atoms, in Kant's system, have no transcendent reality — they are not 'things-in-themselves'. Thus the physicist cannot appeal to the Kantian philosophy; his arguments lead only to the empirical external world that we all acknowledge, not to a transcendent one; his electrons are not metaphysical entities.

Many scientists speak, nonetheless, of the necessity of having to postulate the existence of an external world as a *metaphysical* hypothesis. They never do this, indeed, within their own science (although all the necessary hypotheses of a science ought to occur *within* it), but only at the point where they leave this territory and begin to philosophize. The transcendent external world is actually something that is referred to exclusively in philosophy, never in a science or in daily life. It is simply a technical term, whose meaning we now have to inquire into.

How does the transcendent or metaphysical external world differ from the empirical one? In philosophical systems it is thought of a subsisting somehow behind the empirical world, where the word 'behind' is also supposed to indicate that this world is not *knowable* in the same sense as the empirical, that it lies beyond a boundary that divides the accessible from the inaccessible.

This distinction originally has its ground in the view formerly shared by the majority of philosophers, that to know an object requires that it be immediately given, directly experienced; knowledge is a kind of intuition, and is perfect only if the known is directly present to the knower, like a sensation or a feeling. So what cannot be immediately experienced or intuited remains, on this view, unknowable, ungraspable, transcendent, and belongs to the realm of things-in-themselves. Here, as I have elsewhere had to state on numerous occasions, we simply have a confusion of knowing with mere acquaintance or experiencing. But such a confusion is certainly not committed by modern scientists; I do not believe that any physicist considers knowledge of the electron to consist in its entering bodily, by an act of intuition, into the scientist's consciousness; he will take the view, rather, that for complete knowledge the only thing needed is for the regularity of an electron's behaviour to be so exhaustively stated that all formulae in which its properties occur in any way are totally confirmed by experience. In other words, the electron, and all physical realities likewise, are *not* unknowable things-in-themselves, and do not belong to a transcendent, metaphysical reality, if this is characterized by the fact that it embraces the unknowable.

Thus we again return to the conclusion that all the physicists' hypotheses can relate only to *empirical* reality, if by this we mean the knowable. It would in fact be a self-contradiction to wish to assume something unknowable as a hypothesis. For there must always be specific *reasons* for setting up a hypothesis, since it is, after all, supposed to fulfil a specific purpose. What is assumed in the hypothesis must therefore have the property of fulfilling this purpose, and of being precisely so constituted as to be justified by these reasons. But in virtue of this very fact certain statements are made of it, and these contain *knowledge* of it. And they contain, indeed, *complete* knowledge of it, since *only* that can be hypothetically assumed for which there are reasons in experience.

Or does the scientific 'realist' wish to characterize the talk of not immediately experienced objects as a metaphysical hypothesis for some reason other than the non-existent one of its unknowability? To this, perhaps, he will answer 'yes'. In fact it can be seen from numerous statements in the literature, that the physicist by no means couples his claim of a transcendent world with the claim that it is unknowable; on the contrary, he (quite rightly) takes the view that the nature of extra-mental things is reflected with perfect correctness in his equations. Hence the external world of the physical realist is not that of traditional metaphysics. He employs the technical term of the philosophers, but what he designates by means of it has seemed to us to be merely the external world of everyday life, whose existence is doubted by nobody, not even the 'positivist'.

So what is this other reason that leads the 'realist' to regard his external world as a metaphysical assumption? Why does he want to distinguish it from the empirical external world that we have described? The answer to this question leads us back again to an earlier point in our argument. For the 'realistic' physicist is perfectly content with our description of the external world, except on one point: he thinks that we have not lent it enough *reality*. It is not by its unknowability or any other feature that he takes his 'external world' to differ from the empirical one; it is simply and solely by the fact that another, higher reality attaches to it. This often finds expression even in the terminology; the word 'real' is often reserved for this external world, in contrast to the merely 'ideal', 'subjective' content of consciousness, and the mere 'logical constructions' into which 'positivism' is accused of dissolving reality.

But now even the physical realist has a dim feeling that, as we know, reality is not a 'property'; hence he cannot simply pass from our empirical external world to his transcendent one by attributing to it the feature of 'reality' over and above the features that we, too, ascribe to all physical objects; yet that is how he talks, and this illegitimate leap, whereby he leaves the realm of the meaningful, would in fact be 'metaphysical', and is also felt to be such by himself.

We now have a clear view of the situation, and can judge it on the basis of the preceding considerations.

Our principle, that the truth and falsity of all statements, including those about the reality of a physical object, can be tested only in the 'given', and that *therefore* the meaning of all statements can likewise be formulated and understood only by means of the given – this principle has been wrongly construed as if it claimed or presupposed that only the given is real. Hence the 'realist' feels compelled to contradict the principle, and to set up the counterclaim, that the meaning of a reality-statement is by no means exhausted in mere assertions of the form 'Under these particular circumstances this particular experience will occur' (where these assertions, on our view, are in any case an infinite multitude); the meaning, he says, in fact lies *beyond this* in something else, which must be referred to, say, as 'independent existence', 'trans-cendent being' or the like, and of which our principle provides no account.

To this we ask: Well, then, *how* does one give an account of it? What do these words 'independent existence' and 'transcendent being' mean? In other words, what testable difference does it make in the world, whether an object has transcendent being or not?

Two answers are given here. The first runs: It makes a quite enormous difference. For a scientist who believes in a 'real external world' will feel and work quite differently from one who merely aims at 'describing sensations'. The former will regard the starry heaven, whose aspect recalls to him the inconceivable sublimity and size of the universe, and his own human smallness, with feelings of awe and devotion quite different from those of the latter, to whom the most distant galactic systems are but 'complexes of his own sensations'. The first will be devoted to his task with an enthusiasm, and will feel in his knowing of the objective world a satisfaction, that are denied to the second, since he takes himself to be concerned only with constructions of his own.

To this first answer we have this to say: If, in the behaviour of two thinkers, there should anywhere occur a difference such as has here been described – and it would in fact involve an observable state-of-affairs — and were we to insist upon so expressing this difference as to say that the first believes in a real external world, and the other not — well, even so, the *meaning* of our assertion still consists solely in what we observe in the behaviour of the two. That is to say, the words 'absolute reality', or 'transcendent being', or whatever other terms we may use for it, now *signify* absolutely nothing else but certain states of feeling which arise in the two whenever they contemplate the universe, or make reality-statements, or philosophize. The fact of the matter is, that employment of the words 'independent existence', 'transcendent reality' and so on, is simply and solely the expression of a feeling, a psychological attitude of the speaker (which may in the end, moreover, apply to all metaphysical propositions). If someone assures us that there is a real external world in the supra-empirical sense of the term, he thinks, no doubt, that he has thereby conveyed a truth about the world; but in actuality his words express a quite different state-of-affairs, namely the mere presence of certain feelings, which provoke him to specific reactions of a verbal or other nature.

If the self-evident still needs to be specially dwelt on, I should like to underline — but in that case with maximum emphasis, and with stress upon the *seriousness* of what I am saying — that the non-metaphysician does not differ from the metaphysician by the fact, say, that he lacks those feelings to which the other gives expression by way of the propositions of a 'realistic' philosophy, but only by the fact that he has recognized that these propositions by no means have the meaning that they seem to have, and are therefore to be avoided. He will give expression to the same feelings in a *different* way. In other words, this confrontation of the two types of thinker, set up in the 'realist's' first answer, was misleading and erroneous. If anyone is so unfortunate as not to feel the sublimity of the starry heaven, then the blame lies on something other than a logical analysis of the concepts of reality and the external world. To suppose that the opponent of metaphysics is incapable, say, of justly estimating the greatness of Copernicus, because in a certain sense the Ptolemaic view reflects the empirical situation just as well as the Copernican, seems to me no less strange than to believe that the 'positivist' cannot be a good father to his family, because according to his theory his children are merely complexes of his own sensations, and it is therefore senseless to make provision for their welfare after his death. No, the world of the non-metaphysician is the same world as that of everybody else; it lacks nothing that is needed in order to make meaningful all the statements of science and all the actions of daily life. He merely refuses to add meaningless statements to his description of the world.

We come to the *second* answer that can be given to the question about the meaning of the claim that there is a transcendent reality. It simply consists in admitting that it makes absolutely no difference for experience whether we postulate something else existing behind the empirical world or not; metaphysical realism cannot therefore be actually tested or verified. Thus it cannot be further stated what is meant by this claim; yet something *is* meant thereby, and the meaning can also be understood without verification.

This is nothing else but the view criticized in the previous Section, that the meaning of a proposition has nothing to do with its verification, and it only remains for us to repeat once more our earlier general criticism, as applied to this particular case. We must reply, therefore: Well now! You are giving the name 'existence' or 'reality' here to something that is utterly inexpressible and cannot be explained or stated in any fashion. You think, nonetheless, that these words have a meaning. As to that, we shall not quarrel with you. But this much is certain: by the admission just made, this meaning cannot in any way become manifest, cannot be expressed by any oral or written communication, or by any gesture or act. For if this were possible, a testable empirical situation would exist; there would be something *different* in the world, if the proposition 'There is a transcendent world' were true, from if it were false. This differentness would then signify the meaning of the words 'real external world', and hence it would be an empirical meaning — that is, this real external world would again be merely the empirical world which we, too, acknowledge, like everyone else. Even to speak, merely, of another world, is logically impossible. There can be no discussion about it, for a non-verifiable existence cannot enter as meaning into any possible proposition. Anyone who still believes in such a thing — or imagines he believes — can only do so in silence. There are arguments only for something that can be said.

The results of our discussion can be summarized as follows.

1. The principle, that the meaning of every proposition is exhaustively determined by its verification in the given, seems to me a legitimate, unassailable core of the 'positivist' schools of thought.

But within those schools it has seldom come clearly to light, and has often been mingled with so many untenable principles, that a logical clean-up is necessary. If we want to call the result of this clean-up 'positivism', which might well be justified on historical grounds, we should have, perhaps, to affix a differentiating adjective: the term[3] 'Logical' or 'logistic positivism' is often used; otherwise the expression 'consistent empiricism' has seemed to me appropriate.

2. This principle does not mean, nor does it follow from it, that only the given is real; such a claim would actually be meaningless.

3. Consistent empiricism, therefore, does *not* deny, either, the existence of an external world; it merely points out the empirical meaning of this existence-claim.

4. It is not an 'as if theory'. It does not say, for example, that everything behaves as if there were physical independent bodies; on the contrary, for it, too, everything is real that the non-philosophizing scientist declares to be real. The subject-matter of physics does not consist of sensations, but of laws. The formulation employed by some positivists, that bodies 'are mere complexes of sensations' is therefore to be rejected. The only correct view is that propositions about bodies can be transformed into propositions of like meaning about the regularity of occurrence of sensations.[4]

5. Logical positivism and realism are therefore not opposed; anyone who acknowledges our principle must actually be an empirical realist.

6. There is opposition only between consistent empiricism and the metaphysician, and it is directed as much against the realist as the idealist (the former is designated in our discussion as a 'realist', in quotation-marks).

7. The denial of the existence of a transcendent external world would be just as much a metaphysical proposition as its assertion; the consistent empiricist does not therefore deny the transcendent, but declares both its denial and its affirmation to be equally devoid of meaning.

---

[3] Cf. the article by A. E. Blumberg and H. Feigl ['Logical Positivism'] in *The Journal of Philosophy* 28 (1931); see also E. Kaila ['Der logistische Neupositivismus. Eine kritische Studie'] in *Annales Universitatis Aboensis* **13** (1930), and A. Petzäll ['Logistischer Positivismus'] in *Göteborgs Högskolas Arsskrift* 37 (1931).

[4] On this, as on the content of the whole essay, cf. the article by H. Cornelius ['Zur Kritik der wissenschaftlichen Grundbegriffe'] in *Erkenntnis* 2 (1931). The formulations there are admittedly not free from objection. Cf. also the outstanding discussion by Philipp Frank in chapter X of his book *Das Kausalgesetz und seine Grenzen,* Wien 1932, and Rudolf Carnap, *Scheinprobleme in der Philosophie,* Leipzig and Berlin 1928.

This last distinction is of the greatest importance. I am convinced that the main resistances to our viewpoint stem from the fact that the difference between the falsity and the meaninglessness of a proposition is not heeded. The proposition 'Talk of a metaphysical external world is meaningless' does *not* say 'There is no metaphysical external world', but something *toto coelo* different. The empiricist does not say to the metaphysician: 'Your words assert something false', but 'Your words assert nothing at all!' He does not contradict the metaphysician, but says: 'I do not understand you'.

2 Wittgenstein's Lectures 1930-33

G. E. Moore

... Near the beginning of (I)* he made the famous statement, 'The sense of a proposition is the way in which it is verified'; but in (III) he said this only meant 'You can determine the meaning of a proposition by asking how it is verified' and went on to say, 'This is necessarily a mere rule of thumb, because "verification" means different things, and because in some cases the question "How is that verified?" makes no sense'. He gave as an example of a case in which that question 'makes no sense' the proposition 'I've got toothache', of which he had already said that it makes no sense to ask for a verification of it – to ask 'How do you know that you have?' I think that he here meant what he said of 'I've got toothache' to apply to all those propositions which he had originally distinguished from 'hypotheses' as 'what I call propositions'; although in (II) he had distinguished the latter from 'hypotheses' by saying that they had 'a definite verification or falsification'. It would seem, therefore, that in (III) he had arrived at the conclusion that what he had said in (II) was wrong, and that in the case of 'what he called propositions', so far from their having 'a definite verification', it was senseless to say that they had a verification at all. His 'rule of thumb', therefore, could only apply, if at all, to what he called 'hypotheses'; and he went on to say that, in many cases, it does not apply even to

---

Source: Mind 1954, pp. 266-7, and 1955, p. 103.

*The numbers (I), (II) and (III) were used by Moore to refer to his notes of Wittgenstein's lectures in 1930, 1930-1 and 1932-3 respectively—*Ed.*

these, saying that statements in the newspapers could verify the 'hypothesis' that Cambridge had won the boat-race, and that yet these statements 'only go a very little way towards explaining the meaning of "boat-race" '; and that similarly 'The pavement is wet' may verify the proposition 'It has been raining', and that yet 'it gives very little of the grammar of "It has been raining" '. He went on to say 'Verification determines the meaning of a proposition only where it gives the grammar of the proposition in question'; and in answer to the question 'How far is giving a verification of a proposition a grammatical statement about it?' he said that, whereas 'When it rains the pavement gets wet' is not a grammatical statement at all, if we say 'The fact that the pavement is wet is a *symptom* that it has been raining' this statement is 'a matter of grammar'.

. . . he began the discussion by raising a question, which he said was connected with Behaviourism, namely, the question 'When we say "He has toothache" is it correct to say that his toothache is only his behaviour, whereas when I talk about my toothache I am not talking about my behaviour?'; but very soon he introduced a question expressed in different words, which is perhaps not merely a different formulation of the same question, viz. 'Is another person's toothache "toothache" in the same sense as mine?' In trying to find an answer to this question or these questions, he said first that it was clear and admitted that what verifies or is a criterion for 'I have toothache' is quite different. In this connection he said later, first, that the meaning of 'verification' is different, when we speak of verifying 'I have' from what it is when we speak of verifying 'He has', and then, later still, that there is no such thing as a verification for 'I have', since the question 'How do you know that you have toothache? is nonsensical. He criticized two answers which might be given to this last question by people who think it is not nonsensical, by saying (1) that the answer 'Because I feel it' won't do, because 'I feel it' means the same as 'I have it', and (2) that the answer 'I know it by inspection' also won't do, because it implies that I can 'look to see' whether I have it or not, whereas 'looking to see whether I have it or not' has no meaning. The fact that it is nonsense to talk of verifying the fact that I have it, puts, he said, 'I have it' on 'a different level' in grammar from 'he has it'. And he also expressed his view that the two expressions are on a different grammatical level by saying that they are not both values of a single propositional function 'x has toothache'; and in favour of this view he gave two definite reasons for saying that they are not, namely, (1) that 'I don't know whether I have toothache' is always absurd or nonsense, whereas 'I don't know whether he has toothache' is not nonsense, and (2) that 'It seems to me that I have toothache' is nonsense, whereas 'It seems to me that he has' is not. . . .

3 Logical Foundations of the Unity of Science

Rudolf Carnap

I WHAT IS LOGICAL ANALYSIS OF SCIENCE?

The task of analysing science may be approached from various angles. The analysis of the subject matter of the sciences is carried out by science itself. Biology, for example, analyses organisms and processes in organisms, and in a similar way every branch of science analyses its subject matter. Mostly, however, by 'analysis of science' or 'theory of science' is meant an investigation which differs from the branch of science to which it is applied. We may, for instance, think of an investigation of scientific *activity*. We may study the historical development of this activity. Or we may try to find out in which way scientific work depends upon the individual conditions of the men working in science, and upon the status of the society surrounding them. Or we may describe procedures and appliances used in scientific work. These investigations of scientific activity may be called history, psychology, sociology, and methodology of science. The subject matter of such studies is science as a body of actions carried out by certain persons under certain circumstances. Theory of science in this sense will be dealt with at various other places in this *Encyclopedia;* it is certainly an essential part of the foundation of science.

We come to a theory of science in another sense if we study not the actions of scientists but their results, namely, science as a body of ordered knowledge. Here, by 'results' we do not mean beliefs, images, etc., and the behaviour influenced by them. That would lead us again to psycho-

Source: Foundations of the Unity of Science, edited by Otto Neurath, Rudolf Carnap and Charles Morris, volume I, University of Chicago Press, 1969, pp. 42-62. Copyright 1938, 1939, 1946, 1951, 1952, 1955, and 1969 by The University of Chicago. Originally published as *International Encyclopedia of Unified Science,* edited by O. Neurath et al., University of Chicago Press, 1938.

logy of science. We mean by 'results' certain linguistic expressions, viz., the statements asserted by scientists. The task of the theory of science in this sense will be to analyse such statements, study their kinds and relations, and analyse terms as components of those statements and theories as ordered systems of those statements. A statement is a kind of sequence of spoken sounds, written marks, or the like, produced by human beings for specific purposes. But it is possible to abstract in an analysis of the statements of science from the persons asserting the statements and from the psychological and sociological conditions of such assertions. The analysis of the linguistic expressions of science under such an abstraction is *logic of science*.

Within the logic of science we may distinguish between two chief parts. The investigation may be restricted to the forms of the linguistic expressions involved, i.e., to the way in which they are constructed out of elementary parts (e.g., words) without referring to anything outside of language. Or the investigation goes beyond this boundary and studies linguistic expressions in their relation to objects outside of language. A study restricted in the first-mentioned way is called *formal*; the field of such formal studies is called formal logic or *logical syntax*. Such a formal or syntactical analysis of the language of science as a whole or in its various branches will lead to results of the following kinds. A certain term (e.g., a word) is defined within a certain theory on the basis of certain other terms, or it is definable in such a way. A certain term, although not definable by certain other terms, is reducible to them (in a sense to be explained later). A certain statement is a logical consequence of (or logically deducible from) certain other statements; and a deduction of it, given within a certain theory, is, or is not, logically correct. A certain statement is incompatible with certain other statements, i.e., its negation is a logical consequence of them. A certain statement is independent of certain other statements, i.e., neither a logical consequence of them nor incompatible with them. A certain theory is inconsistent, i.e., some of its statements are incompatible with the other ones. The last sections of this essay will deal with the question of the unity of science from the logical point of view, studying the logical relations between the terms of the chief branches of science and between the laws stated in these branches; thus it will give an example of a syntactical analysis of the language of science.

In the second part of the logic of science, a given language and the expressions in it are analysed in another way. Here also, as in logical syntax, abstraction is made from the psychological and sociological side of the language. This investigation, however, is not restricted to formal analysis but takes into consideration one important relation between linguistic expressions and other objects that of designation. An investigation of this kind is called *semantics*. Results of a semantical analysis of the language of science may, for instance, have the following forms. A certain term designates a certain particular object (e.g., the sun), or a certain property of things (e.g., iron), or a certain relation between things (e.g., fathership), or a certain physical function (e.g., temperature); two terms in different branches of science (e.g., 'homo sapiens' in biology and 'person' in economics, or, in another way, 'man' in both cases) designate (or: do not designate) the same. What is designated by a certain expression may be called its *designatum*. Two expressions designating the same are called *synonymous*. The term 'true,' as it is used in science and in everyday life, can also be defined within semantics. We see that the chief subject matter of a semantical analysis of the language of science are such properties and relations of expressions, and especially of statements, as are based on the relation of designation. (Where we say 'the designatum of an expression', the customary phrase is 'the meaning of an expression'. It seems, however, preferable to avoid the word 'meaning' wherever possible because of its ambiguity, i.e., the multiplicity of its designata. Above all, it is important to distinguish between the semantical and the psychological use of the word 'meaning'.)

It is a question of terminological convention whether to use the term 'logic' in the wider sense, including the semantical analysis of the designata of expressions, or in the narrower sense of logical syntax, restricted to formal analysis, abstracting from designation. And accordingly we may distinguish between logic of science in the narrower sense, as the syntax of the language of science, and logic of science in the wider sense, comprehending both syntax and semantics.

II THE MAIN BRANCHES OF SCIENCE

We use the word 'science' here in its widest sense, including all theoretical knowledge, no matter whether in the field of natural sciences or in the field of the social sciences and the so-called humanities, and no matter whether it is knowledge found by the application of special scientific procedures, or knowledge based on common sense in everyday life. In the same way the term 'language of science' is meant here to refer to the language which contains all statements (i.e., theoretical sentences as distinguished from emotional expressions, commands, lyrics, etc.) used for scientific purposes or in everyday life. What usually is called science is merely a more systematic continuation of those activities which we carry out in everyday life in order to know something.

The first distinction which we have to make is that between *formal science* and *empirical science*. Formal science consists of the analytic statements established by logic and mathematics; empirical science consists of the synthetic statements established in the different fields of factual knowledge. The relation of formal to empirical science will be dealt with at another place; here we have to do with empirical science, its language, and the problem of its unity.

Let us take 'physics' as a common name for the nonbiological field of science, comprehending both systematic and historical investigations within this field, thus including chemistry, mineralogy, astronomy, geology (which is historical), meteorology, etc. How, then, are we to draw the boundary line between physics and biology? It is obvious that the distinction between these two branches has to be based on the distinction between two kinds of things which we find in nature: organisms and nonorganisms. Let us take this latter distinction as granted; it is the task of biologists to lay down a suitable definition for the term 'organism', in other words, to tell us the features of a thing which we take as characteristic for its being an organism. How, then, are we to define 'biology' on the basis of 'organism'? we could perhaps think of trying to do it in this way: biology is the branch of science which investigates organisms and the processes occurring in organisms, and physics is the study of nonorganisms. But these definitions would not draw the distinction as it is usually intended. A law stated in physics is intended to be valid universally, without any restriction. For example, the law stating the electrostatic force as a function of electric charges and their distance, or the law determining the pressure of a gas as a function of temperature, or the law determining the angle of refraction as a function of the coefficients of refraction of the two media involved, are intended to apply to the processes in organisms no less than to those in inorganic nature. The biologist has to know these laws of physics in studying the processes in organisms. He needs them for the explanation of these processes. But since they do not suffice, he adds some other laws, not known by the physicist, viz., the specifically biological laws. Biology presupposes physics, but not vice versa.

These reflections lead us to the following definitions. Let us call those terms which we need – in addition to logico-mathematical terms

– for the description of processes in inorganic nature *physical terms*, no matter whether, in a given instance, they are applied to such processes or to processes in organisms. That sublanguage of the language of science, which contains – besides logico-mathematical terms – all and only physical terms, may be called *physical language*. The system of those statements which are formulated in the physical language and are acknowledged by a certain group at a certain time is called the physics of that group at that time. Such of these statements as have a specific universal form are called *physical laws*. The physical laws are needed for the explanation of processes in inorganic nature; but, as mentioned before, they apply to processes in organisms also.

The whole of the rest of science may be called *biology (in the wider sense)*. It seems desirable, at least for practical purposes, e.g., for the division of labor in research work, to subdivide this wide field. But it seems questionable whether any distinctions can be found here which, although not of a fundamental nature, are at least clear to about the same degree as the distinction between physics and biology. At present, it is scarcely possible to predict which subdivisions will be made in the future. The traditional distinction between bodily (or material) and mental (or psychical) processes had its origin in the old magical and later metaphysical mind-body dualism. The distinction as a practical device for the classification of branches of science still plays an important role, even for those scientists who reject that metaphysical dualism; and it will probably continue to do so for some time in the future. But when the aftereffect of such prescientific issues upon science becomes weaker and weaker, it may be that new boundary lines for subdivisions will turn out to be more satisfactory.

One possibility of dividing biology in the wider sense into two fields is such that the first corresponds roughly to what is usually called biology, and the second comprehends among other parts those which usually are called psychology and social science. The second field deals with the behaviour of individual organisms and groups of organisms within their environment, with the dispositions to such behaviour, with such features of processes in organisms as are relevant to the behaviour, and with certain features of the environment which are characteristic of and relevant to the behaviour, e.g., objects observed and work done by organisms.

The first of the two fields of biology in the wider sense may be called biology in the narrower sense, or, for the following discussions, simply *biology*. This use of the term 'biology' seems justified by the fact that, in terms of the customary classification, this part contains most of what is usually called biology, namely, general biology, botany, and the greater part of zology. The terms which are used in this field in addition to logico-mathematical and physical terms may be called biological terms in the narrower sense, or simply biological terms. Since many statements of biology contain physical terms besides biological ones, the *biological language* cannot be restricted to biological terms; it contains the physical language as a sublanguage and, in addition, the biological terms. Statements and laws belonging to this language but not to physical language will be called *biological statements* and *biological laws*.

The distinction between the two fields of biology in the wider sense has been indicated only in a very vague way. At the present time it is not yet clear as to how the boundary line may best be drawn. Which processes in an organism are to be assigned to the second field? Perhaps the connection of a process with the processes in the nervous system might be taken as characteristic, or, to restrict it more, the connection with speaking activities, or, more generally, with activities involving signs. Another way of characterization might come from the other direction, from outside, namely, selecting the processes in an organism from the point of view of their relevance to achievements in the environment . . . There is no name in common use for this second field. (The term 'mental sciences' suggests too narrow a field and is connected too closely with the metaphysical dualism mentioned before.) The term 'behaviouristics' has been proposed. If it is used, it must be made clear that the word 'behaviour' has here a greater extension than it had with the earlier behaviourists. Here it is intended to designate not only the overt behaviour which can be observed from outside but also internal behaviour (i.e., processes within the organism); further, dispositions to behaviour which may not be manifest in a special case; and, finally, certain effects upon the environment. Within this second field we may distinguish roughly between two parts dealing with individual organisms and with groups of organisms. But it seems doubtful whether any sharp line can be drawn between these two parts. Compared with the customary classification of science, the first part would include chiefly psychology, but also some parts of physiology and the humanities. The second part would chiefly include social science and, further, the greater part of the humanities and history, but it has not only to deal with groups of human beings but also to deal with groups of other organisms. For the following discussion, the terms 'psychology' and 'social science' will be used as names of the two parts because of lack of better terms. It is clear that both the question of boundary lines and the question of suitable terms for the sections is still in need of much more discussion.

III REDUCIBILITY

The question of the unity of science is meant here as a problem of the logic of science, not of ontology. We do not ask: "Is the world one?" "Are all events fundamentally of one kind?" "Are the so-called mental processes really physical processes or not?" "Are the so-called physical processes really spiritual or not?" It seems doubtful whether we can find any theoretical content in such philosophical questions as discussed by monism, dualism, and pluralism. In any case, when we ask whether there is a unity in science, we mean this as a question of logic, concerning the logical relationships between the terms and the laws of the various branches of science. Since it belongs to the logic of science, the question concerns scientists and logicians alike.

Let us first deal with the question of terms. (Instead of the word 'term' the word 'concept' could be taken, which is more frequently used by logicians. But the word 'term' is more clear, since it shows that we mean signs, e.g., words, expressions consisting of words, artificial symbols, etc., of course with the meaning they have in the language in question. We do not mean 'concept' in its psychological sense, i.e., images or thoughts somehow connected with a word; that would not belong to logic.) We know the meaning (designatum) of a term if we know under what conditions we are permitted to apply it in a concrete case and under what conditions not. Such a knowledge of the conditions of application can be of two different kinds. In some cases we may have a merely practical knowledge, i.e., we are able to use the term in question correctly without giving a theoretical account of the rules for its use. In other cases we may be able to give an explicit formulation of the conditions for the application of the term. If now a certain term x is such that the conditions for its application (as used in the language of science) can be formulated with the help of the terms y, z, etc., we call such a formulation a *reduction statement* for x in terms of y, z, etc., and we call x *reducible* to y, z, etc. There may be several sets of conditions for the application of x; hence x may be reducible to y, z, etc., and also to u, v, etc., and perhaps to other sets. There may even be cases of mutual reducibility, e.g., each term of the set x_1, x_2, etc., is reducible to y_1, y_2, etc.; and, on the other hand, each term of the set y_1, y_2, etc., is reducible to x_1, x_2, etc.

A *definition* is the simplest form of a reduction statement. For the formulation of examples, let us use '$\equiv$' (called the symbol of equivalence) as abbreviation for 'if and only if.' Example of a definition for 'ox': 'x is an ox $\equiv x$ is a quadruped and horned and cloven-footed and ruminant, etc.' This is also a reduction statement because it states the conditions for the application of the term 'ox,' saying that this term can be applied to a thing if and only if that thing is a quadruped and horned, etc. By that definition the term 'ox' is shown to be reducible to — moreover definable by — the set of terms 'quadruped,' 'horned,' etc.

A reduction statement sometimes cannot be formulated in the simple form of a definition, i.e., of an equivalence statement, '. . . $\equiv$ . . .,' but only in the somewhat more complex form 'If . . ., then: . . . $\equiv$ . . .' Thus a reduction statement is either a simple (i.e., explicit) definition or, so so speak, a conditional definition. (The term 'reduction statement' is generally used in the narrower sense, referring to the second, conditional form.) For instance, the following statement is a reduction statement for the term 'electric charge' (taken here for the sake of simplicity as a nonquantitative term), i.e., for the statement form 'the body x has has an electric charge at the time t': 'If a light body y is placed near x at t, then: x has an electric charge at $t \equiv y$ is attracted by x at t.' A general way of procedure which enables us to find out whether or not a certain term can be applied in concrete cases may be called a *method of determination* for the term in question. The method of determination for a quantitative term (e.g., 'temperature') is the method of measurement for that term. Whenever we know an experimental method of determination for a term, we are in a position to formulate a reduction statement for it. To know an experimental method of determination for a term, say 'Q_3,' means to know two things. First, we must know an experimental situation which we have to create, say the state Q_1, e.g., the arrangement of measuring apparatuses and of suitable conditions for their use. Second, we must know the possible experimental result, say Q_2, which, if it occurs, will confirm the presence of the property Q_3. In the simplest case — let us leave aside the more complex cases — Q_2 is also such that its nonoccurrence shows that the thing in question does not have the property Q_3. Then a reduction statement for 'Q_3,' i.e., for the statement form 'the thing (or space-time-point) x is Q_3 (i.e., has the property Q_3) at the time t,' can be formulated in this way: 'If x is Q_1 (i.e., x and the surroundings of x are

in the state Q_1) at time t, then: x is Q_3 at $t \equiv x$ is Q_2 at t.' On the basis
of this reduction statement, the term 'Q_3' is reducible to 'Q_1,' 'Q_2',
and spatio-temporal terms. Whenever a term 'Q_3' expresses the disposition of a thing to behave in a certain way (Q_2) to certain conditions
(Q_1), we have a reduction statement of the form given above. If there
is a connection of such a kind between Q_1, Q_2, and Q_3, then in biology
and psychology in certain cases the following terminology is applied:
'To the stimulus Q_1 we find the reaction Q_2 as a symptom for Q_3.' But
the situation is not essential different from the analogous one in physics,
where we usually do not apply that terminology.

Sometimes we know several methods of determination for a certain
term. For example, we can determine the presence of an electric current
by observing either the heat produced in the conductor, or the devia-
tion of a magnetic needle, or the quantity of a substance separated
from an electrolyte, etc. Thus the term 'electric current' is reducible to
each of many sets of other terms. Since not only can an electric current
be measured by measuring a temperature but also, conversely, a temperature can be measured by measuring the electric current produced
by a thermo-electric element, there is mutual reducibility between the
terms of the theory of electricity, on the one hand, and those of the
theory of heat, on the other. The same holds for the terms of the
theory of electricity and those of the theory of magnetism.

Let us suppose that the persons of a certain group have a certain set
of terms in common, either on account of a merely practical agreement
about the conditions of their application or with an explicit stipulation
of such conditions for a part of the terms. Then a reduction statement
reducing a new term to the terms of that original set may be used as a
way of introducing the new term into the language of the group. This
way of introduction assures conformity as to the use of the new term.
If a certain language (e.g., a sublanguage of the language of science,
covering a certain branch of science) is such that every term of it is
reducible to a certain set of terms, then this language can be constructed
on the basis of that set by introducing one new term after the other by
reduction statements. In this case we call the basic set of terms a
sufficient reduction basis for that language.

IV THE UNITY OF THE LANGUAGE OF SCIENCE

Now we will analyse the logical relations among the terms of different
parts of the language of science with respect to reducibility. We have

indicated a division of the whole language of science into some parts. Now we may make another division cutting across the first, by distinguishing in a rough way, without any claims to exactness, between those terms which we use on a prescientific level in our everyday language, and for whose application no scientific procedure is necessary, and scientific terms in the narrower sense. That sublanguage which is the common part of this prescientific language and the physical language may be called physical thing-language or briefly *thing-language*. It is this language that we use in speaking about the properties of the observable (inorganic) things surrounding us. Terms like 'hot' and 'cold' may be regarded as belonging to the thing-language, but not 'temperature' because its determination requires the application of a technical instrument; further, 'heavy' and 'light' (but not 'weight'); 'red', 'blue', etc.; 'large', 'small', 'thick', 'thin', etc.

The terms so far mentioned designate what we may call observable properties, i.e., such as can be determined by a direct observation. We will call them *observable thing-predicates*. Besides such terms the thing-language contains other ones, e.g., those expressing the disposition of a thing to a certain behaviour under certain conditions, e.g., 'elastic', 'soluble', 'flexible', transparent', 'fragile', 'plastic', etc. These terms — they might be called disposition-predicates — are reducible to observable thing-predicates because we can describe the experimental conditions and the reactions characteristic of such disposition-predicates in terms of observable thing-predicates. Example of a reduction statement for 'elastic': 'If the body x is stretched and then released at the time t, then: x is elastic at the time $t \equiv x$ contracts at t,' where the terms 'stretched', 'released', and 'contracting' can be defined by observable thing-predicates. If these predicates are taken as a basis, we can moreover introduce, by iterated application of definition and (conditional) reduction, every other term of the *thing-language*, e.g., designations of substances, e.g., 'stone', 'water', 'sugar', or of processes, e.g., 'rain', 'fire', etc. For every term of that language is such that we can apply it either on the basis of direct observation or with the help of an experiment for which we know the conditions and the possible result determining the application of the term in question.

Now we can easily see that every term of the *physical language* is reducible to those of the thing-language and hence finally to observable thing-predicates. On the scientific level, we have the quantitative coefficient of elasticity instead of the qualitative term 'elastic' of the thing-language; we have the quantitative term 'temperature' instead of the qualitative ones 'hot' and 'cold'; and we have all the terms by means of which physicists describe the temporary or permanent states of things or processes. For any such term the physicist knows at least one method of determination. Physicists would not admit into their language any term for which no method of determination by observations were given. The formulation of such a method, i.e., the description of the experimental arrangement to be carried out and of the possible result determining the application of the term in question, is a reduction statement for that term. Sometimes the term will not be directly reduced by the reduction statement to thing-predicates, but first to other scientific terms, and these by their reduction statements again to other scientific terms, etc.; but such a reduction chain must in any case finally lead to predicates of the thing-language and, moreover, to observable thing-predicates because otherwise there would be no way of determining whether or not the physical term in quesiton can be applied in special cases, on the basis of given observation statements.

If we come to *biology* (this term now always understood in the narrower sense), we find again the same situation. For any biological term the biologist who introduces or uses it must know empirical criteria for its application. This applies, of course, only to biological terms in the sense explained before, including all terms used in scientific biology proper, but not to certain terms used sometimes in the philosophy of biology — 'a whole', 'entelechy', etc. It may happen that for the description of the criterion, i.e., the method of determination of a term, other biological terms are needed. In this case the term in question is first reducible to them. But at least indirectly it must be reducible to terms of the thing-language and finally to observable thing-predicates, because the determination of the term in question in a concrete case must finally be based upon observations of concrete things, i.e., upon observation statements formulated in the thing-language.

Let us take as an example the term 'muscle'. Certainly biologists know the conditions for a part of an organism to be a muscle; otherwise the term could not be used in concrete cases. The problem is: Which other terms are needed for the formulation of these conditions? It will be necessary to describe the functions within the organism which are characteristic of muscles, in other words, to formulate certain laws connecting the processes in muscles with those in their environment, or, again in still other words, to describe the reactions to certain stimuli characteristic of muscles. Both the processes in the environment and those in the muscle (in the customary terminology: stimuli and reactions) must be described in such a way that we can determine them by observations. Hence the term 'muscle', although not definable in terms of the thing-language, is reducible to them. Similar considerations easily show the reducibility of any other biological term – whether it be a designation of a kind of organism, or of a kind of part of organisms, or of a kind of process in organisms.

The result found so far may be formulated in this way: The terms of the thing-language, and even the narrower class of the observable thing-predicates, supply a sufficient basis for the languages both of physics and of biology. (There are, by the way, many reduction bases for these languages, each of which is much more restricted than the classes mentioned.) Now the question may be raised whether a basis of the kind mentioned is sufficient even for the whole language of science. The affirmative answer to this question is sometimes called *physicalism* (because it was first formulated not with respect to the thing-language but to the wider physical language as a sufficient basis). If the thesis of physicalism is applied to biology only, it scarcely meets any serious objections. The situation is somewhat changed, however, when it is applied to psychology and social science (individual and social behaviouristics). Since many of the objections raised against it are based on misinterpretations, it is necessary to make clear what the thesis is intended to assert and what not.

The question of the reducibility of the terms of psychology to those of the biological language and thereby to those of the thing-language is closely connected with the problem of the various methods used in psychology. As chief examples of methods used in this field in its present state, the physiological, the behaviouristic, and the introspective methods may be considered. The *physiological approach* consists in an investigation of the functions of certain organs in the organism, above all, of the nervous system. Here, the terms used are either those of biology or those so closely related to them that there will scarcely be any doubt with respect to their reducibility to the terms of the biological language and the thing-language. For the *behaviouristic approach* different ways are possible. The investigation may be restricted to the external behaviour of an organism, i.e., to such movements, sounds, etc., as can be observed by other organisms in the neighbourhood of the first. Or processes within the organism may also be taken into account so that this approach overlaps with the physiological one. Or, finally, objects in the environment of the organism, either observed or worked on or produced by it, may also be studied. Now it is easy to see that a term for whose determination a behaviouristic method – of one of the kinds mentioned or of a related kind – is known, is reducible to the terms of the biological language, including the thing-language. As we have seen before, the formulation of the method of determination for a term is a reduction statement for that term, either in the form of a simple definition or in the conditional form. By that statement the term is shown to be reducible to the terms applied in describing the method, namely, the experimental arrangement and the characteristic result. Now, conditions and results consist in the behaviouristic method either of physiological processes in the organism or of observable processes in the organism and in its environment. Hence they can be described in terms of the biological language. If we have to do with a behaviouristic approach in its pure form, i.e., leaving aside physiological investigations, then the description of the conditions and results characteristic for a term can in most cases be given directly in terms of the thing-language. Hence the behaviouristic reduction of psychological terms is often simpler than the physiological reduction of the same term.

Let us take as an example the term 'angry'. If for anger we knew a sufficient and necessary criterion to be found by a physiological analysis of the nervous system or other organs, then we could define 'angry' in terms of the biological language. The same holds if we knew such a criterion to be determined by the observation of the overt, external behaviour. But a physiological criterion is not yet known. And the peripheral symptoms known are presumably not necessary criteria because it might be that a person of strong self-control is able to suppress these symptoms. If this is the case, the term 'angry' is, at least at the present time, not definable in terms of the biological language. But, nevertheless, it is reducible to such terms. It is sufficient for the formulation of a reduction sentence to know a behaviouristic procedure which enables us – if not always, at least under suitable circumstances – to determine whether the organism in question is angry or not. And we know indeed such procedures; otherwise we should never be able to apply the term 'angry' to another person on the basis of our observations of his behaviour, as we constantly do in everyday life and in scientific investigation. A reduction of the term 'angry' or similar terms by the formulation of such procedures is indeed less useful than a definition would be, because a definition supplies a complete (i.e., unconditional) criterion for the term in question, while a reduction statement of the conditional form gives only an incomplete one. But a criterion, conditional or not, is all we need for ascertaining reducibility. Thus the result is the following: If for any psychological term we know either a physiological or a behaviouristic method of determination, then that term is reducible to those terms of the thing-language.

In psychology, as we find it today, there is, besides the physiological and the behaviouristic approach, the so-called *introspective method.* The questions as to its validity, limits, and necessity are still more unclear and in need of further discussion than the analogous questions with respect to the two other methods. Much of what has been said about it, especially by philosophers, may be looked at with some suspicion. But the facts themselves to which the term 'introspection' is meant to refer will scarcely be denied by anybody, e.g., the fact that a person sometimes knows that he is angry without applying any of those procedures which another person would have to apply, i.e., without looking with the help of a physiological instrument at his nervous system or looking at the play of his facial muscles. The problems of the practical reliability and theoretical validity of the introspective method may here be left aside. For the discussion of reducibility an answer to these problems is not needed. It will suffice to show that in every case, no matter whether the introspective method is applicable or not, the behaviouristic method can be applied at any rate. But we must be careful in the interpretation of this assertion. It is not meant as saying: 'Every psychological process can be ascertained by the behaviouristic method.' Here we have to do not with the single processes themselves (e.g., Peter's anger yesterday morning) but with kinds of processes (e.g., anger). If Robinson Crusoe is angry and then dies before anybody comes to his island, nobody except himself ever knows of this single occurrence of anger. But anger of the same kind, occurring with other persons, may be studied and ascertained by a behaviouristic method, if circumstances are favourable. (Analogy: if an electrically charged raindrop falls into the ocean without an observer or suitable recording instrument in the neighbourhood, nobody will ever know of that charge. But a charge of the same kind can be found out under suitable circumstances by certain observations.) Further, in order to come to a correct formulation of the thesis, we have to apply it not to the kinds of processes (e.g., anger) but rather to the terms designating such kinds of processes (e.g., 'anger'). The difference might seem trivial but is, in fact, essential. We do not at all enter a discussion about the question whether or not there are kinds of events which can never have any behaviouristic symptoms, and hence are knowable only by introspection. We have to do with psychological terms not with kinds of events. For any such term, say, 'Q', the psychological language contains a statement form applying that term, e.g., 'The person . . . is at the time . . . in the state Q.' Then the utterance by speaking or writing of the statement 'I am now (or: I was yesterday) in the state Q,' is (under suitable circumstances, e.g., as to reliability, etc.) an observable symptom for the state Q. Hence there cannot be a term in the psychological language, taken as an intersubjective language for mutual communication, which designates a kind of state or event without any behaviouristic symptom. Therefore, there is a behaviouristic method of determination for any term of the psychological language. Hence every such term is reducible to those of the thing-language.

The logical nature of the psychological terms becomes clear by an analogy with these physical terms which are introduced by reduction statements of the conditional form. Terms of both kinds designate a state characterized by the disposition to certain reactions. In both cases the state is not the same as those reactions. Anger is not the same as the movements by which an angry organism reacts to the conditions in his environment, just as the state of being electrically charged is not the same as the process of attracting other bodies. In both cases that state sometimes occurs without these events which are observable from outside; they are consequences of the state according to certain laws and may therefore under suitable circumstances be taken as symptoms for it; but they are not identical with it.

The last field to be dealt with is *social science* (in the wide sense indicated before; also called social behaviouristics). Here we need no detailed analysis because it is easy to see that every term of this field is reducible to terms of the other fields. The result of any investigation of a group of men or other organisms can be described in terms of the members, their relations to one another and to their environment. Therefore, the conditions for the application of any term can be formulated in terms of psychology, biology, and physics, including the thing-language. Many terms can even be defined on that basis, and the rest is certainly reducible to it.

It is true that some terms which are used in psychology are such that they designate a certain behaviour (or disposition to behaviour) within a group of a certain kind or a certain attitude toward a group, e.g., 'desirous of ruling', 'shy', and others. It may be that for the definition or reduction of a term of this kind some terms of social science describing the group involved are needed. This shows that there is not a clear-cut line between psychology and social science and that in some cases it is not clear whether a term is better assigned to one or to the other field. But such terms are also certainly reducible to those of the thing-language because every term referring to a group of organisms is reducible to terms referring to individual organisms.

The result of our analysis is that the class of observable thing-predicates is a sufficient reduction basis for the whole of the language of science, including the cognitive part of the everyday language.

V THE PROBLEM OF THE UNITY OF LAWS

The relations between the terms of the various branches of science have been considered. There remains the task of analysing the relations between the laws. According to our previous consideration, a biological law contains only terms which are reducible to physical terms. Hence there is a common language to which both the biological and the physical laws belong so that they can be logically compared and connected. We can ask whether or not a certain biological law is compatible with the system of physical laws, and whether or not it is derivable from them. But the answer to these questions cannot be inferred from the reducibility of the terms. At the present state of the development of science, it is certainly not possible to derive the biological laws from the physical ones. Some philosophers believe that such a derivation is forever impossible because of the very nature of the two fields. But the proofs attempted so far for this thesis are certainly insufficient. This question is, it seems, the scientific kernel of the problem of vitalism; some recent discussions of this problem are, however, entangled with rather questionable metaphysical issues. The question of derivability itself is, of course, a very serious scientific problem. But it will scarcely be possible to find a solution for it before many more results of experimental investigation are available than we have today. In the meantime the efforts toward derivation of more and more biological laws from physical laws — in the customary formulation: explanation of more and more processes in organisms with the help of physics and chemistry — will be, as it has been, a very fruitful tendency in biological research.

As we have seen before, the fields of psychology and social science are very closely connected with each other. A clear division of the laws of these fields is perhaps still less possible than a division of the terms. If the laws are classified in some way or other, it will be seen that sometimes a psychological law is derivable from those of social science, and sometimes a law of social science from those of psychology. (An example of the first kind is the explanation of the behaviour of adults – e.g., in the theories of A. Adler and Freud – by their position within the family or a larger group during childhood; an example of the second kind is the obvious explanation of an increase of the price of a commodity by the reactions of buyers and sellers in the case of a diminished supply.) It is obvious that, at the present time, laws of psychology and social science cannot be derived from those of biology and physics. On the other hand, no scientific reason is known for the assumption that such a derivation should be in principle and forever impossible.

Thus there is at present *no unity of laws*. The construction of one homogeneous system of laws for the whole of science is an aim for the future development of science. This aim cannot be shown to be unattainable. But we do not, of course, know whether it will ever be reached.

On the other hand, there is a *unity of language* in science, viz., a common reduction basis for the terms of all branches of science, this basis consisting of a very narrow and homogeneous class of terms of the physical thing-language. This unity of terms is indeed less far-reaching and effective than the unity of laws would be, but it is a necessary preliminary condition for the unity of laws. We can endeavour to develop science more and more in the direction of a unified system of laws only because we have already at present a unified language. And, in addition, the fact that we have this unity of language is of the greatest practical importance. The practical use of laws consists in making predictions with their help. The important fact is that very often a prediction cannot be based on our knowledge of only one branch of science. For instance, the construction of automobiles will be influenced by a prediction of the presumable number of sales. This number depends upon the satisfaction of the buyers and the economic situation. Hence we have to combine knowledge about the function of the motor, the effect of gases and vibration on the human organism, the ability of persons to learn a certain technique, their willingness to spend so much money for so much service, the development of the general economic situation, etc. This knowledge concerns particular facts and general laws belonging to all the four branches, partly scientific and partly common-sense knowledge. For very many decisions, both in individual and in social life, we need such a prediction based upon a combined knowledge of concrete facts and general laws belonging to different branches of science. If now the terms of different branches had no logical connection between one another, such as is supplied by the homogeneous reduction basis, but were of fundamentally different character, as some philosophers believe, then it would not be possible to connect singular statements and laws of different fields in such a way as to derive predictions from them. Therefore, the unity of the language of science is the basis for the practical application of theoretical knowledge.

D. VERIFICATION AND EXPERIENCE

1 Structure and Content
Moritz Schlick

5* STRUCTURE AND MATERIAL

Thus far we have found that the possibility of expression seems to depend on the possibility of arranging signs in different ways, in other words, that the essential feature of expression is Order. Speech is based on a temporal order of signs, writing on a spatial order. When we read a written sentence aloud, its spatial order is translated into the temporal order of the spoken sentence. The possibility of such a translation proves that the particular spatial or temporal character of different languages is not relevant for the expression; the order which is essential for it must be of a more general or abstract kind, it must be something that belongs to speech just as well as to writing, or indeed to any other kind of language. It is not spatial order that is required, nor temporal order, nor any other particular order, but just Order in general. It is the kind of thing with which Logic is concerned, and we may, therefore, call it Logical Order, or simply Structure.

One and the same fact may be expressed in a thousand different languages, and the thousand different propositions will all have the same structure, and the fact which they express will have the same structure, too, for it is just for this reason that all those propositions express just this particular fact. A language must, in principle, be able to express *any* facts by its propositions, anything that can possibly happen must be capable of being expressed by language. In order to describe the world we must be able to speak of all *possible* facts includ-

Source: Moritz Schlick, *Philosophical Papers*, volume II (1925-1936), edited by H. L. Mulder and B. van de Velde-Schlick, D. Reidel, 1979, pp. 290-307. The lectures entitled 'Form and Content. An Introduction to Philosophical Thinking', of which this is an extract, were first published in Moritz Schlick, *Gesammelte Aufsätze 1926-1936*, Gerold & Co., Vienna, 1938.

*The original section numbers are retained here because of back references later. —Ed.

ing those which do not exist at all, for language must be able to deny their existence.

One might think that in saying this we are making rather bold *a priori* statement about the world. For are we not implying that all possible things or events in the world must conform to certain conditions, must possess a certain kind of order which will enable us to grasp them by means of our expressions? And would this not mean a metaphysical presupposition which can never be justified?

It is of the highest importance to see that in maintaining that all facts must have a structure we are *not* making any presuppositions about the facts at all, we are saying only that facts are facts, which is, as will probably be admitted, saying nothing about them. Some philosophers have discussed the possibility of the world's being 'irrational', which probably means that we could have no knowledge of it, form no true propositions about it. These philosophers might object to my view by asking: How do you know that everything has a logical structure? Is it not possible that the world or part of it may be entirely without order? I answer that this question is the result of a misunderstanding. The order of which I speak is of such a general nature that it would be meaningless to speak of anything as not possessing it. To say that a fact has a structure is to assert nothing of it; it is a mere tautological statement. This will become clearer as we proceed; but I think it will be admitted at the beginning that the possibility of describing or expressing a fact cannot be regarded as a genuine 'property' of the fact which it may possess or not possess.

It seems impossible to speak of Form and of Structure without implying the existence of something that *has* the structure or form. It seems natural to ask: What is the Material which possesses a certain structure? What is the Content which corresponds to the Form?

Very soon we shall feel certain misgivings as to whether there is any sense in a question of this sort, but at present we will put off these doubts and endeavour to understand Structure by trying to distinguish it from that which has the structure. Such a distinction appears to be not only reasonable but even necessary, for our examples seem to show that the same material may take many different structures, or even any structure; and that the same structure may belong to any material, or at least to any number of different materials. A sheet of music with its words and notes is as different as can be from the record on a gramophone disc, and different from the motions of the singer's larynx and the motions of the pianist's fingers: nevertheless all these things may be perfect expressions of one and the same song, which means that the structure of the melody (and of everything else which constitutes the 'song') must in some way be contained in them. On the other hand it goes without saying that a gramophone disc, for instance, must be regarded as a material which is capable of expressing anything that can be expressed, i.e., capable of taking any possible structure.

The difference between structure and material, between form and content is, roughly speaking, the difference between that which can be expressed and that which cannot be expressed. The fundamental importance for philosophy of that which is vaguely indicated by this distinction can hardly be exaggerated. We shall avoid all the typical mistakes of traditional philosophy if we bear in mind that the inexpressible cannot be expressed, not even by the philosopher.

6 COMMUNICABILITY OF STRUCTURE

We have seen that Expression serves as a means of Communication and that the latter is rendered possible by the former. Undoubtedly a thought cannot be communicated without having been expressed before; we may, therefore, regard communicability as a criterion of expressibility, i.e., of structure, and throw some light on the distinction of form and content by examining some particular instances of communication.

There is a green leaf lying on my desk. My fingers touch it, my eyes see it, I am aware of its shape, its colour, its approximate weight, and so on. You, who are not present in my room, are not aware of any of these properties, but it is possible for me to communicate them to you by *describing* the leaf. The description *expresses* its properties; how is it effected, and are there any limits to it? From what has been said before we might be led to think that there must be two kinds of properties: those which can be described and communicated, and those which cannot; the former constituting the structure of the leaf, the latter its material or content. But that would be a mistake, for in a certain sense a complete description can be given of *all* the properties of the leaf, and it is not in this simple way that we arive at the distinction of form and content.

The size of the leaf will be described by giving its various measurements, say, in fractions of inches; its shape will be communicated by mentioning its similarity to the shape of some well known object ('heart-

shaped', etc.) or by giving a drawing of its contour, which, theoretically speaking, could be replaced by a mathematical equation represent-
ing the curve of the contour. Similarly, a description of the colour can
be given by certain combinations of words such as 'dark yellowish green',
'a little darker than the green dress of a certain Madonna by Raphael',
and so forth; and if this does not seem definite enough, I might state
the exact physical circumstances under which light of that particular
green colour is produced; or, finally, I might send you a piece of paper
with a green spot on it and write underneath: 'This colour is exactly
like that of the leaf on my desk.' In this way I could go on and answer
all the questions you could possibly ask about the leaf, without any
exception.

All my answers, all my descriptions of the leaf, are propositions by
which I can communicate to you the whole of my knowledge about the
leaf. This knowledge is knowledge of a certain set of facts, and if our
former arguments are true my propositions express these facts by
conveying to you their logical structure, and nothing but their logical
structure.

Most people will find it difficult to see that this is so; they will be
inclined to believe that my descriptions contain information about the
'material' as well as about the structure of the facts which they express.
Even the statements concerning the shape and the size of the leaf do
not seem to be purely formal in the sense explained, for spatial structure,
although 'space' may justly be considered as a 'form' of natural things
or events, is not itself *logical* structure, for how could it be 'spatial' if
not by virtue of its content? If the shape of the leaf were described by
the equation of its boundary curve it would probably be admitted that
the mere equation as such contained nothing intrinsically spatial and
could, therefore, impart nothing but the logical properties of the curve.
But on the other hand the equation itself does not communicate anything anyway; it pictures the outline of the leaf only in connection with,
and by means of, an explanation of the terms composing the formula,
the terms must be interpreted as signifying spatial quantities (coordin-
ates), and it is in this way that the content 'space' seems to be brought
into the description: indirectly but no less essentially then appears to
be done by actually repeating the contour in a pencil drawing. Under
these circumstances it seems difficult to understand and prove our
assertion that only structure can be communicated and that content is
inexpressible; it does not appear to be true even for the spatial form of
our leaf — how could it be true for its colour!

Later on we shall have occasion to speak of spatial form — so we may put off the consideration of this point and confine ourselves to the analysis of expressions which deal with 'quality', that is, in our case: with the greenness of the leaf. How do those expressions communicate the colour, and in what sense is it true that they communicate nothing but its structure? What can we mean by the 'structure' of a quality?

7 STRUCTURE AND INTERNAL RELATIONS

Let us first examine the verbal expressions of our ordinary language, i.e., the sentences and their words by which I give a description of our particular green colour. We easily discover an essential feature which they all have in common: they assign to the 'green' a certain place within a comprehensive system of shades, they speak of it as belonging to a certain order of colours. They assert, for instance, that it is a bright green, or a rich green, or a bluish green, that it is similar to this, less similar to that, equally dark as that, and so on; in other words, they try to describe the green by *comparing* it to other colours. Evidently it belongs to the intrinsic nature of our green that it occupies a definite position in a range of colours and in a scale of brightness, and this position is determined by relations of similarity and dissimilarity to the other elements (shades) of the whole system.

These relations which hold between the elements of the system of colours are, obviously, *internal* relations, for it is customary to call a relation internal if it relates two (or more) terms in such a way that the terms cannot possibly exist without the relation existing between them — in other words, if the relation is necessarily implied by the very nature of the terms. Thus, all relations between *numbers* are internal: it is in the nature of six and twelve that the one is half of the other, and it would be nonsense to suppose that instances might be found in which twelve would not be twice as much as six. Similarly, it is not an accidental property of green to range between yellow and blue, but it is essential for green to be related to blue and yellow in this particular way, and a colour which was not so related to them could not possibly be called green, unless we decide to give to this word an entirely new meaning. In this way every quality (for instance, the qualities of sensation: sound, smell, heat etc., as well as colour) is interconnected with all others by internal relations which determine its place in the system of qualities.

It is nothing but this circumstance which I mean to indicate by saying that the quality has a certain definite logical structure.

It will help to make matters clearer if I say a few words about 'external' relations. The relation holding between the leaf and the desk is 'external', because it is in no way essential for the leaf to be lying there, nor does it belong to the nature of the desk to have the leaf lying on it. The surface of the desk might just as well be empty, and the leaf might be somewhere else. If the leaf happens to have the same colour as a blotter lying next to it, the colour similarity between the two objects is an external relation, for the blotting paper might just as well have been dyed with a different colour. You will notice this important difference: the relation of similarity between the two coloured objects is external, but the relation of similarity between the particular *colours* as such is internal.

It is clear that in speaking of colours or other 'qualities' we can refer to them only as *external* properties of something: we have to define a certain flavour as the sweetness of *sugar*, a certain colour as the green *of a meadow*, a certain sound as the sound produced *by a tuning fork* of a particular description, and so on.

In this way it becomes evident that propositions express facts in the world by speaking of objects and their external properties and relations. And it would be a serious misunderstanding of our statements if you believed that propositions could *speak of* logical structures or *express* them in the same sense in which we speak of objects and express facts. Strictly speaking none of our sentences about the green leaf expresses the internal structure of the green; nevertheless it is revealed by them in a certain way, or – to use Wittgenstein's term – it is *shown forth* by them. The structure of 'green' shows itself in the various possibilities of using the word 'green', it is revealed by its grammar. A language does not, of course, express its own grammar, but it shows itself in the use of the language.

All the statements that can be made in any language about the colour of our leaf speak only of its external properties and relations. They tell us where to find it (i.e., what position it occupies relatively to other things), how it is distinguished from the colour of other objects, under what circumstances it may be produced, and so forth – in other words, they express certain facts into which the green of the leaf enters as a part or element. And the way in which the word 'green' occurs in these sentences reveals the internal structure of that part or element.

8 INEXPRESSIBILITY OF CONTENT

If it is true that verbal sentences, the propositions of our spoken language, can communicate nothing but the logical structure of the green colour, then they seem to be unable to express the most important thing about it, namely that ineffable quality of greenness which appears to constitute its very nature, its true essence, in short, its Content. Obviously this content is accessible only to beings endowed with eyesight and power of colour perception. It could not possibly be conveyed to a person born blind. Shall we conclude that such a person could not understand any of our statements about the colour of the leaf, that they must be quite meaningless to him because he can never possess the content whose structure they reveal?

This conclusion would not be justified. On the contrary, the propositions describing the greenness can communicate to the blind man just as much as they do to a seeing person, namely, that it is something possessing a certain structure or belonging to a certain system of internal relations. Since Content is essentially incommunicable by language, it cannot be conveyed to a seeing man any more or any better than to a blind one. You will say that nevertheless there is an enormous difference between the two: the seeing man will *understand* the propositions about colour in a way in which the blind man is unable to understand them, and you will add that the first way is the only right way and that the blind man can never grasp the 'true meaning' of those propositions.

Nobody can deny the difference of the two cases, but let us carefully examine its real nature. The different is *not* due to an impossibility of *communicating* to the one something which could be communicated to the other, but it is due to the fact that a different *interpretation* takes place in the two cases. What you call the 'understanding of the true meaning' is an act of interpretation which might be described as the filling in of an empty frame: the communicated structure is filled with content by the understanding individual. The material is furnished by the individual himself, derived from his own experience. The seeing person fills in material supplied by his visual experience, i.e., material he has acquired by the use of his *eyes*, while the blind person will fill in some other 'content', i.e., some material which is acquired by some *other* sense organ, such as the ear, or some of the sense organs located in the skin.

(These different interpretations are possible because, as we pointed out before, any material may take any structure. It is well known that psychologists and physiologists try to represent the system of colours in a spatial picture, e.g., a double cone, each point of which is made to correspond to a particular shade of colour, and the relations of similarity between the colours are represented by relations of spatial neighbourhood between the points. The whole scheme is nothing but the construction of a system of points whose spatial relations have the same structure as the internal relations between the colours. We know that a blind man is perfectly familiar with the structure of 'space', which to him is a certain order of tactual or kinaesthetic sensations. With the help of this material he is able to build up any spatial structures, and, therefore, also the structure of the system of colours, because it can be represented by a spatial picture like that of the double cone or a similar device.)

The description of a coloured object does not *communicate* content to any one, whether blind or seeing, but leaves it to him to provide it from his own stock. You will probably say that only the seeing person will really provide 'colour', whereas a blind man will provide some other content, and you will assert that the latter, although he will think that he understands the description perfectly well, is in reality very far from it, because the 'true' interpretation must be given in terms of 'colours', and nothing else can take their place.

I answer that you are quite right if by 'colour' you mean something which has to do with *vision*, i.e., involves the use of certain particular sense organs called 'eyes'. You are at liberty to say, by way of definition, that an interpretation shall be acknowledged as *correct* only in the case of a person capable of using his eyes in a normal way. This would be perfectly legitimate. If I should ask you whether or not Mr X could properly *understand* a description of, say, a coloured picture, you could subject him to certain experiments (which would consist in observing his reactions to colours presented to his *eyes*), and the results would enable you to answer my question with either yes or no (in the latter case you would declare Mr X to be blind or colourblind).

Nothing can be said against this procedure, which, as we know, is actually used in certain tests, but I cannot agree with you if you think that it is based on anything more than an arbitrary, though very sensible, definition. I suspect that you are inclined to argue somewhat on the following line: 'If I observe a man using his eyes in a similar way in which I use my own I am justified in believing that he experiences in his consciousness exactly the same kind of sensations as I do when the same objects are presented to my eyes, so that he will be able to fill a given structure with *the same content* which I have in mind when I try to communicate to him what I have seen. I must necessarily regard his interpretation as the *only* correct one, because only he can use the right content for it'.

This argument speaks of visual sensations not only as of something which has certain relations to sense organs (or, which would amount to the same, to certain brain centres), but as of something that is made up of content, which is evidently regarded as the intrinsic nature of certain 'states of consciousness'. Later on we shall see that this whole argument is really meaningless; but before we proceed to show this we will for some time remain on a level on which there seems to be some sense in phrases of this sort. This will involve the use of incorrect language on our part, but for the sake of clarity we shall not be afraid of it and shall add the necessary corrections in due time.

The above argument, or a similar one, occurs in many metaphysical discussions, and we shall have to explain later that it must be regarded as *the* typical argument in metaphysics. The metaphysicians who use it ascribe to it the character of an inference by analogy and are therefore willing to admit that the conclusion is not absolutely certain. They say that it is just 'highly probable' that the visual perceptions of two individuals have practically *the same content* when they look at the same object and are both in possession of sound eyes and optical nerves and brain centres. We declare ourselves satisfied with this admission and call our philosopher's attention to the fact that, according to him, there is a possibility, however faint, that the content of one person's visual perception may be altogether different from that of another person's. He would have to admit that possibly the content which arises in the first man's mind when he is looking at something might be similar to, or even the same as, the content of the perceptions which arise in the second man's mind when he is listening to something. In other words: what the first person calls 'colour' would be called 'sound' by the second person, if he could experience the content of the first one. If the second man could suddenly enter into the first one's mind he might exclaim: 'Oh, now I am hearing with my eyes and seeing with my ears!' (The reader will bear in mind that I am speaking as if there were real meaning in the metaphysician's first argument.)

Now, since such an exchange of personalities cannot possibly take place (and this impossibility is not just an empirical or a practical one, but, as we shall understand later, a logical impossibility, i.e., there is no sense in the assumption), the supposed difference of content could never be discovered as long as we assume the order and structure of all the perceptions to remain the same. For this assumption means that all reactions by which the perceptive faculties could be tested (including utterances of speech) would be exactly the same for the two individuals. Both of them would say that they were seeing with their eyes and hearing with their ears, they would call the objects and their qualities by the same names, their judgements about all similarities and differences of sounds, colours, sizes etc. would agree in every respect, in short, they would understand each other perfectly. And yet in spite of all this the content of all their experiences and thoughts would be absolutely and incomparably different (I am always using the language of the metaphysician), they would be living in two entirely different world of content.

Thus we see that there may be complete understanding between individuals even if there is no similarity between the contents of their minds, and we conclude that understanding and meaning are quite independent of Content and have nothing whatever to do with it.

This result remains valid (although it should be formulated in more correct language), and we see that wherever words like 'colour', 'sound', 'feeling' etc. occur in our sentences they can never stand for Content. They have meaning only in so far as they stand for certain structures. The structures corresponding to the word 'colour' occur, as we know empirically, in connection with the use of the organs called 'eyes'. People who do not possess these organs or lack the capacity of using them in the ordinary way are called 'blind' or 'colour blind' etc. And if we assert that, e.g., colour blind persons are not able properly to understand a proposition about colours, we assert nothing but that certain structures do not occur in their experience – a fact which is revealed by the set of their responses, and we do *not* assert anything about their inability to fill structures with the 'right content'.

In so far as a blind man is actually capable of building up structures identical with those of the colour system, he does understand communications concerning coloured things, and in so far he is in possession of the logical form of colours. He is not able to *use* his knowledge in the same way as a normal person – he cannot, for instance, be a painter – but that is not on account of lack of some particular content, but because the different structures which play important parts in his life do not have the same connections and relationships among each other as exist in the life of a seeing person. We must not fall into the error of saying that this is so *because* his optical apparatus (eyes and optical centres) does not function properly; for in reality the statement that there is something wrong with his perceptive faculties is *identical* with the statement that the structures which determine the general character of his conscious life are connected or disconnected in a way which differs in a well defined manner from the lives of normal human beings. The latter statement might be formulated more shortly by saying that the structure of the world of experience shows a well defined typical difference in the two cases. All these assertions, in spite of their different wording, have exactly the same meaning.

In this way we are always confronted with the same result: wherever it may at first seem necessary or possible to speak of content a closer examination shows that it is unnecessary and impossible. Everything we can possibly say and – which is more – everything we can possibly want to say is always said without mentioning content. Content cannot be mentioned, it is inexpressible.

If you should object that in this very sentence and in all the explanations presented on these pages I myself have continually been trying to say something about content, I may remind you that I am deliberately using incorrect language at present, hoping to convince you in the end that I am not guilty of such a very crude contradiction.

It would be nonsense to regard the inexpressibility of content as a wonderful discovery or as a new deep insight. On the contrary, I am convinced that nobody seriously denies it. It may not be stated *expressis verbis*, but it is revealed in our everyday actions. Even the man in the street would not try to explain to a blind person the essence of colour. The man in the street knows that the content which, e.g., he believes to be indicated by the word 'fear' cannot be communicated but must be learned by the experience of being afraid (one of Grimm's fairy tales treats of this subject), and so forth. It is important to notice that he knows such communication or expression to be impossible, not because he has tried to do it in many ways and has failed each time, but because he cannot even try it, he can see no possible way of going about it; he is like a man who is asked to translate a sentence into a language with which he is not acquainted: the impossibility of this is not an empirical, but a logical one.

9 WHY IS CONTENT INEXPRESSIBLE?

I can imagine that beginners in philosophy (but, when we come to think of it, can anyone really be more than a beginner in philosophy?) may still entertain doubts in regard to our assertions, and it would be natural for them to ask: 'You are making very categorical statements, but must they really be true? How do you know that content might not be expressed after all, if one went about it in the right way? Why could not some means of doing it be discovered in the future? Even if it is impossible for human beings, could it not be achieved by beings of higher intellectual powers? Perhaps it is all a mistake, and a better philosopher might give us a different conviction? So where is your final proof?'

I answer that no proof is needed, because I have not asserted anything which can be believed or doubted. Our 'assertion' of the inexpressibility of Content is a mere truism, it may be regarded as a tautology; and a tautology, properly speaking, does not assert anything. It does not impart any *knowledge*. As a matter of fact, I am not claiming to convey any knowledge to you when I say that content cannot be expressed; I am only trying to agree with you on the way in which we use our terms, especially the questionable word 'content' itself. It is, if you like to put it that way, a matter of definition. Inexpressibility is not an accidental property of content which to our surprise we discover it to possess after we have been acquainted with it for some time; we cannot get acquainted with it at all without knowing that this property belongs to its very nature.

All the insight we have gained thus far we have gained by simply considering carefully what we mean when we use the term 'expression'. Expression implies two facts: one that expresses and one that is being expressed. The former is a sort of picture of the latter, it repeats its structure in a different material. A picture must differ from the original in some way, otherwise it would not be a picture at all, but simply the original itself, or perhaps an exact duplicate of it. Now there are cases in which the picture serves as a substitute for the original, we should prefer to have the original, but because for some reason or other it is unattainable we have to be satisfied with a picture (as a lover kisses the picture of his sweetheart during her absence); but there are also other cases where we do not care for the original at all — it may even be in our possession — but where we want the picture for the picture's sake, our whole interest is turned to the expression and is turned away from that which is expressed.

It is these latter cases with which we are concerned in our present analysis: we are not interested in facts but in the way in which facts can be expressed. This means that we have nothing to do with content. To express *is* to leave content out of consideration. It is by its content that the original is distinguished from all its possible pictures, reproductions or representations. If we were to use oldfashioned philosophical terms we might compare it to the *'haecceitas'* of the scholastics or speak of it as the *'principium individuationis'*. The picture could not have the same content as the original (the reader must again excuse my incorrect language) without being the original itself, it would no longer be an *expression* of it. And it is the nature of expression into which we are inquiring here.

10 TRANSPORTATION AND EXPRESSION

There is still another way of formulating the insight we have gained. In ordinary life we may distinguish between communication by transportation and communication by expression. The first consists in simply taking the thing or fact in question and putting it in the presence of the person to whom it is to be communicated; the second consist in describing it to him or her, or sending a photograph or drawing of it, or telling about it in some way or other.

This distinction can well be made in everyday life, but it may prove misleading when we try to apply it to the subtle problem with which we are concerned. If I take the green leaf from my desk and send it to a friend, he will see and touch *the same* leaf that I have seen and touched before, the leaf 'itself' will have been transported to him. And yet it will not be quite the same leaf, as it certainly will have undergone certain changes in the meantime, and even if it had not changed, there would be no identity in the logical sense, for some sentences about the leaf which were true propositions when the leaf was lying on my desk will not be so any more after it is in the hands of my friend (e.g., those referring to its place). In the strictest sense there is no transportation of an entity 'remaining identically itself'. Even the motion of a physical body through space is nothing but the transmission of a comparatively constant structure, or, still more correctly, it is a continuous series of events having approximately the same structures.

If (in the language of traditional metaphysics) I could take the greenness of a colour which I am experiencing out of my consciousness and put it into somebody else's, then he would have the green itself, and not an expression of it. We do not use the word 'expression' unless there is some other material which, as it were, carries the meaning of the expression, and this 'other' excludes the original content. Expression involves some means of communication which does not (if it were at all possible) seize the fact or object itself, does not do anything to it, but leaves it entirely as it is and where it is, conveying to us only those of its features which it may share with other materials. I might be tempted to say: well, those features are the structure, and the rest (whether it be called 'material' or otherwise) is Content, but such a figure of speech would be entirely misleading, as it seems to give an indirect description of content — which we know to be impossible. And I might be tempted to say that content cannot be expressed by language because the nature of language is expression, not transportation; but again this would give the wrong impression as if there were any sense in speaking of the transportation of content, and we know that there is not.

We can say that we express a fact by another fact (a sentence, a gesture, etc.), but to speak of expressing content is a contradiction in itself, like making music without sounds or painting without dyes. These things cannot be done, not because they are too difficult and beyond human faculties, but because there are no such things; the sentences in which we seem to be speaking of them are meaningless in the same sense in which it is meaningless to speak of a 'round square'. (I need not remind the reader that the sentence 'there is no round square' cannot be interpreted as asserting the non-existence of a certain thing called a round square, but must be understood as saying that the *combination of words* 'round square' makes no sense.)

11 IS THERE NO ESCAPE FROM LANGUAGE?

Thus far we have been discussing the nature of expression chiefly in regard to our ordinary language of words, at least we have taken from it most of our illustrations. Nevertheless our arguments have been of such a general nature that they hold for any kind of language, they include every possible sort of expression. I think this will be admitted readily, and there would be no reason for dwelling on it if we did not have to take precautions against certain misunderstandings which might arise from a failure to grasp the true function of expression.

One might be tempted to say: What, after all, is the final aim of language and expression? Is it not to make the listener or reader *acquainted* with the fact which is to be communicated to him? And is not language only an indirect and roundabout way of doing this? Could it not be achieved in a more direct way by avoiding language and bringing the listener or beholder into immediate contact with the fact?

Thus one might think (and we shall see in our second lecture that most philosophers have thought it) that expression was just a means to an end which could also be attained in some other way. If, for instance, instead of describing our green leaf and talking so much about it, we produce the leaf itself: does not this act fulfil the same purpose as any expression, only much more perfectly? Does it not provide content itself (e.g., the green of the leaf) which, as we had to admit, cannot be grasped by any expression? In this way the only effect of all our arguments against the incommunicability of content might be the desire to avoid language and replace it by real acts of presentation which would have the advantage of making us acquainted with content as well as form.

You will notice that the act of making a person directly perceive a certain object or witness a certain fact is nothing but what we called 'transportation' a little while ago. And we have treated it as not essentially different from the case of a verbal description. It is important to see that we were right in doing this. There can be no doubt that for many purposes this procedure of presenting the object itself is by far the best method of communication, but we must insist that from our point of view it is also a sort of language, or part of a language. It either has all the properties of expression (its advantages and defects), or it is no communication at all.

If one morning the mail should bring you a letter containing nothing but a green leaf, you would not be able to make anything of it; you could record it as a simple fact, but it would not 'mean' anything to you. On the other hand, the curious occurrence would have the character of a communication, it would be an actual message, if the leaf were accompanied by some explanation or if you had received some instruction concerning it. It might be a leaf someone promised to send to you from his garden, or there might be a note saying 'I found this on my desk' or 'please observe the colour of this leaf' or 'this is the colour I spoke of yesterday', etc. In all these cases the object itself enters into language as part of it, it has exactly the same function that a picture or a description or any other sign would have: it is itself a symbol in the symbolism called 'language'. The only peculiarity of this case is that the symbol has the greatest possible similarity to the signified object.

Nothing can prevent us from making the signs out of which we construct our language as similar to the signified objects as we wish; this is even the most natural procedure, and when the human mind first invented writing, it consisted of little pictures (hieroglyphics, Chinese characters). Gradually it was seen that similarity between object and symbol is quite superfluous and that convenience and practical utility are the only things which matter. If in order to denote a certain shade of green we use a little patch of colour together with our written words, we use the same method as those ancient writings: we avail ourselves of the similarity of colour in the same way as they did of the similarity of shape.

It would be a mistake to think that by using samples as symbols in the way just described we had succeeded in communicating content and had avoided the indirect method of expression. This can be seen by referring to the arguments of Section 8, and if you agree with them you will admit that we have no possibility of saying that the reader of the 'sample writing' will have 'the same content' in his mind as the writer of it. Although the 'sample symbolism' is very useful for certain purposes, it cannot be said to be in every respect the most perfect language, it does not fulfil its functions any more correctly than a verbal language can. There can be no doubt, for instance, that a scientific description of a colour in terms of wave lengths and other physical data (perhaps including the physiological state of the percipient) must be regarded as ever so much safer and more accurate than the presentation of a sample or the coloured object itself, for the latter may have undergond all kinds of changes when we were not looking (or, for that matter, even while we were looking), and the physiological condition of the percipient may not be at all what we expected it to be. The colour sample language can be understood only by people with normal eyesight, it will produce a certain colour perception in their minds, but it will not 'communicate' any 'colour content' to them.

Thus we may say in conclusion that we need language for communication, there is no escape from it and consequently no possibility of 'communicating content'. We can introduce *samples* into our language, i.e., speak with colours about colours, with sounds about sounds etc., but Content refuses to enter into it. In so far as a sample can communicate anything it does not do so by its content, but because it is used as a symbol (i.e., as something whose signification must be indicated) and it functions in the same way as all symbols do. Signs remain signs, no matter how we fix their meaning. We can relate the symbol to the object we want it to symbolize by pointing at both of them simultaneously, or by agreeing that the sign shall exhibit a well defined similarity to its object (as in the case of 'samples'), or in some other way: in all cases it is entirely a matter of arbitrary agreement.

No fact can be an 'expression' except by agreement. Nothing expresses anything *by itself*. No series of signs, whether consisting of human sounds, or marks on paper, or any other natural or artificial elements, is a 'proposition' simply by its own nature, if by this word we denote something which 'says' anything or has a 'meaning'. A series of marks can become a proposition only by virtue of some agreement which assigns a signification to the single signs and a grammar to the way in which they are combined.

12 ON 'SAMENESS OF QUALITY'

Several times during the course of the foregoing considerations I had to warn the reader that I was not expressing myself correctly, and had to ask his pardon for it. We shall now examine one of the most important cases in which our language was imperfect, and then see in general how we can guard ourselves against falling into error on account of such imperfections.

We have continually been speaking of 'content' (although often with some hesitation) and we have discussed the possibility of two separate minds experiencing 'the same' content. It is usually admitted – on the strength of arguments like those presented in Section 8 – that it is forever impossible to *find out* whether or not two people have the same 'data of consciousness' in their minds; at the same time it is generally believed that two data in different minds must either be alike or not alike, and that the question concerning their sameness has a definite meaning, although, unfortunately, it cannot be answered with absolute certainty. Usually it is added that only a high degree of probability is attainable for the answer, because sameness or diversity of mental states of different individuals 'cannot be observed directly but must be inferred by analogy'.

What are we to think of these current opinions? They seem to me to be very ambiguously expressed, and it is necessary to become perfectly clear about the meaning which the phrase 'sameness of quality' can possibly have in these assertions. I think it is perfectly legitimate to say that two individuals experience 'the same' of 'different' feelings or qualities of sensation as long as the truth or falsity of such statements can actually be tested. Such tests are carried out by the physiologist who can examine and compare the perceptive powers of different individuals. He discovers, for instance, that most people exhibit a difference in their responses (e.g., their verbal utterances) when confronted with two different shades of colour, but that a certain percentage of individuals cannot be made to react differently in the two cases. These latter persons are called 'colour blind' by the physiologist; he says that the quality of their sense perception is not the same as that of people with normal eyesight. He is perfectly right in maintaining this, and his statement is by no means based on an inference by analogy, it is an empirical judgement of the same kind of validity as any proposition in chemistry or physics. It asserts the existence of certain structures in the personality of the individuals in question: there is a difference in the multiplicity of reactions between a colour blind person and a normal one, there is a great variety in the perceptions of a normal individual, and this is, of course, a purely *formal* property. This is all that can be said, and nothing else *is* said by the proposition 'the qualities of the sensations in the two cases differ in such and such a way'. The system of colours is more complicated in a normal person than in a colour blind one, the internal relations are less simple, and this is a difference of structure.

Thus the assertions of the physiologist are ordinary statements of fact and contain *everything* that can be said about the qualities. If the statements cannot be made with absolute certainty but only with a lesser or greater degree of probability this is not because the qualities 'cannot be observed directly but must be inferred by analogy'; it is because those statements share the fate of all empirical assertions: the observations on which they are based are never complete and always subject to error, they may be corrected by subsequent, and perhaps more careful, investigations of reactions of the same individuals.

These reactions reveal the structure of the sense perceptions, and everything that can possibly be said about their qualities can be said in terms of those responses. As soon as you try to say anything *more*, as soon as you think that there *is* anything more to be said, namely about the 'content' of the qualities, your assertions will *not* become less probable or more hypothetical, but they will cease to be assertions at all, the word 'quality' will simply have become meaningless, you will not be making an intelligible use of it. The reason for this lies in the fact that no series of words will actually form a proposition, will have actual *meaning*, unless we can indicate a way of testing its truth, at least in principle. This will be explained later (Section 14*); at present we confine ourselves to saying that statements about the Sameness or Diversity of Qualities must by no means be interpreted as dealing with Content. Like all other propositions, they express the facts they communicate by showing forth their structure; Content is not touched upon in any way.

This is not because content is too difficult to get at, or because the right method of investigating it has not yet been found, but simply because there is no sense in asking any questions about it. There is no proposition about content, there cannot be any. In other words: it would be best not to use the word 'content' at all, there is no need for it, and my only excuse for using the word (even in the title of these lectures) is that this forbidden road seemed to me to be the easiest way of taking the reader to a point which will allow him to get a first view of the land before him. He will now be able to turn back and find the right road which will actually take him to the promised land. I shall continue to use the term 'content' now and then for the sake of convenience, but the reader will understand that a sentence in which this word occurs must not be regarded as a proposition about something called 'content', but as a sort of abbreviation of a more complicated sentence in which the word does not occur. . . .

---

*Reprinted here as the first part of item A2—*Ed.*

2 Protocol Statements and the Formal Mode of Speech
Rudolf Carnap

LANGUAGES

In formulating the thesis of the unity of Science as the assertion that objects are of a single kind, that states of affairs are of a single kind, we are using the ordinary fashion of speech in terms of 'objects' and 'states of affairs'. The correct formulation replaces 'objects' by 'words' and 'states of affairs' by 'statements', for a philosophical, i.e. a logical, investigation must be an analysis of language. Since the terminology of the analysis of language is unfamiliar we propose to use the more usual mode of speech (which we will call *'material'*) side by side with the correct manner of speaking (which we will call the *'formal'*). The first speaks of 'objects', 'states of affairs', of the 'sense', 'content' or 'meaning' of words, while the second refers only to linguistic forms.[1]

In order to characterize a definition *language* it is necessary to give its *vocabulary* and *syntax*, i.e. the words which occur in it and the rules in accordance with which (1) sentences can be formed from those words and (2) such sentences can be transformed into other sentences, either of the same or of another language (the so-called rules of inference and rules for translation). But is it not also necessary in order to understand the 'sense' of the sentences, to indicate the 'meaning' of the words? No; the demand thereby made in the material mode is satisfied by specifying the formal rules which constitute its syntax. For the

---

Source: Rudolf Carnap, *The Unity of Science,* translated by M. Black, Kegan Paul, 1934, pp. 37-52, 76-84. This monograph, originally entitled 'Die physikalische Sprache als Universalsprache der Wissenschaft', first appeared in *Erkenntnis,* vol. II, 1932.

[1] A strictly formal theory of linguistic forms ('logical syntax'), will be developed later. The 'thesis of syntax' which has only been sketched in the above will there be explained in detail and justified. It asserts that all propositions of philosophy which are not nonsense are syntactical propositions, and therefore deal with linguistic forms. (So-called propositions in metaphysics, on the other hand, can be only the subject-matter of syntactical statements, e.g. of a statement which asserts their syntactical invalidity, i.e. which asserts that they are nonsense.)

(The book here announced is *Logische Syntax der Sprache,* Vienna, 1934; translated as *Logical Syntax of Language,* London, 1937.)

'meaning' of a word is given either by translation or by definition. A translation is a rule for transforming a word from one language to another, (e.g. 'cheval' = 'horse'); a definition is a rule for mutual transformation of words in the same language. This is true both of so-called nominal definitions (e.g. 'Elephant' = animal with such and such distinguishing characteristics) and also, a fact usually forgotten, for so-called ostensive definitions (e.g. 'Elephant' = animal of the same kind as the animal in this or that position in space-time); both definitions are translations of words.

At the expense of some accuracy we may also characterize a language in a manner other than in the formal mode above and, using the more 'intuitive' material mode, say a language is such that its statements describe such and such (here would follow a list of the objects named in the language). The alternative formulation is permissible provided the writer and the reader are clear that the material mode is only a more vivid translation of the previous description in the formal mode. If this is forgotten the danger may arise of being diverted by the material mode of speech into considering pseudo-questions concerning the essence or reality of the objects mentioned in the definition of a language. Nearly all philosophers and even many Positivists have taken the wrong turning and gone astray in this way.

As an example we may take the language of arithmetic. In the formal mode, this particular language might be characterized as follows:—

Arithmetical statements or sentences are compounded of signs of such and such a kind put together in such and such a way; such and such (specified) rules of transformation apply to them.

Alternatively, using now the material mode, we could say:—

Arithmetical theorems state certain properties of numbers and certain relations between numbers.

Though such a formulation is inexact it can be clearly understood and is permissible if carefully handled. One must not, however, be led by this formulation into considering pseudo-questions about what kind of objects these 'numbers' are, whether they are 'real' or 'ideal', extramental or intra-mental, etc. If the formal mode is used, in which 'numbers' are replaced by 'numerical symbols', such pseudo-questions vanish.

In the rest of the paper we shall at all times help the reader by using both modes of expression and write the formal, and, strictly speaking, only correct, expression of our thought in a parallel column on the left of the more usual formulation.

Various 'languages' can be distinguished in science. Let us for example consider the language of economics which can be characterized in somewhat the following fashion: i.e., by the fact

that its sentences can be constructed from expressions: 'supply and demand', 'wage', 'price', etc. ... put together in such and such a way.

that its propositions describe economic phenomena such as supply and demand, etc.

We will call a language a *universal* language

if every sentence can be translated into it,

if it can describe every state of affairs,

and if this is not the case, a 'partial' language. The language of economics is a 'partial' language since e.g.

a theorem in physics concerning the vectors of an electro-magnetic field cannot be translated into the language of economics.

the state of an electro-magnetic field in some region cannot be described in economic terms.

PROTOCOL LANGUAGE

Science is a system of statements based on direct experience, and controlled by experimental verification. Verification in science is not, however, of single statements but of the entire system or a sub-system of such statements. Verification is based upon 'protocol statements', a term whose meaning will be made clearer in the course of further discussion. This term is understood to include statements belonging to the basic protocol or direct record of a scientist's (say a physicist's or psychologist's) experience. Implied in this notion is a simplification of actual scientific procedure as if all experiences, perceptions, and feelings, thoughts, etc., in everyday life as well as in the laboratory, were first recorded in writing as 'protocol' to provide the raw material for a subsequent organization. A 'primitive' protocol will be understood to exclude all statements obtained indirectly by induction or otherwise and postulates therefore a sharp (theoretical) distinction between the raw material of scientific investigation and its organization. In practice, the laboratory record of a physicist may have approximately the following form: 'Apparatus set up as follows: . . . ; arrangement of switches: . . . ; pointer readings of various instruments at various times: . . . ; sparking discharge takes place at 500 volts'. Such a set of statements is not a primitive protocol in view of the occurrence of statements

deduced with the help of other statements from the protocol.	which describe states of affairs not directly observed.

A primitive protocol would perhaps run as follows: 'Arrangement of experiment: at such and such positions are objects of such and such kinds (e.g., "copper wire"; the statement should be restricted perhaps to "a thin, long, brown body" leaving the characteristics denoted by "copper" to be deduced from previous protocols in which the same body has occurred): here now pointer at 5, simultaneously spark and explosion, then smell of ozone there'. Owing to the great clumsiness of primitive protocols it is necessary in practice to include terms of derivative application in the protocol itself. This is true of the physicist's protocol and true in far greater measure of the protocols made by biologists, psychologists and anthropologists. In spite of this fact, questions of the justification of any scientific statement, i.e. of its origin in protocol statements, involve reference back to the primitive protocol.

From now onwards 'protocol statements' will be used as an abbreviation for 'statements belonging to the primitive protocol'; the language to which such statements belong will be called the *'protocol-language'*. (Sometimes also termed 'language of direct experience' or 'phenomenal language'; the neutral term 'primary language' is less objectionable.) In the present state of research it is not possible to characterize this language with greater precision, i.e. to specify its vocabulary, syntactical forms and rules. This is, however, unnecessary for the subsequent arguments of this paper. The analysis which follows is a sketch of some of the views as to the form of protocol statements held at the present day by various schools of thought. Though the author will take no sides in the issues involved the incidental discussion will elucidate still further the meaning of the term 'protocol-language'.

The simplest statements in the *protocol-language* are protocol-statements i.e. statements needing no justification and serving as foundation for all the remaining statements of science.	The simplest statements in the *protocol-language* refer to the given, and describe directly given experience or phenomena, i.e. the simplest states of which knowledge can be had.

Question: What kinds of word occur in protocol statements?

First answer: Protocol statements are of the same kind as: 'joy now', 'here, now, blue; there, red'.

Second answer: Words like 'blue' do not occur in protocol statements but appear first of all in derived propositions (they are words of higher type). Protocol statements on the other hand are of forms similar to the following:—

(a) 'Red circle, now'

or (b) . . .

or (c). . . .

Third answer: Protocol statements have approximately the same kind of form as 'A red cube is on the table'.

Question: What objects are the elements of given, direct experience?

First answer: The elements that are directly given are the simplest sensations and feelings.

Second answer: Individual sensations are not given directly but are the result of isolation. Actually given are more complex objects such as:—

(a) Partial *gestalts* of single sensory fields, e.g. a visual gestalt,

or (b) Entire sensory fields, e.g. the visual fields as a unity,

or (c) The total experience during an instant as a unity still undivided into separate sense-regions.

Third answer: Material things are elements of the given: a three dimensional body is perceived as such directly and not as a series of successive two-dimensional projections.

These are three examples of contemporary opinions which are, of course, usually expressed in the material mode. The first can be termed 'atomistic Positivism' and is approximately Mach's standpoint. Most present-day critics regard it as inadequate, for objections brought against it by subsequent psychologists and especially followers of Gestalt psychology are to a great extent justified. Opinion on the whole tends to choose between the variations included in the second of the answers given above. The third view in our classification is not often held to-day; it is however more plausible than it appears and deserves more detailed investigation, for which this is however not the place.

Statements of the system constituted by science (statements in the language of that system) are not, in the proper sense of the word, derived from protocol statements. Their relation to these is more complicated. In considering scientific statements, e.g. in physics, it is necessary to distinguish in the first place between 'singular' statements (referring to events at a definite place and time, e.g. 'the temperature was so much at such and such a place and time') and the so-called 'laws of nature', i.e. general propositions from which singular propositions or combinations of such can be derived (e.g. 'the density of iron is 7.4 (always and everywhere'). In relation to singular statements a 'law' has the character of an *hypothesis*; i.e. cannot be directly deduced from any finite set of singular statements but is, in favourable cases, increasingly supported by such statements. A singular statement (expressed in the vocabulary of the scientific systems) has again the character of an hypothesis in relation to other singular statements and in general the same character in its relation to protocol statements. From no collection of protocol statements, however many, can it be deduced, but is in the most favourable case continually supported by them. In fact deduction is possible but in the converse direction. For protocol statements can be deduced by applying the rules of inference to sufficiently extensive sets of singular statements (in the language of the scientific system) taken in conjunction with laws of nature. Now the verification of singular statements consists of performing such deductions in order to discover whether the protocol statements so obtained do actually occur in the protocol. Scientific statements are not, in the strict sense, 'verified' by this process. In establishing the scientific system there is therefore an element of convention, i.e. the form of the system is never completely settled by experience and is always partially determined by conventions.

We will now consider the case of a person A undertaking, with the help of his protocol, verifications of scientific statements in the manner described above. The question whether each person has his own protocol language will be discussed later. For the present A's own protocol language will be referred to as 'the' protocol language.

Whenever the rules of transformation state the conditions under which statements in the protocol	If a state of affairs described by p can be reduced to facts about given, i.e. direct, experience of A,

language can be deduced from a statement p, it is always possible, in principle, for A to verify p. Whether A can actually do this depends on empirical circumstances. If, however, there is no such inferential relationship between a statement p and statements of the protocol language then p is not verifiable for A; p has no sense, is formally incorrect.

A has in theory the possibility of verifying p. A then knows the 'sense' of p, for the 'sense' of p, or what is expressed by p, consists of the method of verification, i.e. in the reduction to the given. If some statement p is not in this inferential relation to statements concerning the given, p cannot be understood by A, i.e. p is nonsense.

In such a case A cannot understand the statement p, for to 'understand' means to know the consequences of p, i.e. to know the statements of the protocol language which can be deduced from p.

For if A is to understand a statement he must know what states of affairs involving the given (what possible direct experiences) are the case if p is true.

If an inferential relation of the kind described holds between a statement p and each of the protocol languages of several persons,

If the state of affairs expressed by a statement p is verifiable in the manner described by several persons,

p has sense for each such person. In such a case p will be said to have sense (for those persons) *inter-subjectively*. This term of course is relative to the persons who understand the statement in the manner described. By a language 'inter-subjective' (for certain persons) will be understood a language whose statements are inter-subjective (for those persons). A statement p, which is inter-subjective (for certain persons), is said to be inter-subjectively valid if p is valid for each person, i.e. if it is supported, in sufficient measure, by the protocol statements of each such person. . . .

PROTOCOL LANGUAGE AS A PART OF PHYSICAL LANGUAGE

To what extent do statements in protocol language conform to our thesis of the universality of the physical language? That thesis demands that statements in protocol language, e.g. statements of the basic protocol, can be translated into physical language.

given, direct experiences are physical facts, i.e. spatio-temporal events.

Objections will certainly be raised to these assertions. It will be said

'Rain may be a physical event but not my present memory of rain. My perception of water which is falling at this moment and my present joy are not physical events'.

This objection is in the spirit of usual views on this question, and would be accepted by most writers on the Theory of Knowledge. If this objection is considered more closely it will be remarked, in the first place, that it is directed only against the material formulation of our thesis (in the right hand column). We have previously seen that the material mode is a mere transformation of the correct formal mode of speech and easily leads to pseudo-problems. We shall therefore, regard this objection critically in view of the fact that it can be formulated only in the terminology of the right hand column i.e. in the material form, but for the moment, however, we will leave such criticisms on one side and adopt the (fictitious) procedure of regarding the matter from the standpoint of our opponent: we shall, in the first place, use the material mode quite freely and, secondly, suppose that the objection and the grounds on which it is based in its material formulation are justified. It will then appear that we are led into insoluble difficulties and contradictions. This fact will disprove the supposition and dispose of the objection.

Let p be a singular statement in the protocol language of a person S_1, i.e. a statement about the content of one of S_1's experiences, e.g. 'I (i.e. S_1) am thirsty' or, briefly, 'Thirst now'. Can the same state of affairs be expressed also in the protocol language of another person S_2? The statements of the latter language speak of the content of S_2's experiences. An experience in the sense in which we are now using the word is always the experience of a definite person and cannot at the same time be the experience of another person. Even if S_1 and S_2 were, by chance, thirsty simultaneously the two protocol statements 'Thirst now' though composed of the same sounds would have different senses when uttered by S_1 and S_2 respectively. For they refer to different situations, one to the thirst of S_1, the other to the thirst of S_2. No statement in S_2's protocol language can express the thirst of S_1. For all such statements express only what is immediately given to S_2; and S_1's thirst is a *datum* for S_1 only and not for S_2. We do say of course that S_2 can 'recognize' the thirst of S_1 and can therefore also refer to it. What S_2 is actually recognizing however is, strictly speaking, only the physical state of S_1's body which is connected for S_2 with the idea of his own thirst. All that S_2 can verify when he asserts 'S_1 is thirsty' is that S_1's body is in such and such a state, and a statement asserts no more than can be verified. If by 'the thirst of S_1' we understand not the physical state of his body but his sensations of thirst, i.e. something non-material, then S_1's thirst is fundamentally beyond the reach of S_2's recognition.

A statement about S_1's thirst would then be fundamentally un-verifiable by S_2, it would be for him in principle impossible to understand, void of sense.

In general, every statement in any person's protocol language would have sense for that person alone, would be fundamentally outside the understanding of other persons, without sense for them. Hence every person would have his own protocol language. Even when the same words and sentences occur in verious protocol languages, their sense would be different, they could not even be compared. *Every protocol language could therefore be applied only solipsistically; there would be no intersubjective protocol language. This is the consequence obtained by consistent adherence to the usual view and terminology* (rejected by the author).

But even stranger results are obtained by using, on the basis of our supposition, the material terminology which we regard as dangerous. We have just considered the experiences of various persons and were forced to admit that they belong to completely separated and mutually disconnected realms. We will now consider the relations between the content of my own experiences say, as described by statements in my protocol, and the corresponding physical situation as described by singular statements in physical language, e.g. 'Here the temperature is 20 degrees centigrade now'. We have on the one side the content of experience, sensations, perceptions, feelings, etc., and on the other side constellations of electrons, protons, electro-magnetic fields, etc.; that is, two completely disconnected realms in this case also. Nevertheless an inferential connection between the protocol statements and the singular physical statements must exist for if, from the physical statements, nothing can be deduced as to the truth or falsity of the protocol statements there would be no connection between scientific knowledge and experience. Physical statements would float in a void disconnected, in principle, from all experience. If, however, an inferential connection between physical language and protocol language does exist there must also be a connection between the two kinds of facts. For one statement can be deduced from another if, and only if, the fact described by the first is contained in the fact described by the second. Our fictitious supposition that the protocol language and the physical language speak of completely different facts cannot therefore be reconciled with the fact that the physical descriptions can be verified empirically.

In order to save the empirical basis of the physical descriptions the hypothesis might perhaps be adopted that although protocol language does not refer to physical events the converse is true and physical language refers to the content of experiences and definite complexes abstracted from such content. Difficulties then arise however on considering the relation between the several persons' protocol languages and physical language. S_1's protocol language refers to the content of S_1's experience, S_2's protocol language to the content of S_2's experience. What can the intersubjective physical language refer to? It must refer to the content of the experiences of both S_1 and S_2. This is however impossible for the realms of experience of two persons do not overlap. There is no solution free from contradictions in this direction.

We see that the use of the material mode leads us to questions whose discussion ends in contradiction and insoluble difficulties. The contradictions however disappear immediately we restrict ourselves to the correct, formal mode of speech. The questions of the kinds of facts and objects referred to by the various languages are revealed as pseudo-questions. These led us, in turn, to further unanswerable pseudo-questions such as the question how the reciprocal convertibility of physical language and protocol language is compatible with the 'fact' that the first refers to physical situations and the second to experienced content. *The pseudo-questions are automatically eliminated by using the formal mode.* If, instead of speaking of the 'content of experience', 'sensations of colour' and the like, we refer to 'protocol statements' or 'protocol statements involving names of colours' no contradiction arises in connection with the inferential relation between protocol language and physical language. Should then, those expressions in the material mode not be used at all? Their use is in itself no mistake, nor are they senseless, but we see that the danger involved is even greater than previously stated. For complete safety it would be better to avoid the use of the material mode entirely, although it is the terminology usual throughout the whole of Philosophy (also in the Viennese circle). If this mode is still to be used particular care must be taken that the statements expressed are such as might also be expressed in the formal mode. That is the criterion which distinguishes statements from pseudo-statements in Philosophy. . . .

3 Protocol Sentences*

Otto Neurath

With the progress of knowledge, the number of expressions which are formulated with a high degree of precision in the language of Unified Science is continually on the increase. Even so, no such scientific term is wholly precise; for they are all based upon terms which are essential for *protocol sentences;* and it is immediately obvious to everyone that these terms must be vague.

The fiction of an ideal language constructed out of pure atomic sentences is no less metaphysical than the fiction of Laplace's demon. The language of science, with its ever increasing development of symbolic systems, cannot be regarded as an approximation to such an ideal language. The sentence 'Otto is observing an angry person' is less precise than the sentence 'Otto is observing a thermometer reading 24 degrees', insofar as the expression 'angry person' cannot be so exactly defined as 'thermometer reading 24 degrees'. But 'Otto' itself is in many ways a vague term. The phrase 'Otto is observing' could be replaced by the

Source: A. J. Ayer (ed.), *Logical Positivism,* Allen & Unwin, 1959, pp. 199-207. This paper, originally entitled 'Protokollsätze', first appeared in *Erkenntnis,* vol. III, 1932-33. Reprinted with permission of George Allen and Unwin and Macmillan Publishing Co., Inc., copyright © 1959 by the Free Press, a Corporation.

*At the beginning of his article Neurath had the following note: 'References will be to Rudolf Carnap's article, "Die Physikalische Sprache als Universalsprache der Wissenschaft', *Erkenntnis,* 1932, vol. II, p. 432 ff. Since there is widespread agreement with Carnap, we shall adopt his terminology. So that I need not repeat what I have already written elsewhere, I refer the reader to my articles "Physikalismus", *Scientia,* 1931, pp. 297 ff. and "Soziologie im Physikalismus", *Erkenntnis,* Vol. II, 1932, pp. 393 ff.'–*A.J.A.*

Extracts from Carnap's paper, in translation, appear as item D2 above–*Ed.*

phrase 'The man, whose carefully taken photograph is listed no. 16 in the file, is observing'; but the term 'photograph listed no. 16 in the file' still has to be replaced by a system of mathematical formulae, which is unambiguously correlated with another system of mathematical formulae, the terms of which take the place of 'Otto', 'angry Otto', 'friendly Otto', etc.

What is originally given to us is our *ordinary natural language* with a stock of imprecise, unanalysed terms. We start by purifying this language of metaphysical elements and so reach the *physicalistic ordinary language*. In accomplishing this we may find it very useful to draw up a list of proscribed words.

There is also the *physicalistic language of advanced science* which we can so construct that it is free from metaphysical elements from the start. We can use this language only for special sciences, indeed only for parts of them.

If one wished to express all of the unified science of our time in one language, one would have to combine terms of ordinary language with terms of the language of advanced science, since, in practice, the two overlap. There are some terms which are used only in ordinary language, others which occur only in the language of advanced science, and still others which appear in both languages. Consequently, in a scientific treatise concerned with the entire field of unified science only a 'slang' comprising words of both languages will serve.

We believe that every word of the physicalistic ordinary language will prove to be replaceable by terms taken from the language of advanced science, just as one may also formulate the terms of the language of advanced science with the help of the terms of ordinary language. Only the latter is a very unfamiliar proceeding, and sometimes not easy. Einstein's theories are expressible (somehow) in the language of the Bantus – but not those of Heidegger, unless linguistic abuses to which the German language lends itself are introduced into Bantu. A physicist must, in principle, be able to satisfy the demand of the talented writer who insisted that: 'One ought to be able to make the outlines of any rigorously scientific thesis comprehensible in his own terms to a hackney-coach-driver.'

The language of advanced science and ordinary language coincide today primarily in the domain of arithmetic. But, in the system of radical physicalism, even the expression '2 times 2 is 4', a *tautology*, is linked to protocol sentences. Tautologies are defined in terms of sentences which state how tautologies function as codicils appended to

certain commands under certain circumstances. For instance: 'Otto says to Karl "Go outside when the flag waves *and* when 2 times 2 is four." '
The addition of the tautology here does not alter the effect of the command.

Even considerations of rigorous scientific method restrict us to the use of a *'universal slang.'* Since there is as yet no general agreement as to its composition, each scholar who concerns himself with these matters must utilize a universal slang to which he himself has contributed new terms.

There is no way of taking conclusively established pure protocol sentences as the starting point of the sciences. No *tabula rasa* exists. We are like sailors who must rebuild their ship on the open sea, never able to dismantle it in dry-dock and to reconstruct it there out of the best materials. Only the metaphysical elements can be allowed to vanish without trace. Vague linguistic conglomerations always remain in one way or another as components of the ship. If vagueness is diminished at one point, it may well be increased at another.

We shall, from the very first, teach children the universal-slang — purged of all metaphysics — as the language of the historically transmitted unified science. Each child will be so trained that it starts with a simplified universal-slang, and advances gradually to the use of the universal-slang of adults. In this connection, it is meaningless to segregate this children's language from that of the adults. One would, in that case, have to distinguish several universal-slangs. The child does not learn a *primitive* universal-slang from which the universal-slang of the adults derives. He learns a 'poorer' universal-slang, which is gradually filled in. The expression 'ball of iron' is used in the language of adults as well as in that of children. In the former it is defined by a sentence in which terms such as 'radius' and 'π' occur, while in the children's definition words such as 'nine-pins', 'present from Uncle Rudi', etc. are used. But 'Uncle Rudi' also crops up in the language of rigorous science, if the physical ball is defined by means of protocol sentences in which 'Uncle Rudi' appears as 'the observer who perceives a ball'.

Carnap, on the other hand, speaks of a *primitive* protocol language.[1] His comments on the primitive protocol language — on the protocol sentences which 'require no verification' — are only marginal to his significant anti-metaphysical views, the mainspring of which is not

[1]*Op. cit., Erkenntnis,* Vol II, pp. 437 ff. and 453 ff. (Above, pp. 152 ff. and 156 ff.–*Ed.*)

affected by the objections here brought forward. Carnap speaks of a primary language, also referred to as an experiential or as a pheno-menalistic language. He maintains that 'at the present stage of inquiry, the question of the precise characterization of this language cannot be answered.' These comments might induce younger men to search for a protocol language of the sort described: and this might easily lead to metaphysical deviations. Although metaphysical speculation cannot altogether be restrained by argument, it is important, as a means of keeping waverers in line, to maintain physicalism in its most radical version.

Apart from tautologies, unified science consists of factual sentences. These may be subdivided into

(a) protocol sentences
(b) non-protocol sentences.

Protocol sentences are factual sentences of the same form as the others, except that, in them, a personal noun always occurs several times in a specific association with other terms. A complete protocol sentence might, for instance, read: 'Otto's protocol at 3:17 o'clock: [At 3:16 o'clock Otto said to himself: (at 3:15 o'clock there was a table in the room perceived by Otto)].' This factual sentence is so constructed that, within each set of brackets, further factual sentences may be found, viz.: 'At 3:16 o'clock Otto said to himself: (At 3:15 o'clock there was a table in the room perceived by Otto)' and 'At 3:15 o'clock there was a table in the room perceived by Otto.' These sentences are, however, not protocol sentences.

Each term occurring in these sentences may, to some extent, be replaced at the very outset by a group of terms of the language of advanced science. One may introduce a system of physicalistic designa-tions in place of 'Otto', and this system of designations may, in turn, further be defined by referring to the 'position' of the name 'Otto' in a group of signs composed of the names 'Karl', 'Heinrich', etc. All the words used in the expression of the above protocol sentence are either words of the universal-slang or may without difficulty be replaced at any moment by words of the universal-slang.

For a protocol sentence to be complete it is essential that the name of some person occur in it. 'Now joy', or 'Now red circle', or 'A red die is lying on the table' are not complete protocol sentences.[2] They are

---

[2] Cf. Carnap, *op. cit., Erkenntnis*, Vol. II, pp. 438 ff. (Above, p. 154—*Ed.*)

not even candidates for a position within the innermost set of brackets. For this they would, on our analysis, at least have to read 'Otto now joy', or 'Otto now sees a red circle', or 'Otto now sees a red die lying on the table' – which would roughly correspond to the children's language. That is, in a full protocol sentence the expression within the innermost set of brackets is a sentence which again features a personal noun and a term from the domain of perception-terms. The relative extent to which terms of ordinary language and of the language of advanced science are used is of no significance, since the universal-slang may be used with considerable flexibility.

The expression 'said to himself', after the first bracket, recommends itself when, as above, one wants to construct various groups of sentences, as, for instance, sentences incorporating reality-terms, or hallucination-terms, or dream-terms, and especially when one wants to identify unreality as such. For instance, one could say: 'Otto actually said to himself, "There was nothing in the room but a bird perceived by Otto" but, in order to amuse himself, he wrote, "There was nothing in the room but a table perceived by Otto." ' This is especially pertinent to the discussion in the next section, in which we reject Carnap's thesis to the effect that protocol sentences are those 'which require no verification'.

The transformation of the sciences is effected by the discarding of sentences utilized in a previous historical period, and, frequently, their replacement by others. Sometimes the same form of words is retained, but their definitions are changed. *Every law and every physicalistic sentence of unified-science or of one of its sub-sciences is subject to such change. And the same holds for protocol sentences.*

In unified science we try to construct a non-contradictory system of protocol sentences and non-protocol sentences (including laws).[3] When a new sentence is presented to us we compare it with the system at our disposal, and determine whether or not it conflicts with that system. If the sentence does conflict with the system, we may discard it as useless (or false), as, for instance, would be done with 'In Africa lions sing only in major scales.' One may, on the other hand, *accept* the sentence and so change the system that it remains consistent even after the adjunction of the new sentence. The sentence would then be called 'true'.

The fate of being discarded may befall even a protocol sentence. No sentence enjoys the *noli me tangere* which Carnap ordains for protocol

---

[3] Cf. Carnap, *op. cit., Erkenntnis,* Vol. II, pp. 439 ff. (Above, pp. 155 ff.–*Ed.*)

sentences. Let us consider a particularly drastic example. We assume that we are acquainted with a scholar called 'Kalon', who can write with both hands simultaneously. He writes with his left hand, 'Kalon's protocol at 3:17 o'clock: [At 16 minutes 30 seconds past 3 o'clock Kalon said to himself: (There was *nothing* in the room at 3:16 o'clock except a table perceived by Kalon)] .' At the same time, with his right hand, he writes, 'Kalon's protocol at 3:17 o'clock: [At 16 minutes 30 seconds past 3 o'clock Kalon said to himself: (There was *nothing* in the room at 3:16 o'clock except a bird perceived by Kalon)] .' What is he — and what are we — to make of the conjunction of these two sentences? We may, of course, make statements such as 'Marks may be found on this sheet of paper, sometimes shaped this way and sometimes that.' With respect to these marks on paper, however, Carnap's word 'verification' finds no application. 'Verification' can only be used with reference to sentences, that is, with reference to sequences of marks which are used in a context of a reaction-test and which may systematically be replaced by other marks.[4] Synonymous sentences may be characterized as stimuli which under specific reaction-tests evoke the same responses. Chains of ink-marks on paper and chains of air-vibrations which may under specific conditions be co-ordinated with one another are called 'sentences'.

Two conflicting protocol sentences cannot both be used in the system of unified science. Though we may not be able to tell which of the two is to be excluded, or whether both are not to be excluded, it is clear that not both are verifiable, that is, that both do not fit into the system.

If a protocol sentence must in such cases be discarded, may not the same occasionally be called for when the contradiction between protocol sentences on the one hand and a system comprising protocol sentences and non-protocol sentences (laws, etc.) on the other is such that an extended argument is required to disclose it? On Carnap's view, one could be obliged to alter only non-protocol sentences and laws. *We also allow for the possibility of discarding protocol sentences. A defining condition of a sentence is that it be subject to verification, that is to say, that it may be discarded.*

Carnap's contention that protocol sentences do not require verification, however it may be understood, may without difficulty be related to the belief in *immediate experiences* which is current in traditional

---

[4]Cf. my article in *Scientia*, p. 302.

academic philosophy. According to this philosophy there are, indeed, certain *basic elements* out of which the world-picture is to be constructed. On this academic view, these *atomic experiences* are, of course, above any kind of critical scrutiny; they do not require verification.

Carnap is trying to introduce a kind of *atomic protocol,* with his demand that 'a clear-cut distinction be made in scientific procedure between the adoption of a protocol and the interpretation of the protocol sentences', as a result of which 'no indirectly acquired sentences would be accepted into the protocol'.[5] The above formulation of a complete protocol sentence shows that, insofar as personal nouns occur in a protocol, interpretation must *always* already have taken place. When preparing scientific protocols, it may be useful to phrase the expression within the innermost set of brackets as simply as possible, as, for instance, 'At 3 o'clock Otto was seeing red', or — another protocol — 'At 3 o'clock Otto was hearing C sharp', etc. But a protocol of such a sort is not primitive in Carnap's sense, since one cannot, after all, get around Otto's act of perception. There are no sentences in the universal-slang which one may characterize as 'more primitive' than any others. All are of equal primitiveness. Personal nouns, words denoting perceptions, and other words of little primitiveness occur in all factual sentences, or, at least, in the hypotheses from which they derive. All of which means that *there are neither primitive protocol sentences nor sentences which are not subject to verification.*

The universal-slang, in the sense explained above, is the same for the child as for the adult. It is the same for a Robinson Crusoe as for a human society. If Crusoe wants to relate what he registered ('protokolliert') yesterday with what he registers today, that is, when he wants to have any sort of recourse to a language, he cannot but have recourse to the inter-subjective language. The Crusoe of yesterday and the Crusoe of today stand to one another in precisely the relation in which Crusoe stands to Friday. Consider a man who has both lost his memory and been blinded, who is now learning afresh to read and to write. The notes which he himself took in the past and which now, with the aid of a special apparatus, he reads again are for him as much the notes of some other man as notes actually written by someone else. And the same would still be the case after he had realized the tragic nature of his circumstances, and had pieced together the story of his life.

---

[5] *Op. cit.,* p. 437. (Above, p. 152—*Ed.*)

In other words, *every* language *as such* is inter-subjective. The protocols of one moment must be subject to incorporation in the protocols of the next, just as the protocols of A must be subject to incorporation in the protocols of B. *It is therefore meaningless to talk, as Carnap does, of a private language,* or of a set of disparate protocol languages which may ultimately be drawn together. The protocol languages of the Crusoe of yesterday and of the Crusoe of today are as close and as far apart from one another as are the protocol languages of Crusoe and of Friday. If, under certain circumstances, the protocol languages of yesterday's Crusoe and of today's are called the *same* language, then one may also, under the same circumstances, call the protocol language of Crusoe and that of Friday the same language.

In Carnap's writings we also encounter an emphasis on the 'I' familiar to us from idealistic philosophy. In the universal-slang it is as meaningless to talk of a *personal* protocol as to talk of a *here* or a *now*. In the physicalistic language personal nouns are simply replaced by co-ordinates and coefficients of physical states. One can distinguish an *Otto-protocol* from a *Karl-protocol*, but not a protocol of one's own from a protocol of others. The whole puzzle of *other minds* is thus resolved.

Methodological solipsism and *methodological positivism*[6] do not become any the more serviceable because of the addition of the word 'methodological'.[7]

For instance, had I said above, 'Today, the 27th of July, I examine protocols both of my own and of others', it would have been more correct to have said 'Otto Neurath's protocol at 10:00 a.m., July 27, 1932; [At 9:35 o'clock Otto Neurath said to himself: (Otto Neurath occupied himself between 9:40 and 9:57 with a protocol by Neurath and one by Kalon, to both of which the following two sentences belong: ...)].' Even though Otto Neurath himself formulates the protocol concerning the utilization of these protocols, he does not link his own protocol with the system of unified science in any different way from that in which he links Kalon's. It may well happen that Neurath discards one of Neurath's protocols, and adopts in its stead one of Kalon's. The fact that men generally retain their own protocol sentences more obstinately than they do those of other people is a historical accident which is of no real significance for our purposes. Carnap's contention that 'every

---

[6] Cf. Carnap, *op. cit., Erkenntnis,* Vol. II, p. 461.

[7] Cf. my article in *Erkenntnis,* Vol. II, p. 401.

individual can adopt only his own protocol as an epistemological basis' cannot be accepted, for the argument presented in its favour is *not* sound: 'S$_1$ can, indeed, also utilize the protocol of S$_2$ — and the incorporation of both protocol languages in physicalistic language makes this utilization particularly easy. The utilization is, however, indirect: S$_1$ must first state in his own protocol that he sees a piece of writing of such and such a form.'[8] *But Neurath must describe Neurath's protocol in a manner analogous to that in which he describes Kalon's!* He describes how Neurath's protocol looks to him as well as how Kalon's does.

In this way we can go on to deal with everyone's protocol sentences. Basically, it makes no difference at all whether Kalon works with Kalon's or with Neurath's protocols, or whether Neurath occupies himself with Neurath's or with Kalon's protocols. In order to make this quire clear, we could conceive of a sorting-machine into which protocol sentences are thrown. The laws and other factual sentences (including protocol sentences) serving to mesh the machine's gears sort the protocol sentences which are thrown into the machine and cause a bell to ring if a contradiction ensues. At this point one must either replace the protocol sentence whose introduction into the machine has led to the contradiction by some other protocol sentence, or rebuild the entire machine. *Who* rebuilds the machine, or *whose* protocol sentences are thrown into the machine is of no consequence whatsoever. Anyone may test his own protocol sentences as well as those of others.

SUMMING UP

Unified science utilizes a universal-slang, in which terms of the physicalistic ordinary language necessarily also occur.

Children can be trained to use the universal-slang. Apart from it we do not employ any specially distinguishable 'basic' protocol sentences, nor do different people make use of different protocol languages.

We find no use in unified science for the expressions 'methodological solipsism' and 'methodological positivism'.

One cannot start with conclusively established, pure protocol sentences. Protocol sentences are factual sentences like the others, containing names of persons or names of groups of people linked in specific ways with other terms, which are themselves also taken from the universal-slang. . . .

---

[8]Cf. Carnap, *op. cit., Erkenntnis,* Vol. II, p. 461.

4 The Foundations of Empirical Knowledge

A. J. Ayer

THE ERRORS OF FORMALISM

. . . The position of those who deny the possibility of expressing propositions that refer to empirical facts, in the sense in which 'reference to a fact' is ordinarily understood, may be summarized as follows. They hold that all that is necessary for the specification of a language is an account of what Professor Carnap has called its formation and transformation rules. The formation rules determine what combinations of signs are to constitute proper sentences of the language; the transformation rules prescribe the ways in which these sentences may legitimately be derived from one another. Both these sets of rules are held to be purely formal in character; and this means that they contain 'no reference to the meaning of the symbols (for example, the words) or to the sense of the expression (*e.g.* the sentences), but simply and solely to the kinds and order of the symbols from which the expressions are constructed'.[1] Consequently, if a distinction is made between the sentences that express *a priori* and those that express empirical propositions, it can be only in virtue of a difference in the form of the symbols which they contain, or in the nature of the formal relations which they have to other sentences. In the case of languages which allow the expression of empirical propositions, it is thought possible to mark out a special class of sentences, which are referred to as 'observation' or 'protocol' or 'basic' sentences; and it is held to be a necessary and sufficient condition of the admissibility of any sentence that is intended to express an empirical proposition that some observation-sentence should be derivable from it in accordance with the established rules of the language. One must not, however, be misled by the name of these observation-sentences into supposing that they refer to observable facts; or that the test which they provide for the validity of empirical propositions is one of correspondence with fact, as this is ordinarily understood. For the

---

Source: A. J. Ayer, *The Foundations of Empirical Knowledge,* Macmillan, 1940, sections 9 and 13, pp. 84-92, 146-53. Reprinted by permission of Macmillan, London and Basingstoke.

[1] Rudolf Carnap, *The Logical Syntax of Language,* p. 1.

properties by which these sentences are essentially distinguished are intended to be purely formal; and the only criterion that is allowed for determining the truth or falsity of any 'observation-statement' is the formal possibility of incorporating it in a given system. Nor does this criterion give them any advantage over statements of other kinds. For it is held that even when a hypothesis 'proves to be logically incompatible with certain protocol-sentences, there always exists the possibility of maintaining the hypothesis and renouncing acknowledgement of the protocol-sentences'.[2] All that is required is that the system of propositions which is accepted as true should be formally self-consistent. And this is supposed to be the sole criterion of their truth.

I do not think that any very elaborate argument is needed to show that this theory is altogether untenable. In the first place, it is not true that we are able to use or understand a language when we are acquainted only with its formation and transformation rules. These rules are indeed sufficient for the characterization of a purely abstract system of logic or mathematics, so long as no attempt is made to give the system a material interpretation; but they are not sufficient for the characterization of any language that serves to communicate propositions about matters of fact. From the transformation rules we can learn that in any situation in which we are entitled to use a given sentence of the language, we are also entitled to use certain others; but neither they nor the formation rules afford us any means of knowing what are the situations in which any single sentence can legitimately be used. But until this is determined the 'language' in question is not, in the ordinary sense, a language at all. For it does not serve to communicate anything. It is merely a formal calculus which we do not know how to apply. For it to become a language it is necessary that some at least of the expressions that it contains should be given a meaning. And this is effected by the method of ostensive definition, that is, by correlating these expressions, not with other expressions, but with what is actually observed. Professor Carnap has indeed asserted that these 'so-called ostensive definitions' are themselves 'translations of words'. According to him, to define, for example, an elephant, ostensively, is merely to lay down the transformation rule ' "elephant" = animal of the same kind as the animal in this or that position in space-time'.[3] But this is clearly a

---

[2] *Ibid.* p. 318.

[3] *The Unity of Science*, p. 39. (Reprinted above, p. 151—*Ed.*)

mistake. It is true that if I teach someone the meaning of the English word 'elephant' by pointing to a particular animal, the information he receives is that an elephant is an animal of the same kind as that which he is observing at a particular place and time. But this is not to say that the word 'elephant' is synonymous in English with any such expression as 'animal of the same kind as that which, on July 2nd, 1939, was standing 30 yards south-west of the bandstand at the London Zoo'. For even if it is a fact that an elephant was actually to be observed at that particular place and time, it is not a necessary fact. I may be expressing a false proposition if I say that there was no animal standing 30 yards south-west of the bandstand at the London Zoo on July 2nd, 1939, or that there was such an animal but it was not an elephant; but I shall certainly not be contradicting myself. The spatio-temporal description may serve to indicate the context in which some word has been, or is being, ostensively defined, but it is not in itself a substitute for that context. And it is only by reference to an empirical context that any ostensive definition is to be understood.

Having allowed the possibility of ostensive definitions, we might then consider that we required a special name for the class of sentences whose constituents were defined in this way; and it would be reasonable for us to call them observation-sentences, on the ground that they were intended to refer to what could be directly observed. But this cannot be what those who uphold the theory I am now considering mean by an observation-sentence. For, in effect, they deny the possibility of using any sentence to refer to what can be directly observed. As they use it, the term 'observation-sentence' is purely syntactical. The sentences to which it is applied are distinguished from other sentences merely by the fact that they contain different words and obey different transformation rules. But what is the point of this conventional distinction? It seems to be intended to furnish a principle of empiricism. The theory is that one excludes metaphysics by asserting that every proposition that is not analytic must be 'empirically testable' and by defining this 'testability' in terms of the derivation of observation-sentences. But this use of the term 'empirically testable' is again very misleading. For what sort of empirical test is provided by the fact that the conventional rules of a language allow one sentence to be formally derived from another, when neither sentence is to be understood as recording what can be actually experienced? One does not become an empiricist merely by a free use of the word 'empirical' or the word 'observation'.

If we were to take this view of the nature of observation-sentences, it clearly would not matter whether we agreed with Carnap that 'every concrete sentence belonging to the physicalistic system-language can in suitable circumstances serve as an observation-sentence',[4] or whether we required that these sentences should have a special form. For it would only be a question of how we chose to apply a syntactical designation; and in either case it would be an arbitrary choice. It has, indeed, been argued[5] that the form in which we choose to cast these sentences may make a difference to the 'stability' of the propositions they express, in the sense that it may give them a greater or lesser chance of being retained in the accepted system of propositions, and so of being 'true' in the only sense in which the exponents of this theory recognize the notion of truth. But this must be a mistake. For if the only possible criterion of the truth of a proposition is its logical compatibility with other propositions, then it cannot be necessary to devise a special form for its expression in order to secure its retention in the accepted system. It is sufficient for us, if we wish to retain it, simply to decide to exclude all propositions that are inconsistent with it. This is admittedly an arbitrary procedure; but so would be any other procedure that we could adopt. Provided that it is internally self-consistent we may, on this view, regard as 'true' any system of propositions that we choose. And so long as the suggestion of an appeal to the observable facts is ruled out as meaningless, no question of justification can arise.

But suppose now, what is admitted to be possible, that we are confronted with two mutually exclusive sets of propositions, each of which is internally self-consistent. Are we to say that both are independently true? If we do, we contradict ourselves, according to the meaning that we ordinarily give to 'truth'. We must look therefore for some method of deciding between these incompatible systems. But what method can there be if the only criterion of the truth of any system is its internal self-consistency? I believe that this objection is unanswerable. An attempt has indeed been made to answer it by saying that the true system is that which happens to be accepted by accredited observers, such as the

---

[4] 'Über Protokollsätze', *Erkenntnis*, vol. 3, p. 224.

[5] Cf. Otto Neurath, 'Protokollsätze', *Erkenntnis*, vol. 3; and for criticism, my article on 'Verification and Experience', *Proceedings of the Aristotelian Society*, 1936-7, where I put forward a more detailed refutation of the whole of this version of the coherence theory of truth. (A translation of Neurath's paper appears above as item D3–*Ed.*)

scientists of our era.[6] But now we may ask whether the true system is merely that which contains in itself the proposition that it alone is accepted by these scientists, or whether it is that which is so accepted, as a matter of fact. In the former case the proposed criterion does not effect what is required of it. For each of several incompatible systems might contain the proposition that it alone was the accepted one, without being internally inconsistent. But to adopt the other alternative is to abandon the coherence theory of truth. For it involves, what the advocates of the theory hold to be impossible, a comparison of a proposition about the behaviour of contemporary scientists, why not in other cases also? Is it not conceivable even that actual observation might show that contemporary scientists sometimes made mistakes? . . .

PUBLIC AND PRIVATE LANGUAGES

An alternative way of formulating this problem,* which has recently come into favour, is to treat it as question of the inter-relationship of languages. There is, we are told, on the one hand the 'physical language' which is said to be 'characterized by the fact that statements of the simplest form attach to a specific set of co-ordinates a definite value or range of values of a coefficient of physical state', or, in other words, 'express a quantitatively determined property of a definite position at a definite time'[7]; and on the other hand there is the 'protocol language', which consists of 'statements belonging to the basic protocol or direct record'[8] of an individual's experience. It is assumed that the physical language is inter-subjective; and the question then is to determine how the protocol language is related to it. The answer that is given by those who use these terms is that the protocol language is a sub-language of the physical language. There is, in their view, no problem involved in making the transition from the realm of the individual's direct experience to the realm of public, physical facts; for they hold that reports of

---

*Concerning the privacy of experience—*Ed.*

[6]Cf. Carnap, 'Erwiderung auf die Aufsätze von E. Zilsel und K. Duncker', *Erkenntnis*, vol. 3, pp. 179-80; and Carl Hempel, 'Some Remarks on Empiricism', *Analysis*, vol. iii, No. 3.

[7]Rudolf Carnap, *The Unity of Science*, pp. 52-3.

[8]*Ibid.* p. 42. (And above, p. 152—*Ed.*)

direct experience themselves already refer to such facts. In considering this view, I may refer once again to the work of Professor Carnap, who has given the fullest and clearest exposition of it. To prove that the protocol language is a part of the inter-subjective physical language, he uses the following argument. He affects to adopt the standpoint of an opponent who maintains that when he asserts a protocol proposition such as 'I am thirsty' he is referring not to a physical event but to the content of one of his experiences. In that case, argues Carnap, the same state of affairs cannot also be expressed in the protocol language of any other person. 'No statement in S2's protocol language', he says,

> can express the thirst of S_1. For all such statements express only what is immediately given to S_2; and S_1's thirst is a datum for S_1 only and not for S_2.... All that S_2 can verify when he asserts 'S_1 is thirsty' is that S_1's body is in such and such a state, and a statement asserts no more than can be verified. If by 'the thirst of S_1' we understand not the physical state of his body but his sensations of thirst, *i.e.* something non-material, then S_1's thirst is fundamentally beyond the reach of S_2's recognition. A statement about S_1's thirst would then be fundamentally unverifiable by S_2, it would be for him in principle impossible to understand, void of sense.

The same thing would, it is held, be true of every other protocol statement, and the general consequence would be that 'every protocol language could be applied only solipsistically'.[9]

The next step in the argument is to consider what, on this view, must be the relationship between protocol and physical statements. If scientific statements are to be capable of being verified empirically there must be some 'inferential connexion' between the two; but how is this possible if 'the protocol language and the physical language speak of completely different facts'? Suppose that we adopt the hypothesis that 'although protocol language does not refer to physical events the converse is true and physical language refers to the content of experiences'. Then, it is argued,

> difficulties arise on considering the relation between the several persons' protocol languages and physical language. S_1's protocol language refers to the content of S_1's experience, S_2's protocol language to the content of S_2's experience. What can the inter-

---

[9] *Ibid.* pp. 79-80. (And above, p. 158.—*Ed.*)

subjective physical language refer to? It must refer to the content of the experiences of both S_1 and S_2. This is, however, impossible, for the realms of experience of two persons do not overlap.

And so it is concluded that 'there is no solution free from contradictions in this direction'.[10]

The solution Carnap himself puts forward is that every protocol statement is equivalent to a statement about the subject's body. For instance, the protocol statement 'red now', made by a subject S, is said to be equivalent to 'the body S is now seeing red' where 'seeing red'

> denotes that state of the human body characterized by the fact that certain specified (physical) reactions appear in answer to certain specified (physical) stimuli. (For example: Stimulus, the sounds, 'What do you see now?'; reaction, the sound, 'red'. Stimulus, the sounds, 'Point out the colour you have just seen on this card'; reaction, the finger points to some definite part of the card . . .).[11]

In this way every protocol statement is given an interpretation that allows it to be incorporated in the physical language. The protocol languages of various persons are said to be mutually exclusive only in the sense that 'they are non-overlapping sub-sections of the physical language'.[12] Each person's protocol statements are supposed to refer to the states of his own body, and so to a special class of physical facts.

It is Carnap's view that the problem of the egocentric predicament, which he solves in this fashion, would never have troubled philosophers if they had expressed it, in 'formal' terminology, as a question about the relationship of languages instead of speaking, in 'material' terms, about the contents of people's experiences and their relation to the public world. But in this instance his predilection for the formal terminology has led him into confusion. His argument rests, as we have seen, upon the assumption that if the sentences of the protocol language referred, not to physical events, but to the contents of experiences, it would follow, in view of the privacy of personal experience, that each person would have his own private protocol language which could

---

[10] *The Unity of Science*, pp. 81-2. (And above, p. 159.–*Ed.*)

[11] *Ibid.* p. 86.

[12] *Ibid.* p. 88.

have no meaning for anybody else. But this assumption is false. It is due to a mistranslation from the material into the formal mode of speech. A correct formal rendering of the proposition that each person's experiences are private to himself might run as follows: 'For any experience E, and personal histories $H1$ and $H2$, "E belongs to $H1$" implies that E does not belong to $H2$'. And this is by no means equivalent, as Carnap seems to suppose, to saying that each person has his own protocol language, when this is taken to mean that 'for any protocol sentence s, and persons A and B, "s occurs in the language used by A" implies that s does not occur in the language used by B'. Nor does this proposition asserting the privacy of each person's protocol language follow from the proposition that the sentences of the protocol language refer to the contents of experiences. It is indeed possible to have a private protocol language, just as it is possible to have a private physical language. If, for example, I were to express propositions about the contents of my experiences by executing the movements of a dance, and no one else made these movements in order to express such propositions, I might correctly be said to be using a private protocol language; and similarly, if I were to whistle snatches of popular tunes in order to express propositions about physical events, and no one else expressed such propositions in this way, I might correctly be said to be using a private physical language. But it is no more necessary for me to express protocol propositions in a private language than it is for me to express physical propositions in a private language. When I employ expressions like 'this is red' or 'I am thirsty' to refer to the contents of my experiences, I am using English sentences in the way that other English people use them. And, as such sentences are ordinarily used, they are not equivalent to the sentences referring to physical events into which it is proposed that we should translate them. There may indeed be a *de facto* connexion between my feeling of thirst and such physical facts as that my throat is parched or that I utter certain words, or a *de facto* connexion between my sensing a red sense-datum and my being in the physical state that the sentence 'my body is seeing red' is intended to describe. But in all such cases, the dependence of the facts referred to by the protocol propositions upon the facts referred to by the physical propositions is logically a contingent and not a necessary relation. Even if one assumed, what is by no means fully established, that to every fact described by a protocol proposition there was a physical correlate, there would still be no logical contradiction involved in asserting the protocol proposition and denying the physical proposition which was empirically conjoined with it. In other words, it is logically conceivable that the protocol proposition should be true when the corresponding physical proposition was false; and if this is so, the sentences that express them are not equivalent.

We have seen that the ground on which it is assumed that sentences which seem to refer to the contents of experiences must really refer to physical events is that only thus could they serve as a means of communication between one person and another. But if there is a philosophical problem concerning the possibility of such communication it applies just as much to propositions about physical events as it does to propositions about people's states of mind, or about the sense-data wich they directly experience. For it is only in terms of what we individually experience that these physical propositions can be understood by us at all. Suppose, for example, that I wish to ascertain the temperature of the room in which I am sitting, and that, taking up a Fahrenheit thermometer, I observe that the top of the column of mercury coincides with the figure 70. In that case I may put forward the physical proposition that the temperature of the room is 70 degrees Fahrenheit. And if someone else then takes the thermometer and also observes that the top of the mercury column coincides with the figure 70, it may be said that this physical proposition has been inter-subjectively verified. But this inter-subjective verification amounts to no more than what may be described by saying that each of us apprehends a spatial coincidence of two sense-data in his own sense-field. Consequently, since the truth of every physical proposition depends upon the truth of protocol propositions, if the privacy of experience made it impossible for two people to communicate by means of protocol propositions, it would equally be impossible for them to communicate by means of physical propositions. But the fact is that if what is meant by 'inter-subjective understanding' is understanding in the same way by a number of different people, both these types of propositions are capable of being inter-subjectively understood.

5 On the Foundation of Knowledge
Moritz Schlick

I

All great attempts at establishing a theory of knowing arise from the problem of the reliability of human cognition, and this question again arises from the wish for absolute certainty of knowledge.

That the statements of everyday life and of science can ultimately lay claim only to probable status, and that even the most universal findings of inquiry, confirmed in all experience, can only have the character of hypotheses — this is an insight that has repeatedly spurred philosophers from the time of Descartes, and less clearly, indeed, from antiquity onwards, to seek for an unshakeable foundation, immune from all doubt and forming the firm basis on which the tottering edifice of our knowledge is reared. The unsafeness of the structure has mostly been put down to the fact that it was impossible — perhaps in prinicple — to build anything more solid by the power of human thought; but this did not prevent a search for the natural bedrock which is there *before* building commences, and does not itself sway.

This search is a praiseworthy honest endeavour, and also exerts an influence among 'relativists' and 'skeptics' who would dearly like to be ashamed of it. It makes its appearance in various forms and leads to strange differences of opinion. The question of 'protocol propositions', their function and structure, is the latest form in which philosophy, or rather the radical empiricism of our day, invests the problem of the ultimate ground of knowledge.

As the name implies, 'protocol propositions' originally meant those propositions which in absolute simplicity, without any forming, change or addition, set forth the *facts*, whose elaboration constitutes the substance of all science, and which are prior to all knowledge, to every claim about the world. It makes no sense to speak of uncertain facts — it is only statements, only our knowledge that can be uncertain; and if

Source: Moritz Schlick, *Philosophical Papers,* volume II (1925-1936), ed. H. L. Mulder and B. van de Velde-Schlick, D. Reidel, 1979, pp. 370-87. Copyright © 1979 by Albert M. Schlick and Barbara F. B. van de Velde-Schlick. Reprinted by permission of D. Reidel Publishing Company. This paper, originally entitled 'Über das Fundament der Erkenntnis', first appeared in *Erkenntnis,* vol. III, 1932-33.

it is therefore possible to reproduce the raw facts quite purely in 'protocol propositions', the latter seem to be the absolute indubitable starting-points of all knowledge. They are indeed again left behind, the moment we go over to propositions which are really useable in life or science (such a transition appears to be that from 'singular' to 'general' statements), but they constitute, for all that, the firm basis to which all our knowledge owes the whole of whatever validity it may still possess.

It makes no difference here whether these so-called protocol propositions are ever indeed formulated, i.e., actually uttered, written or even merely explicitly 'thought'; it is important only to know what propositions the designations actually made are based on, and to be able at any time to reconstruct them. If a research worker, for example, records that 'under such and such circumstances the pointer stands at 10.5', he knows that this means 'two black lines coincide', and that the words 'under such and such circumstances' (which we here suppose to be enumerated), are likewise to be resolved into particular protocol propositions, which he could also state exactly in principle if he wanted to, though it might be a trouble to do so.

The fact is clear, and to my knowledge has not been contested by anyone, that knowledge in life and in the research situation *begins* in *some* sense with the establishing of facts, and that 'protocol propositions', in which this establishment takes place, stand in a like sense at the *beginning* of science. What is this sense? Is the 'beginning' to be understood in a temporal sense or a logical one?

Here already we find a great deal of wavering and unclarity. When I said above that it did not matter whether the crucial propositions were also uttered or enunciated as protocols, this obviously implies that they do not have to stand at the beginning *in time*, but can equally well be brought in afterwards, if this should be required. And required it will be, whenever we wish to make clear the real meaning of the sentence actually written down. So is the talk about protocol propositions to be understood in a *logical* sense? In that case they would be marked out by specific logical properties, by their structure, their position in the system of science, and the task would arise of actually specifying these properties. In fact, this is the form in which Carnap, for example, expressly posed the problem of protocol propositions at an earlier stage, whereas later[1] he declared it a question to be settled by arbitrary decision.

---

[1] *Erkenntnis* **3**, pp. 216 and 223 ['Über Protokollsätze'].

On the other side we find numerous arguments apparently presupposing that we are to count as 'protocol propositions' only such statements as also take precedence in time over the other assertions of science. And is this not correct? For we have to remember that we are dealing here with the ultimate foundation of our knowledge of *reality*, and that it cannot suffice for this purpose to treat the propositions merely as if they were 'ideal structures' (as in Platonizing fashion it was earlier the custom to say). On the contrary, we have to concern ourselves with real happenings, with the temporally occurring events in which the passing of judgement consists, and hence with mental acts of 'thinking' or physical acts of 'speaking' or 'writing'. Since the mental acts of judgement appear fitted to serve as a basis for intersubjectively valid knowledge only after having been translated into oral or written expression (i.e., into a physical sign-system), it was proposed to regard as 'protocol propositions' certain spoken, written or printed sentences, i.e., certain sign-complexes consisting of sounds, writing fluid or printer's ink, which if rendered out of the customary abbreviations into a fully articulate language would signify somewhat as follows: 'Mr So-and-so, at such-and-such a time and place, is observing this or that'. (This view was particularly upheld by Otto Neurath.) And in fact, if we retrace the road whereby we have actually arrived at all our knowledge, we undoubtedly always come upon these same sources: printed sentences in books, words from the mouth of the teacher, and our own observations (in the latter case we are ourselves Mr So-and-so).

According to this view, protocol propositions would be real occurrences in the world, and would have to be prior in time to the other real processes constituting the 'construction of science', or even the production of knowledge in an individual.

I don't know how far the distinction here drawn between the logical and temporal priority of protocol propositions may correspond to differences in the view actually taken by particular authors — but that is no part of our present concern. For our purpose is not to determine who has said the right thing, but what the right thing *is*. And in this our distinction of the two standpoints will serve us well.

De facto, both views might be compatible, for the propositions recording simple data of observation and standing at the beginning in time could at the same time be those which, in virtue of their structure, must constitute the logical starting-point of science.

II

The question which ought first to interest us is this: what progress is attained by formulating the problem of the ultimately foundation of knowledge with the aid of the concept of 'protocol proposition'? The answering of this question should prepare us for the solution of the problem itself.

It seems to me to signify a great improvement in method, to try to arrive at the foundation of knowledge by searching, not for the primary *facts*, but for the primary *propositions*. But it seems to me also that there has been no understanding of how to make proper use of this advantage, and this perhaps because there has been no real awareness that at bottom the issue was none other than this old problem of the foundation of knowledge. I believe, in fact, that the view arrived at by these considerations about protocol propositions is untenable. They lead towards a peculiar relativism, which seems to be a necessary consequence of the view that regards protocol propositions as empirical facts, on which, as time goes on, the edifice of knowledge is raised.

For as soon as one asks about the certainty with which one may maintain the truth of protocol propositions regarded in this fashion, one has to admit that it is exposed to all manner of doubt.

There is a sentence in a book which says, for example, that So-and-so made such-and-such an observation with such-and-such an instrument. Although, given certain assumptions, one may have the utmost confidence in this statement, it, and hence the observation, can never be regarded as *absolutely* assured. For the possibilities of error are innumerable. So-and-so can inadvertently or deliberately have noted down something which fails to give a correct report of the fact observed; in writing or printing an error may have crept in — indeed the very assumption that the letters in a book preserve their shape even for a minute and do not rearrange themselves 'on their own' into new sentences, is an empirical hypothesis, which as such can never be strictly verified, since every verification would depend on similar assumptions, on the presupposition that our memory does not deceive us at least over short periods, and so forth.

This means of course — and some of our authors have been almost triumphant in pointing it out — that protocol propositions so conceived are in principle exactly the same in character as all other statements of science: they are hypotheses and nothing else. They are anything but irrefutable and can be employed in the construction of the knowledge-system only so long as they are supported, or at least not contradicted, by other hypotheses. We therefore reserve the right to make corrections at any time even to protocol propositions, and such corrections are often enough made, indeed, whenever we eliminate certain protocol data and maintain afterwards that they must have been due to some kind of error.

Even in propositions asserted by ourselves, we never in principle exclude the possibility of error. We admit that at the moment of passing judgement our mind was perhaps utterly confused, and that an experience we now claim to have had two seconds ago might be declared on subsequent examination to have been a hallucination, or even to have never happened at all.

It is clear, then, that for anyone in search of a firm foundation for knowledge the view outlined provides, in its 'protocol propositions', *nothing* of the kind. On the contrary, its only real outcome is that the distinction at first introduced between protocol and other propositions is subsequently done away with again as meaningless. We may therefore understand how the view was arrived at[2] that any propositions we please may be picked out from science and designated as 'protocol propositions', and that it is merely a matter of expediency which ones we care to choose for the purpose.

But can we agree to this? Are there really only grounds of expediency? Is it not rather a question of where the particular propositions come from, of what their origin and history may be? What meaning, in any case, does expediency have here? What is the purpose pursued in setting up and selecting the propositions?

The purpose can only be that of science itself, namely to provide a *true* account of the facts. We think it self-evident that the problem of the foundation of all knowledge is nothing else but the question of the criterion of truth. The term 'protocol propositions' was undoubtedly first introduced so that by means of it certain propositions might be singled out, by whose truth it should then be possible to measure, as if by a yardstick, the truth of all other statements. According to the view described, this yardstick has now turned out to be just as relative as, say, all the standards of measurement in physics. And that view with its consequences has been commended, also, as an eviction of the last remnant of 'absolutism' from philosophy.[3]

---

[2] K. Popper, cited in Carnap, *Erkenntnis* 3, p. 223.

[3] Carnap, *op. cit.* p. 228.

But then what do we have left as a criterion of truth? Since we are not to have it that all statements of science are to accord with a specific set of protocol propositions, but rather that all propositions are to accord with all others, where each is regarded as in principle corrigible, truth can consist only in the *mutual agreement of the propositions with one another.*

III

This doctrine (expressly stated and defended in the above context by Otto Neurath, for example) is well known in the history of modern philosophy. In England it is commonly referred to as the 'coherence theory of truth' and contrasted with the older 'correspondence theory' (on which it should be noted that the term 'theory' is by no means appropriate here, since remarks about the nature of truth are quite different in character from scientific theories, which always consist of a system of hypotheses).

The two views are usually contrasted by saying that on the first or traditional theory the truth of a proposition consists in its agreement with the facts, whereas on the second or 'coherence' theory it consists in its agreement with the system of all other propositions.

I shall not here investigate in general whether the formulation of the latter doctrine cannot also be so interpreted as to draw attention to something perfectly correct (namely that there is a quite specific sense in which, as Wittgenstein puts it, we 'cannot get out of language'); my business here is to show, rather, that in the interpretation that must be given to it in our present context, the doctrine is wholly untenable.

If the truth of a proposition is to consist in its coherence or agreement with other propositions, we have to be clear about what is meant by 'agreement', and *which* propositions the 'others' are supposed to be.

The first point should be easy enough to dispose of. Since it cannot be intended that the statement under examination says the *same* as the others, the only alternative is that it merely has to be *consistent* with them, and hence that no contradiction shall obtain between them and it. Truth would thus consist simply in absence of contradiction. But now the question of whether truth can be straightforwardly identified with freedom from contradiction, ought no longer to be a matter of discussion. It should long since have been generally recognized that non-contradiction and truth (if one wishes to employ this word at all) can be equated only in propositions of a tautological character, e.g., in those of pure geometry. But in propositions of that kind all connection with reality is deliberately severed; they are merely formulae within an established calculus. Of the statements of *pure* geometry it makes no sense to ask whether they agree with the facts of the world or not; in order to be called true or correct, they merely have to be consistent with the axioms arbitrarily laid down at the outset (though it is customarily also required that they should *follow* from these). Here we are confronted with precisely what in earlier days was designated *formal* truth and distinguished from *material* truth.

The latter is the truth of synthetic propositions or factual statements, and if it is desired to describe them by means of the concept of non-contradiction or consistency with other propositions, this can be done only by saying that they may not stand in contradiction to certain *quite specific* statements, namely those very statements which record 'facts of immediate observation'. It is not consistency with *any* sort of propositions you please that can serve as the criterion of truth; what is required, rather, is conformity with certain very particular statements which can be no means be chosen at will. In other words, the criterion of non-contradiction alone is utterly inadequate for material truth; it is wholly a matter, rather, of consistency with very special statements of a peculiar kind; and for *this* consistency there is nothing to prevent — indeed everything, in my view, to justify — our employment of the good old phrase 'agreement with reality'.

The astonishing error of the 'coherence theory' can only be explained by the fact that, in setting up and elaborating this theory, attention was invariably paid only to propositions actually occurring in science, and that these alone were employed as examples. The non-contradictory connection between them was then in fact sufficient, but only because these propositions are already of a quite definite kind. For in a certain sense (yet to be described) they have their 'origin' in observational propositions, and derive, as one may confidently say in the traditional terms, 'from experience'.

Anyone who takes coherence seriously as the sole criterion of truth must consider any fabricated tale to be no less true than a historical report or the propositions in a chemistry text-book, so long as the tale is well enough fashioned to harbour no contradictions anywhere. With the aid of fantasy I can portray a grotesque world of adventure; the coherence philosopher has to believe in the truth of my account, provided only that I have a care for the mutual consistency of my claims and discreetly avoid any collision with the customary description of the world, by laying the sense of my recital on a distant star, where observation is no longer possible. Indeed, strictly speaking, I have no need at all of such discretion; I can equally well insist that others have to adjust themselves to my story, and not the other way round. The others cannot even object, in that case, that this procedure conflicts with observation, for according to the coherence theory no 'observations' of any kind are involved here, but only the consistency of the statements in question.

Since it does not occur to anybody to suppose the propositions in a storybook true, and those in a physics book false, the coherence view is a total failure. Something else must be added to coherence, namely a principle whereby consistency is to be established, and this alone would then be the actual criterion.

If I am given a set of statements, some of which are also contradictory, I can indeed achieve consistency in various ways, in that on one occasion, for example, I pick out certain statements and abandon or correct them, while on another I do the same with those which contradict the first.

This brings out the logical impossibility of the coherence view; it provides absolutely no unambiguous criterion of truth, for by means of it I can arrive at as many internally non-contradictory proposition-systems as I like, although they are not consistent with each other.

The absurdity is avoided only by not permitting the abandonment or correction of any statements you please, but rather by specifying those which are to be upheld, and to which the remainder have to conform.

IV

The coherence theory is now disposed of, and we have long ago arrived in the meantime at the second point of our critical deliberations, namely the question whether *all* propositions are corrigible, or whether there are also some which cannot be shaken. The latter would in fact form the 'foundation' of all knowledge that we were in search of, and towards which we have so far advanced not a single step.

By what rule, then are we to seek out those propositions which themselves remain unaltered, and with which all others must be brought into agreement? In what follows we shall speak of them not as 'protocol propositions', but as 'fundamental propositions', since it is in fact doubtful whether they occur at all in the protocols of science.

The first thing, no doubt, would be to look for the desired rule in a sort of economy-principle, and to say, in other words, that those propositions are to be chosen as fundamental whose adoption requires a *minimum* of changes in the entire system of statements, in order to free it from all contradiction.

It deserves to be noted that such a rule of economy would not establish some particular set of statements once and for all as fundamental propositions; it might happen, rather, that with the progress of knowledge the fundamental propositions that had hitherto served as such were again downgraded, since it had turned out more economical to drop them in favour of newly discovered propositions which from then on – until further notice – would play the part of a foundation. So while the standpoint would indeed be no longer that of pure coherence, but rather one of economy, it would be equally prone to 'relativism'.

It seems to me beyond question that the supporters of the view just criticized were in fact taking the economy principle as their true guideline, whether they stated this or left it unsaid; I have therefore already assumed above (p. 182) that in the relativistic theory it is grounds of expediency that determine the choice of 'protocol propositions', and I asked: 'Can we agree to this?'

To this question I now give the answer 'No!'. It is not in fact economic expediency, but properties of a wholly different kind, which mark out the truly fundamental propositions.

The process of choosing these propositions could be called economic if it consisted, say, in an accommodation to the opinions (or 'protocol propositions') of the majority of inquirers. Now it is indeed the case that we accept a fact, e.g., of geography or history, or even a natural law, as indubitably established, if we very often find its existence mentioned in the places appropriate to such reports. It then simply does not occur to us to want to check it again for ourselves. We therefore concur with what is universally acknowledged. But the reason for this is that we know precisely in what way such factual statements ordinarily come to be made, and this way inspires our confidence; it is not because it corresponds to the majority view. On the contrary, it could only attain to universal acknowledgement because each individual feels the same confidence. Whether and to what extent we declare a statement to be corrigible or capable of annulment depends entirely *on its origin*, and (apart from quite special cases) in no way on whether its retention requires the correcting of very many other statements, and perhaps a rearrangement of the whole system of knowledge.

Before the economy-principle can be applied, we have to know: *which* propositions is it to apply to? And if the principle were to be the *only* decisive rule, the answer could only be: well, to *all* propositions that are advanced, or ever have been advanced, with the claim to validity. In point of fact, the clause 'with the claim to validity' should be left out, for how are we to distinguish such propositions from those advanced purely arbitrarily, having been thought up as a joke, or in order to mislead? This distinction simply cannot be formulated, without taking the *origin* of the statements into account. So we find ourselves repeatedly referred back to the question of their source. Without having classified the statements according to their origin, any application of the economic principle of compatibility would be utterly absurd. But once we have investigated the propositions in respect of their origin, we notice right away that in so doing we have already at the same time ranged them in an order of validity, that — apart from certain special cases in still uncompleted areas of science — there is simply no room for any application of the economy-principle, and that the order in question simultaneously points the way to the foundations we are seeking.

V

At this point, indeed, the most extreme caution is called for. For here we hit upon the very path which has been followed from time immemorial, by all who have embarked on the journey to the ultimate grounds of truth. And the goal has always failed of achievement. For in this ordering of propositions according to their origin, which I attempt in order to judge their certainty, an exceptional position is immediately taken by those which I advance *myself*. And of these, a secondary position is again occupied by those lying in the past, since we believe that their certainty can be impaired by 'deceptions of memory' — and the more so, in general, the further back in time they lie. At the forefront, however, as immune from all doubt, stand those propositions which give expression to a matter of personal 'perception' or 'experience' (or whatever the term may be) that lies *in the present*. And however clear and simple this may appear to be, the philosophers have fallen into a hopeless labyrinth as soon as they have actually tried to employ propositions of the last-mentioned kind as the foundation of all knowledge. Some puzzling alleys in this labyrinth include, for example, those formulae and arguments which, under such names as 'evidence of inner perception', 'solipsism', 'solipsism of the moment', 'self-certainty of consciousness', and so on, have been at the heart of so many philosophical disputes. The most famous destination to which pursuit of this path has led is the Cartesian *cogito ergo sum*, already reached beforehand, as it happens, by St. Augustine. And as to the *cogito ergo sum*, our eyes have nowadays been sufficiently opened by logic: we know that it is simply a pseudo-proposition, which again does not become a genuine statement through being expressed in the form: *cogitatio est* — 'contents of consciousness exist'[4]. Such a proposition, which itself says nothing, can in no sense serve as the foundation of anything; it is not itself a piece of knowledge, and none is based upon it; it can lend no assurance to anything we know.

There is therefore the utmost danger that in pursuing the path recommended we may arrive at nothing but empty word-patterns, instead of the foundation we seek. It was, indeed, from the wish to obviate this danger that the critical theory of protocol propositions arose. But its chosen way out was unable to satisfy us; its *essential* defect consists in failing to recognize the differing status of propositions, most clearly revealed in the fact that for the system of knowledge which anyone accepts as the 'correct' one, his *own* propositions still ultimately play the only decisive role.

It is theoretically conceivable that the statements made by everyone else about the world should be in no way confirmed by my own observations. It might be the case that all the books I read and all the pronouncements I hear are in perfect agreement among themselves and never contradict one another, but that they are utterly irreconcilable with a large part of my own observation propositions. (In this case, the problem of language-learning and its use for communication would create certain difficulties, but they are soluble by means of certain assumptions as to whereabouts alone the contradictions are to appear.) According to the theory under criticism, in such a case I would simply have to sacrifice my own 'protocol propositions', since they are certainly at odds with the overwhelming mass of the others, which do harmonize together, and which there can be no possible expectation of correcting by reference to my own limited and fragmentary experience.

But what would really happen in the case supposed? Well, I would not give up my own observation propositions under any circumstances,

---

[4]Cf. *Erkenntnis* **3**, p. 20. (Item C1 above, p. 100–*Ed.*).

for I find, rather, that I can only adopt a system of knowledge which they fit into without mutilation. And such a system I should always be able to construct. I need only regard other people as dreaming fools, whose madness has uncommon method in it — or to put it more concretely — I would say that the others are actually living in a different world for mine, which has only just so much in common with the latter as to permit communication in the same languge. In any event, and whatever the world-picture I construct, I would always test its truth only by my own experience; this support I would never allow to be taken from me, my own observation propositions would always be the final criterion. I would proclaim, as it were: 'What I see, I see!'.

VI

In the light of these critical preliminaries, it is clear in what direction we have to seek for the solution of the difficulties that bewilder us; we must utilize stretches of the Cartesian road, so far as they are sound and passable, but then must beware of losing ourselves in the *cogito ergo sum* and similar absurdities. This we may do by attaining clarity as to the meaning and role which are in fact possessed by propositions stating what is 'immediately observed'.

What actually lies behind the statement that they are 'absolutely certain'? And in what sense can they be designated as the ultimate ground of all knowledge?

Let us first consider the second question. If we suppose that I at once take note of every observation — it makes no difference in principle whether I do so on paper or in memory — and now start out from thence to construct science, I would have before me genuine 'protocol propositions', standing temporally at the outset of knowledge. From them the remaining propositions of science would gradually be evolved through the process which we call 'induction', and which consists simply in the fact that, stimulated or incited by the protocol propositions, I tentatively set up general propositions ('hypotheses'), from which these first propositions, along with innumerable others, logically follow. Now if these others say the *same* as later observation-statements, obtained under quite specific circumstances that have to be exactly stated in advance, then the hypotheses continue to rank as confirmed so long as observation-statements do not crop up which are in contradiction to the propositions derived from the hypotheses, and hence to the hypotheses themselves. So long as this does not happen, we believe ourselves to have guessed correctly at a law of nature. Induction is therefore nothing else but a methodically guided guessing, a psychological, biological process whose execution has certainly nothing to do with 'logic'.

Here we have a schematic description of the actual procedure of science. It is clear what role is played in it by assertions about the 'immediately perceived'. They are not identical with statements written or remembered, i.e., with what could properly be called 'protocol propositions', but are the *occasion* for framing them. As we have long since conceded, the protocol propositions preserved in a book or in memory are doubtless to be compared in their validity with *hypotheses*, for if we have such a proposition before us, it is a mere assumption that it is true, that it accords with the observation statement which gave rise to it. (Perhaps, indeed, it was not occasioned by any observation statement, but arose out of some game or other.) What I call an observation statement cannot be identical with a real protocol proposition, if only because in a certain sense it cannot be noted down at all — a point to be dealt with shortly.

In the schema of knowledge-construction that I have described, therefore, the role of the observation statements is firstly that of standing in time at the outset of the whole process, occasioning it and setting it to work. How much of their content enters into knowledge, remains as first essentially undecided. With some justice the observation statements can therefore be regarded as the ultimate origin of all knowledge, but ought they to be designated as its foundation, its ultimate certain ground? This is scarcely advisable, for this 'origin' is still connected in too questionable a manner with the edifice of knowledge. Moreover, we have certainly conceived the true process in a schematically simplified fashion. In reality, what is actually stated in a protocol is less closely connected with the observed as such, and in general we should not even assume that pure observation statements are interpolated at all between the observation and the 'protocol'.

But now it seems that these propositions, the statements about the immediately perceived, or 'affirmations' [*Konstatierungen*], as we might also call them, have yet another function to perform, namely in confirming hypotheses, or in *verification*.

Science makes prophecies that are tested by 'experience'. It is in making predictions that its essential function lies. It says, for example: 'If, at such and such a time, you look through a telescope focussed in such and such a manner, you will see a speck of light (a star) coinciding with a black line (cross-wires).' Let us assume that on following these instructions the event prophesied actually occurs; this means, of course, that we make an affirmation for which we are prepared; we pass an observational judgement that we *expected*, and have in doing so a sense of *fulfilment*, a wholly characteristic satisfaction; we are *content*. It is quite proper to say that the affirmations or observation statements have fulfilled their true mission, as soon as this peculiar satisfaction is obtained.

And we obtain it at the very moment in which the affirmation occurs, the observation statement is made. This is of the utmost importance, for it means that the function of propositions about the *presently* experienced itself lies in the present. We saw, indeed, that they have, as it were, no duration, that as soon as they are over we have available in their stead only designations or memory traces, which can play only the role of hypotheses and are thereby lacking in ultimate certainty. Upon affirmations no logically tenable structure can be erected, for they are already gone at the moment building begins. If they stand in time at the outset of the process of knowledge, they are logically of no use. It is quite otherwise, however, when they come at the end; they complete the act of verification (or falsification), and at the moment of their appearance have already performed their duty. Nothing else is logically deduced from them, no conclusions are drawn from them, they are an absolute end.

Psychologically and biologically, of course, the satisfaction they produce is the beginning of a new process of knowledge: the hypotheses whose verification concludes in them are regarded as confirmed, the framing of more extensive hypotheses is attempted, and the seeking and guessing after universal laws resumes its progress. For these temporally subsequent processes the observation statements therefore form the origin and incentive, in the sense already described.

By means of these considerations it seems to me that a new and vivid light is thrown upon the question of the ultimate foundation of knowledge; we get a clear picture of how the system of our knowledge is built up, and of the role that 'affirmations' play in it.

Knowledge is originally a means in the service of life. In order to fit into his environment and to accommodate his actions to events, man must in some degree be able to foresee these events. For this he needs universal propositions, findings of knowledge, and these he can make use of only insofar as the prophecies really come to pass. Now in science this character of knowledge remains completely intact; the only difference is that it no longer serves the purposes of life, and is not pursued for the sake of utility. Once the prediction comes to pass, the aim of science is achieved: the joy in knowledge is joy in verification, the exaltation of having guessed correctly. And this it is that the observation statements convey to us; in them science, as it were, attains its goal, and for their sake it exists. The question concealed behind the problem of the absolutely certain foundation of knowledge is, so to speak, that of the legitimacy of the satisfaction which verification fills us with. Are our predictions actually realized? In every single case of verification or falsification an 'affirmation' answers unambiguously with yes or no, with joy of fulfilment or disillusion. The affirmations are final.

Finality is a very suitable word to describe the significance of observation statements. They are an absolute end, and in them the current task of knowledge is fulfilled. That the joy in which they culminate, and the hypotheses they leave behind, are then the beginning of a new task, is no longer their affair. Science does not rest on them, but leads to them, and they show that it has led aright. They are really the absolutely fixed points; we are glad to reach them, even if we cannot rest there.

VII

What does this fixity consist in? We come here to the question earlier postponed for the time being: In what sense can we speak of the 'absolute certainty' of observation statements?

I should like to elucidate this by first saying something about a quite different kind of proposition, namely *analytic propositions*, and then comparing these with 'affirmations'. In analytic judgements the question of their validity notoriously poses no problem. They are valid *a priori*, we must not and cannot be convinced of their correctness by experience, because they say nothing whatever about the objects of experience. Hence, too, they possess only 'formal truth' (see above, p. 184), i.e., they are not 'true' because they correctly express any facts; their truth, rather, consists solely in the fact that they are framed with formal correctness, i.e., conform to our arbitrarily established definitions.

But now some philosophical authors have felt obliged to ask: 'Well, how do I know in the given case whether a proposition is really in accordance with the definitions, and so is really analytic and therefore indubitable? Must I not bear in mind the proposed definitions, the meaning of all the words employed, while I utter, hear or read the proposition? But can I be sure that my mental capacities are equal to this? Is it not possible, for example, that by the end of the proposition, were it to last only for a second, I might have forgotten the beginning or wrongly remembered it? Must I not therefore admit that for psychological reasons I am never sure of the validity even of an analytic judgement?'

To this it must be replied that the possibility of malfunction in the mental mechanism must naturally always be conceded, but that the consequences that follow from it are not correctly described in the skeptical questions just propounded.

It can happen that through weakness of memory, and a thousand other causes, we fail to understand a proposition, or understand it wrongly (i.e., otherwise than it was intended) — but what is the significance of that? Well, so long as I have not understood a proposition, it is for me no statement at all, but a mere string of words, sounds or characters. In this case there is no problem, for only of a proposition can one ask if it is analytic or synthetic, not of an uncomprehended string of words. If, however, I have interpreted a series of words wrongly, but at all events as some sort of proposition — then I know of *this* particular proposition whether it is analytic, and so valid *a priori*, or not. It should not be thought that I could have grasped a proposition as such and then still be in doubt about its analytic character, for if it is analytic, I have only just then understood it, when I have understood it as analytic. For to understand means in fact nothing else but to be clear about the rules for employment of the words involved; but it is precisely such rules which make the proposition analytic. If I do not know whether a word-complex constitutes an analytic proposition or not, this means simply that at this moment I am without rules for employment of the words, and thus have failed entirely to understand the proposition. The situation is, therefore, that either I have understood nothing whatever, and then there is no more to be said, or else I know whether the proposition that I *have* understood is analytic or synthetic (which is not to assume, of course, that in so doing these words hover before me, or are even known to me). In the case of an analytic proposition, I then know at the same time that it is valid and possesses formal truth.

The foregoing doubts about the validity of analytic propositions were thus misplaced. I can indeed doubt whether I have correctly grasped the meaning of some sign-complex, and even whether I shall ever understand the meaning of a given word-series at all; but I cannot ask whether I am also really able to discern the correctness of an analytic proposition. For in an analytic judgement, to understand its meaning and to discern its *a priori* validity, are *one and the same process*. A synthetic statement, by contrast, is characterized by the fact that if I have merely discerned its meaning, I have no notion whether it is true or false; its truth is established only by a comparison with experience. The process of discerning the meaning is here entirely different from that of verification.

There is only one exception to this. And here we return to our 'affirmations'. For these are always of the form 'Here now so-and-so', e.g., 'Here now two black spots coincide', or 'Here now blue is bounded by yellow', or even 'Here now pain . . .', etc. What is common to all these statements is that they contain *demonstrative* terms having the meaning of a present gesture, i.e., their rules of use stipulate that in making the statement in which they occur, an experience occurs, attention is directed to something observed. The meaning o the words 'here', 'now', 'this here', etc. cannot be stated by means of general definitions in words, but only through such words assisted by pointings and gesticulations. 'This here' makes sense only in combination with a gesture. In order, therefore, to understand the significance of such an observation statement, one must simultaneously make the gesture, one must in some way point to reality.

In other words, I can understand the meaning of an 'affirmation' only on and by way of a comparison with the facts, i.e., a carrying-out of the process required for the verification of all synthetic propositions. But whereas in all other synthetic statements, establishing the meaning and establishing the truth are separate, clearly distinguishable processes, in observation statements they coincide, just as they do in analytic judgements. However different the 'affirmations' may be from analytic propositions, they have this in common, that in both the process of understanding is at the same time the process of verification. Along with their meaning I simultaneously grasp their truth. To ask of an affirmation whether I might perhaps be mistaken about its truth, makes no more sense than with a tautology. Both have absolute validity. The analytical or tautological proposition, however, is at the same time devoid of content, whereas the observation statement gives us the satisfaction of a genuine acquaintance with reality.

It has now become clear, let us hope, that everything here turns upon the character of immediacy which is peculiar to observation statements, and to which they owe their value both positive and negative; the positive value of absolute validity, and the negative value of being useless as an enduring foundation.

The misunderstanding of this character is in large part responsible for the unfortunate issue concerning protocol propositions which formed the starting-point of our inquiry. When I make the affirmation 'Here now blue', that is *not* the same as the protocol proposition 'On such-and-such a date in April 1934, at such-and-such a time and place, Schlick perceived blue'. For the latter proposition is a hypothesis, and as such is always fraught with uncertainty. It is equivalent to the statement '(at the given time and place) . . . Schlick made the affirmation "Here now blue" '. And clearly this statement is not identical with the affirmation occurring in it. In protocol propositions the reference is *always* to perceptions (or they are to be supplied mentally; the personal identity of the perceiving observer is important for a scientific protocol), while in affirmations they are *never* mentioned. A genuine affirmation cannot be written down, for as soon as I put down the demonstrative terms 'here' and 'now', they lose their meaning. Nor can they be replaced by an indication of time and place, for as soon as this is attempted, the observation statement is unavoidably replaced, as we have seen, by a protocol proposition, which as such has an altogether different nature.

VIII

The problem of the foundation of knowledge has now, I believe, been elucidated.

If we look on science as a system of propositions, whose logical interconnection is the only feature of interest to us as logicians, then the question of their foundation, which in that case would be a 'logical' one, can be answered as we please, for we are free to define the foundation at will. In an abstract proposition-system, after all, there is intrinsically no priority and no posteriority. The most general propositions of science, i.e., those which are most commonly selected as 'axioms', could be designated, for example, as its ultimate foundation; but the name could equally well be reserved for the most specific propositions of all, which would then in fact actually correspond to the protocols written down; or some other choice would be possible. But the propositions of science are one and all *hypotheses,* the moment they are seen from the standpoint of their truth-value, or validity.

If we turn our attention to the connection of science with reality, and see in the system of its propositions what it really is, namely a means of orienting oneself among the facts, of attaining to the joy of confirmation, the feeling of finality, then the problem of the 'foundation' will automatically transform itself into that of the unshakeable points of contact between knowledge and reality. These absolutely fixed points, the affirmations, we have come to know in their particularity; they are the only synthetic propositions *which are not hypotheses.* In no sense do they lie at the basis of science, but knowledge, as it were, flickers out to them, reaching each one for a moment only, and at once consuming it. And newly fed and strengthened, it then flares on toward the next.

These moments of fulfilment and combustion are of the essence. From them comes all the light of knowledge. And it is this light for whose source the philosopher is actually asking, when he seeks the foundation of all knowledge.

6 Facts and Propositions

Moritz Schlick

When in the spring of last year I wrote my short paper on 'Das Fundament der Erkenntnis',* sitting leisurely on a balcony overlooking the blue bay of Salerno, it did not occur to me that I was arousing a violent discussion of the 'logical positivists' theory of truth'. I regarded my little article as nothing but a gentle warning of a true empiricist against certain tendencies towards what seemed to me a rather dogmatic or rationalistic formulation of positivistic principles. I was, therefore, a little surprised when, on account of that paper, I was accused of being a metaphysician and a poet. Finding it impossible, however, to take this indictment seriously, I was neither shocked by the one nor flattered by the other and did not intend to take up the discussion. I hoped my article would speak for itself in spite of the objections raised.

The appearance of Dr Hempel's clever article in *Analysis* (vol. 2, no. 4) has changed my mind. He has shaped his arguments clearly and

Source: Analysis, 1935, pp. 65-70.

*Reprinted above as 'On the Foundation of Knowledge'–*Ed.*

nicely, and I feel it my duty to point out once more, as simply as possible, why I cannot be satisfied with some of the views professed by some of my friends. I shall restrict myself to what seems to me to be the most critical point, i.e. the relationship of 'propositions' to 'reality'.

I have been accused of maintaining that statements can be compared with facts. I plead guilty. I have maintained this. But I protest against my punishment: I refuse to sit in the seat of the metaphysicians. I have often compared propositions to facts; so I had no reason to say that it couldn't be done. I found, for instance, in my Baedeker the statement: 'This cathedral has two spires,' I was able to compare it with 'reality' by looking at the cathedral, and this comparison convinced me that Baedeker's assertion was true. Surely you cannot tell me that such a process is impossible and that there is a detestable metaphysics involved in it. You say you did not mean it that way? But I assure you that I meant nothing but a process of this kind when I spoke of testing propositions by comparing them with facts. No one who is familiar with my recent writings can suppose that I used the term 'reality' for anything but empirical objects like churches, trees, clouds, etc.[1] not for any 'metaphysical' entities. A cathedral is not a proposition or a set of propositions, therefore I felt justified in maintaining that a proposition could be compared with reality.

Perhaps you say: 'But if we analyse the process of verification of Baedeker's assertion we shall find that it amounts to a comparison of propositions.' I answer: I don't know; it will depend on what you mean by "analysis". But whatever the result of your analysis may be, at any rate we can distinguish between cases in which a written, printed or spoken sentence is compared with some other written, printed or spoken sentence, and cases like our example, where a sentence is compared with the thing of which it speaks. And it is this latter case which I took the liberty of describing as a 'comparison of a proposition with a fact'. If you don't like to use this expression for the case described it will merely be a difference of terminology.

You insist that a statement cannot or must not be compared to anything but statements. But why? It is my humble opinion that we can compare anything to anything if we choose. Do you believe that propositions and facts are too far removed from each other? Too different? Is it a mysterious property of proposition that they cannot be

---

[1] See e.g. *Les énoncés scientifiques*, chap. IV, Paris 1934.

compared with anything else? That would seem to be a rather mystical view. We are assured that the 'cleavage' between statements and facts 'is nothing but the result of a redoubling metaphysics'.[2] That may be true. But who believes in such a cleavage? Those who say that the one cannot be compared to the other, or the humble empiricist like myself, for whom propositions are facts among other facts and who sees no difficulty, no 'embarrassing consequences' in comparing them?

What is a proposition, after all? In my opinion it is a series of sounds or other symbols (a "sentence") *together with the logical rules belonging to them*, i.e. certain prescriptions as to how the sentence is to be *used*. These rules, culminating in "deictic" definitions, constitute the "meaning" of the proposition. In order to verify the proposition I have to ascertain whether those rules have actually been obeyed — why should that be impossible? In our example it is done by looking at the cathedral and at the sentence in the book and by stating that the symbol "two" is used in connection with the symbol "spires", and that I arrive at the same symbol when I apply the rules of counting to the towers of the cathedral.

You will reproach me for using again the 'material mode of speech', instead of the 'formal mode'. I fully acknowledge the importance of the distinction between these two, and I have admitted that in epistemological analysis we should endeavour to use the formal mode. But I think it is wrong to say that the use of this mode is 'much more correct'. I am convinced, with Carnap, that the material mode as such is not faulty, only it is apt to engender pseudo-problems *if it is employed without sufficient precaution.* Dr Hempel says: 'Saying that empirical statements "express facts" . . . is a typical form of the material mode of speech.' Perhaps so; but what harm is there in it? This particular phrase is an innocent tautology — for what on earth could statements express except facts? On the other hand: saying that certain black marks in my Baedeker express the fact that a certain cathedral has two spires is a perfectly legitimate empirical assertion. By the way, it is easy to express in a purely 'formal' way my opinion that facts and propositions can be compared: words denoting symbols and words denoting other things may occur in the some sentence.

Sometimes we are told that it is in 'a logical respect' that propositions cannot be compared to anything but propositions. This may be true,

---

[2] *Ibid.* p. 51.

but I don't know whether it is true or not, because I don't know what is meant by a comparison in a 'logical respect'.

Is it true that we are unable 'to give a precise account of how a comparison between statements and facts may possibly be accomplished, and how we may possibly ascertain the structure of facts'?[3] I think it is not true. Or was the description faulty which I gave of such a comparison a little while ago? It consisted of the simplest empirical prescriptions of a kind which we carry out many times almost every day. You can easily make the description more precise by adding details, but that is not even necessary, because it would not change the principle of the matter.

If you assert, as you seem to do, that we cannot 'possibly ascertain the structure of facts', I must confess that such a statement reminds me a little of the metaphysics of 'things in themselves' which, it is alleged, must for ever remain unknown to us. Since you do not deny the existence of facts[4] why should you deny that we can know their structure? I should say, for instance, that by counting the spires of a cathedral I get acquainted with the structure of a certain fact. Perhaps you merely want to say that it is nonsense to speak of 'structures of facts' at all? I answer: that may be so if you adopt certain rules for the use of your words, but it is not so if the words are employed in the way in which I used them. It must be remembered that no sentence is meaningful or meaningless *per se*, but only in regard to the definitions and rules which have been stipulated for the use of words occurring in it.

This applies to the whole issue in discussion. If it is true that 'facts' and 'propositions' cannot be compared, then those words are used in a way which differs from the way I used them. They have a different meaning, and the dispute is merely verbal.

The simplest way of maintaining the impossibility of the comparison in question would be to say *that there are no 'facts'* (in the formal mode: the rule for the word "fact" is simply that it shall not be employed at all). But I see no reason why this convenient word should be banished and, if I understand rightly, you do not actually want to go so far.

Perhaps you mean to say that although the facts which we call propositions *may* be compared with other facts, it is actually *never done in science*? I think that this is true for the purely theoretical work

---

[3] *loc. cit.* p. 51.

[4] *Ibid.* p. 54.

of science, e.g. for the mathematical physicist whose business consists in formulating and comparing natural laws and also 'protocol statements', uniting them into a coherent system and computing the consequences. His work is done by means of pencil and paper. But I assert most emphatically that it is *not* true for the experimenting scientist whose work consists in making observations and comparing the predictions of the mathematician with – I do beg your pardon – the observed facts.

It is at this point, I believe, that the psychological source of the criticized view reveals itself: its advocates are theoretically minded men who take their stand *within* science. Science is a system of propositions; and – without being aware of it – these thinkers substitute science for reality; for them facts are not acknowledged before they are formulated in propositions and taken down in their notebooks. But Science is not the World. The universe of discourse is not the whole universe. It is a typical rationalistic attitude which shows itself here under the guise of the most subtle distinctions.

Our good friends and opponents think of the system of truths as the mathematician thinks of theoretical physics: for him it is quite true that his only task is to make all scientific statements *coherent* among each other; and it is also true that if there are several coherent systems his choice of the 'true' one is solely determined by 'the scientists of his culture circle'[5]; he has no other canon because they furnish the 'protocol statements' which he uses as his material without submitting them to an experimental test. It is true, therefore, that the system of protocol statements which he calls 'true' is 'the system which is actually adopted by mankind'.

But the matter is different for the experimenting observer and for unrelenting empiricists like myself. It is one thing to ask how the system of science has been built up and why it is generally believed to be true, and another thing to ask why I myself (the individual observer) accept it as true. You may regard my article on 'Das Fundament der Erkenntnis' as an attempt to answer the last question. It is a psychological question. If anyone should tell me that I believe in the truth of science ultimately because it has been adopted 'by the scientists of my culture circle', I should – smile at him. I do have trust in those good fellows, but that is only because I always found them to be trustworthy

---

[5] *Ibid.* p. 57.

wherever I was able to test their enunciations. I assure you most emphatically that I should *not* call the system of science true if I found its consequences incompatible with my own observations of nature, and the fact that it is adopted by the whole of mankind and taught in all the universities would make no impression on me. If all the scientists in the world told me that under certain experimental conditions I must see three black spots, and if under those conditions I saw only one spot, no power in the universe could induce me to think that the statement 'there is now only one black spot in the field of vision' is false.

In other words: the *only ultimate* reason why I accept any proposition as true is to be found in those simple experiences which may be regarded as the final steps of a comparison between a statement and a fact and which I have spoken of as 'Konstatierungen' — without attaching any importance to the word. One can perhaps give a better description of them than I have done, but no one can convince me that they are not the only ultimate basis of all my beliefs.

7 Some Remarks on "Facts" and Propositions

Carl G. Hempel

1 In a recent article in *Analysis** Prof. Schlick traces the outlines of his view concerning the relationship of propositions to "facts". In this account, Prof. Schlick makes a contribution for which we must be grateful to elucidating some essential points of his article 'Das Fundament der Erkenntnis'† which occasioned a logical controversy, the fundamental ideas of which I tried to characterize in my note 'On the Logical Positivists' Theory of Truth' (*Analysis*, vol 2, no 4).

In his paper, Prof. Schlick raises certain objections to some of the considerations which I sketched in my article and which correspond to Dr. Neurath's and Prof. Carnap's view; he gives his objections the form of questions, which may be summed up by asking: What harm is there in saying that propositions are compared with "facts", and that true propositions express "facts"? To this question I shall try to reply.

Source: Analysis, 1935, pp. 93-6.

*'Facts and Propositions', reprinted above–*Ed.*

†Reprinted above as 'On the Foundation of Knowledge'–*Ed.*

2 Prof. Schlick illustrates the character of the comparison between a proposition and "facts" by means of a very instructive example. But I think that in an essential respect his account is not quite adequate.

For on the one hand Prof. Schlick expressly describes propositions as empirical objects (of a special kind) which may be compared with any other empirical object. So far I fully agree with him. But if we take him at his word, we must expect that the proposition he chooses as an example will be tested by comparing the *physical object* (consisting of ink-symbols) 'This cathedral has two spires' (or a similarly shaped physical object which is to be found in Prof. Schlick's Baedeker), with another physical object called the cathedral. Such a comparison may very well be realized (it would lead to such statements as: The proposition contains more parts, called 'words', than the cathedral has spires); but evidently it does not permit us to test the proposition (indeed, there is no specific "correspondence" between the two compared physical objects). But here Prof. Schlick introduces a second interpretation of the comparison, saying that 'it is done by looking at the cathedral and at the sentence in the book and by stating that the symbol "two" is used in connection with the symbol "spires", and that I arrive at the same symbol when I apply the rules of counting to the towers of the cathedral' (p. 198). Here, he evidently compares the proposition in his Baedeker with *the result* (not with the act!) *of his counting* the spires; this result may have the form 'I now see two spires' or something like that, but in any case it is a second *proposition* with which the first is compared. (And now there really is a certain congruence, both the propositions containing the word "two".)

Thus Prof. Schlick's example reveals that speaking of a 'comparison between a proposition and "fact" ' is nothing but an abbreviated and convenient method of describing a comparison between certain propositions; (and just this is meant by saying that in 'a logical respect' 'propositions cannot be compared to anything but propositions'). Such a comparison *refers to the logical relations* which hold between the compared propositions.

In order to find out, e.g., if a certain hypothesis *h* is confirmed or falsified by the "observed facts" with which it is compared, one has to ascertain, if the observation-statements are *compatible* with (or even *deducible* from) *h*, or if they *contradict h*. Such a logical (syntactical) examination of propositions may be performed, as Carnap has shown in his 'Logische Syntax der Sprache' (cf. also 'Philosophy and Logical Syntax', London, 1934), without knowing the meaning of the propositions, by a mere comparison of the symbols which the propositions are composed of. (Stating that both the propositions mentioned above contain a sign shaped "two" is an example of this kind of comparison.)

3 But furthermore, Carnap has shown that the logical relations which hold between two propositions depend upon the syntactical rules of the language which we choose. A proposition *p* may be deducible from a proposition *h* with respect to one system of rules, and not deducible from *h* with respect to another one. Therefore the result of what is called a 'comparison between propositions and "facts" ' depends upon the syntax of scientific language – a circumstance which need not necessarily, but will at least very easily be veiled by the material mode of speech, the latter evoking the imagination that the "facts" with which propositions are to be confronted are substantial entities and do not depend upon the scientist's choice of syntax-rules.

4 This point is also fundamentally connected with the question of the "structure of facts". If one admits this expression, it seems to be legitimate, e.g. to ask, if the structure of facts admits only the occurrence of rational values of the different coefficients of physical state, or if, on the contrary, the old principle 'natura non facit saltus' is valid in the sense that also irrational values are physically possible? And if one thinks, further, that the structure of propositions must be in a certain way isomorphous to the structure of facts, one has to ask: Have we to introduce the system of real numbers in order to give a true image of the structure of facts? But both these questions are pseudoproblems; for it is impossible to imagine an experience which might furnish a decision by falsifying one of the two possibilities. It is a question of syntactical convention whether to admit or to exclude the occurrence of irrational-number-symbols, and thereby to stipulate a rational or irrational metrical structure for "facts".

5 In Carnap's and Neurath's theory of science, the empirical character of scientific research is fully maintained. It is expressed by emphasizing that scientific propositions are tested by such statements (often observation-statements) as have been produced or adopted by instructed observers or 'scientists'. (Giving someone 'deictic definitions', of the kind Prof. Schlick speaks of, is a special way of instructing or 'conditioning' him for the production of observation-statements.)

But I think it is not quite harmless (though, of course, not 'false' either) to say that those observation-statements (and the statements supported by them) 'express "facts" '; for this term indicates something which is once for ever fixed with all its characteristics, whilst it is

204 Verification and Experience

essential for the system of scientific statements that it may always be
changed again, that no proposition is adopted once and for all, and in
addition that the adoption of any observation-statement has, after all,
the character of a *convention*. But even if one denies this, as Prof.
Schlick does, it is not harmless to say that 'propositions express "facts" '.
For one system of observation statements (or other basic statements) is
compatible with many different systems of physical statements (see
Analysis 2, 4, p. 52), so that any of the ordinary physical statements,
even such as 'This is a piece of iron', is a hypothesis the adoption of
which depends in the end upon a convention.

And the character of statements which are adopted by a convention
evidently does not admit of such questions as: Are there statements
which express facts adequately, which are absolutely true (are perhaps
the 'Konstatierungen' of this kind)? Prof. Schlick had dealt with
questions of this type, and I therefore put forward in the paper which
has been mentioned certain scruples concerning the formulation that
'propositions express "facts" '.

E. ETHICS

1 Ethics

Rudolf Carnap

One division of philosophy, which by some philosophers is considered the most important, has not been mentioned at all so far, namely, the philosophy of values, with its main branch, moral philosophy or *Ethics*. The word 'Ethics' is used in two different senses. Sometimes a certain empirical investigation is called 'Ethics,' viz. psychological and socio- logical investigations about the actions of human beings, especially regarding the origin of these actions from feelings and volitions and their effects upon other people. Ethics in this sense is an empirical, scientific investigation; it belongs to empirical science rather than to philosophy. Fundamentally different from this is ethics in the second sense, as the philosophy of moral values or moral norms, which one can designate normative ethics. This is not an investigation of facts, but a pretended investigation of what is good and what is evil, what it is right to do and what it is wrong to do. Thus the purpose of this philosophical, or normative, ethics is to state norms for human action or judgements about moral values.

It is easy to see that it is merely a difference of formulation, whether we state a norm or a value judgment. A norm or rule has an imperative form, for instance: 'Do not kill!' The corresponding value judgment would be: 'Killing is evil.' This difference of formulation has become practically very important, especially for the development of philo- sophical thinking. The rule, 'Do not kill', has grammatically the impera- tive form and will therefore not be regarded as an assertion. But the value statement, 'Killing is evil', although, like the rule, it is merely an expression of a certain wish, has the grammatical form of an assertive proposition. Most philosophers have been deceived by this form into thinking that a value statement is really an assertive proposition, and

Source: Rudolf Carnap, *Philosophy and Logical Syntax,* Kegan Paul, 1935, chapter 1 (extract).

must be either true or false. Therefore they give reasons for their own value statements and try to disprove those of their opponents. But actually a value statement is nothing else than a command in a misleading grammatical form. It may have effect upon the actions of men, and these effects may either be in accordance with our wishes or not; but it is neither true nor false. It does not assert anything and can neither be proved nor disproved.

This is revealed as soon as we apply to such statements our method of logical analysis. From the statement 'Killing is evil' we cannot deduce any proposition about future experiences. Thus this statement is not verifiable and has no theoretical sense, and the same thing is true of all other value statements.

Perhaps somebody will contend in opposition that the following proposition is deducible: 'If a person kills anybody he will have feelings of remorse.' But this proposition is in no way deducible from the proposition 'Killing is evil'. It is deducible only from psychological propositions about the character and the emotional reactions of the person. These propositions are indeed verifiable and not without sense. They belong to psychology, not to philosophy; to psychological ethics (if one wishes to use this word), not to philosophical or normative ethics. The propositions of normative ethics, whether they have the form of rules or the form of value statements, have no theoretical sense, are not scientific propositions (taking the word scientific to mean any assertive proposition).

To avoid misunderstanding it must be said that we do not at all deny the possibility and importance of a scientific investigation of value statements as well as of acts of valuation. Both of these are acts of individuals and are, like all other kinds of acts, possible objects of empirical investigation. Historians, psychologists, and sociologists may give analyses and causal explanations of them, and such historical and psychological propositions about acts of valuation and about value statements are indeed meaningful scientific propositions which belong to ethics in the first sense of this word. But the value statements themselves are here only objects of investigation; they are not propositions in these theories, and have, here as elsewhere, no theoretical sense. Therefore we assign them to the realm of metaphysics.

2 What is the Aim of Ethics?
Moritz Schlick

1 ETHICS SEEKS NOTHING BUT KNOWLEDGE

If there are ethical questions which have meaning, and are therefore capable of being answered, then ethics is a science. For the correct answers to its questions will constitute a system of true propositions, and a system of true propositions concerning an object is the 'science' of that object. Thus ethics is a system of *knowledge*, and nothing else; its ony goal is the truth. Every science is, as such, purely theoretical; it seeks to understand; hence the questions of ethics, too, are purely theoretical problems. As philosophers we try to find their correct solutions, but their practical application, if such is possible, does not fall within the sphere of ethics. If anyone studies these questions in order to apply the results to life and action, his *dealing* with ethics has, it is true, a practical end; but ethics itself never has any other goal than the truth.

So long as the philosopher is concerned with his purely theoretical questions, he must forget that he has a human interest as well as a cognitive interest in the object of his investigation. For him there is no greater danger than to change from a philosopher into a moralist, from an investigator into a preacher. Desire for the truth is the only appropriate inspiration for the thinker when he philosophizes; otherwise his thoughts run the danger of being led astray by his feelings. His wishes, hopes, and fears threaten to encroach upon that objectivity which is the necessary presupposition of all honest inquiry. Of course, the prophet and the investigator can be one and the same person; but one cannot at the same moment serve both interests, for whoever mixes the two problems will solve neither.

A glance at the great ethical systems will show how necessary these remarks are. There is hardly one in which we do not occasionally find an appeal to the feeling or the morality of the reader where a scientific analysis would have been appropriate.

Source: Moritz Schlick, *Problems of Ethics,* trans. D. Rynin, Dover, 1962, chapter 1. This book, originally entitled *Fragen der Ethik,* was first published by J. Springer Verlag, Vienna, 1930.

Nevertheless, I do not point out the purely theoretical character of ethics merely to warn my reader, and myself. I do it also because it will help us to define the problems with which ethics is concerned and which we shall try to solve.

2 THE SUBJECT-MATTER OF ETHICS

To what object, or realm of objects, do the questions of ethics relate? This object has many names, and we use them so often in daily life that one might think we should know exactly what we mean by them. The ethical questions concern 'morality', or what is morally 'valuable', what serves as a 'standard' or 'norm' of human conduct, what is 'demanded' of us; or, finally, to name it by the oldest, simplest word, ethical questions concern the 'good'.

And what does ethics do with this object? We have already answered this question: ethics seeks to *understand* it, to gain knowledge of it, and would and can under no circumstances do anything else with it. Since ethics is, in essence, theory or knowledge, its task cannot be to produce morality, or to establish it, or call it to life. It does not have the task of producing the good — neither in the sense that its business is to invest the good with reality in human affairs, nor in the sense that it has to stipulate or decree what the word 'good' ought to signify. It creates neither the concept nor the objects which fall under the concept, nor does it provide the opportunity of applying the concept to the objects. All this it finds, as every science finds the materials it works with, in experience. It is obvious that no science can have any other beginning. The misleading view (introduced by the 'Neo-Kantians') according to which objects of a science are not simply 'given' to it but are themselves always 'given as problems' will not lead anyone to deny that whoever wishes to understand anything must first know *what* it is he wishes to understand.

Where and how, then, is 'the good' of ethics given?

We must from the outset be clear on the point that here there is only *one* possibility, the same that lies before all other sciences. Wherever an instance of the object to be known occurs, there must be exhibited a certain mark (or group of marks) which characterizes the thing or event as one of a certain definite kind, thus distinguishing it from all others in a special way. If this were not so we would have no opportunity and no motive to call it by a special name. Every name which is used in discourse for communication must have a meaning capable of being indicated. This is indeed self-evident, and it would not be doubted of the object of any other science — only in ethics has it sometimes been forgotten.

Let us consider some examples outside the field of ethics. Biology, the science of life, finds its sphere limited by a group of characteristics (a special kind of motion, regeneration, growth, and so forth) which belong to all living things, and stand out so clearly for every-day observation that — apart from certain critical instances — the difference between the animate and inanimate is very sharply distinguished, without the use of any scientific analysis. It is only because of this that the concept of life could have first been formed, and obtained its special name. If the biologist succeeds, with progressive knowledge, in establishing new and sharper definitions of life, in order better to bring the events of life under general laws, this means only more precision in, and perhaps extension of, the concept, without however altering its original meaning.

Similarly the word 'light' had a definite meaning before there was a science of light, that is, optics, and this meaning determined the subject-matter of optics. The distinguishing mark was in this case that immediate experience which we call 'light-sensation', that is, a not-further-definable datum of consciousness, known only to the perceiver, the occurrence of which — again apart from critical instances — indicates the presence of those events which constitute the subject-matter of optics. The fact that optics in its modern developed form is the science of Roentgen rays and radio-telegraphic waves as well (because their laws are identical with the laws of light) enlarges the meaning of the word 'optics' without changing its basis.

As certainly, then, as the expression 'moral good' makes good sense, just as certainly must we be able to discover it in a way analogous to that by which one discovers the meaning of the word 'life' or 'light'. But many philosophers see in this a serious difficulty of ethics, indeed *the* difficulty, and they are of the opinion that the sole task of ethics is the discovery of the definition of 'good'.

3 ON THE DEFINITION OF GOOD

This view can be interpreted in two ways. In the first place, it could mean that the task of the philosopher is exhausted in describing exactly the sense in which the word 'good' — or *bon* or *gut* or *buono* or ἀγαθόν — in its moral signification is actually used. It would concern itself merely with making clear the already well-known meaning, by a strict formulation of it in other words (were it not already well known one would not know that, for example, 'good' is the translation of *bonum*). Is this really the goal of ethics? The statement of the meaning of words by definitions is (as G. E. Moore in his *Principia Ethica* has pointed out in a similar connection) the business of the science of language. Ought we really to believe that ethics is a branch of linguistics? Perhaps a branch that has split off from it because the definition of 'good' harbours special difficulties we meet in no other word? A very peculiar case, that a whole science should be necessary to find merely the definition of a concept! And in any case, who is interested in mere definitions? They are, after all, only means to an end; they stand at the *beginning* of the real cognitive task. If ethics ended with a definition it would be at most the introduction to a science, and the philosopher would interest himself only in what comes after it. No, the real problems of ethics are certainly of a very different sort. Even though the task of ethics could be formulated as that of stating what the good 'really is', this could not be understood as consisting in the mere determination of the meaning of a concept (as also, in our example, optics does not strive for a mere definition of 'light'). Rather it would have to be understood as the task of explanation, of complete cognition of the good — which presupposes that the meaning of the concept is already known and then relates it to something else, orders it in more general connections (just as optics does with light, which tells us what light 'really is' by pointing out the place in the sphere of natural events to which the well-known phenomenon belongs, by describing to the last detail its laws, and by recognizing their identity with the laws of certain electrical events).

Secondly, the view according to which the goal of ethics consist of a correct determination of the concept 'good' could be interpreted as not being concerned with the formulation of the content of the concept, but rather with giving it a content. This would, however, be exactly that view which we have from the start recognized to be quite senseless. It would mean that the philosopher made, or created, the concept of the good, while without him there existed merely the word 'good'. He would of course have to invent it quite arbitrarily. (But inasmuch as in formulating his definition he could not act completely arbitrarily, since he would be bound by some norm, some guiding principle, the concept of the good would already be determined by these norms. The philosopher would have merely to find a formulation of it, and we should have before us the previously considered case.) However, it would be quite absurd to demand of ethics nothing but the arbitrary establishment of the meaning of a word. That would be no achievement at all. Even the prophet, the creator of a new morality, never forms a new concept of morality, but presupposes one, and asserts only that other modes of behaviour are subsumed under it than those which people have believed up to that time. In logical terms, the prophet holds that the acknowledged content of the concept has a different range from that supposed. This alone can be the meaning when he declares: 'Not that is "good" which you have held as such, but something else!"

Thus we see the view confirmed that in no way is the formulation of the concept of the moral good to be considered as the final task of ethics; it cannot be regarded as anything but a mere preparation.

To be sure, this preparation is not to be neglected; ethics ought not to spare itself the task of determining the meaning of its concept, even though, as we have said, the meaning of the word 'good' may in one sense be assumed as known.

4 IS THE GOOD INDEFINABLE?

It is very dangerous to withdraw from this task under the pretext that the word 'good' is one of those whose meaning is simple and unanalysable, of which therefore a definition, a statement of the connotation, is impossible. What is demanded here need not be a definition in the strictest sense of the word. It is sufficient to indicate how we can get the content of the concept; to state what must be done in order to become acquainted with its content. It is, strictly speaking, also impossible to define what the word 'green' means – but we can nevertheless fix its meaning unambiguously, for example, by saying it is the colour of a summer meadow, or by pointing to the foliage of a tree. We mentioned above that a 'light-sensation' which furnishes us with the fundamental concept of optics is not definable; however, we know exactly what is meant by it, because we can give the exact conditions under which we have a light-sensation. In the same way, in ethics we must be able to give the exact conditions under which the word 'good' is applied, even though its fundamental concept be indefinable. In this manner it must be possible to give the meaning of any word, for otherwise it would have no meaning at all. It must even be capable of being given easily; profound philosophical analysis cannot be necessary for this, for the matter concerns merely a question of fact, namely, a description of those conditions under which the word 'good' (or its equivalent in other languages, or its contrary, 'evil') is actually used.

It is difficult for many philosophers to stick to the realm of fact even temporarily, without immediately inventing a theory to describe the facts. And thus the theory has been frequently propounded that the fundamental concept of ethics is given as is the fundamental concept of optics. Just as we possess a special sense, namely the sense of sight, for the perception of light, so it is supposed that a special 'moral sense' indicates the presence of good or evil. Accordingly, good and evil would be objective characters, to be determined and investigated as are the physical events which optics investigates, and which it considers to be the causes of light-sensations.

This theory is of course wholly hypothetical. The moral sense is merely assumed; its organs cannot be pointed out as can the human eye. But the hypothesis is also false; it fails to account for the variations in moral judgement among men, since the further assumption that the moral sense is poorly developed in many persons, or completely absent, does not suffice to explain these variations.

No, it is not the distinguishing characteristic of the subject-matter of ethics that it is the object of a special kind of perception. Its characteristics must be capable of exhibition by simply pointing to certain known facts, without any artifice. This can happen in different ways. Two ways are here distinguished: first, one can seek for an external, formal characteristic of good and evil; and, second, one can search for a material characteristic, one of content.

5 THE FORMAL CHARACTERISTIC OF THE GOOD

The formal characteristic, on which Kant placed the whole weight of his moral philosophy, and which he made prominent by his greatest eloquence, is this: the good always appears as something that is demanded, or commanded; the evil, as something forbidden. Good conduct is such as is demanded or desired of us. Or, as it has generally been expressed since Kant: those actions are good which we *ought to do*. Now, to a demand, a claim, or a desire there belongs someone who demands, claims, or desires. This author of the moral law must also be given in order that the characterization by means of the formal property of the command be unambiguous.

Here opinions differ. In theological ethics this author is God, and according to one interpretation the good is good because God desires it; in this case the formal characteristic (to be a command of God) would express the very essence of the good. According to another, perhaps profounder, interpretation, God desires the good because it is good. In this case its essence must be given by certain material characters previously to and independently of those formal determinations. In traditional philosophical ethics the opinion prevails that the author is, for example, human society (utilitarianism) or the active self (eudaimonism) or even no one (the categorical imperative). From this last proceeds Kant's doctrine of the 'absolute ought', that is, a demand without a demander. One of the worst errors of ethical thought lies in his belief that the concept of the moral good is completely exhausted by the statement of its purely formal property, that it has no content except to be what is demanded, 'what should be'.

6 MATERIAL CHARACTERISTICS

In opposition to this, it is clear that the discovery of the formal characters of the good constitutes only a preliminary step in the determination of the content of the good, in the statement of material characteristics. If we know that the good is what is demanded, we must still ask: What is it then that is actually demanded? In answer to this question we must turn to the author of the command and investigate his will and desire, for the content of his desire is that which he wishes to happen. When I recommend an action to someone as being 'good', I express the fact that I *desire* it.

So long as the lawgiver is not known with certainty, we must stick to the laws as they are generally observed, to the formulations of moral rules as we find them among men. We must discover which ways of acting (or dispositions, or whatever be the term used) are called 'good' by different people, at different times, by different wise men or religious writers. Only in this way do we come to know the content of this concept. From the content it may then be possible to infer the lawgiving authority, if it cannot be ascertained otherwise.

In grouping together the individual cases in which something is designated as morally good, we must search for the common elements,

the characters in which these examples agree or show similarities. These
similar elements are the characters of the concept 'good'; they constitute
its content, and within them must lie the reason why one and the same
word, 'good', is used for the several cases.

To be sure, one will at once come upon cases in which nothing
common can be found, in which there seems to be a complete incom-
patibility; one and the same thing – for example, polygamy – will be
considered moral in one community, and in another a crime. In such a
situation there are two possibilities. First, there could be several ir-
reducibly different concepts of 'good' (which agree in the purely formal
property of being somehow 'demanded'); if this were so there would
not be a single morality, but many. Or, second, it could be that the
divergence in moral judgements was only apparent and not final; that,
namely, in the end one and the same goal was approved, but that a
difference of opinion prevailed as to which way leads to it, which
actions should therefore be demanded. (For instance, polygamy and
monogamy are not in themselves judged morally. The real object of
valuation is perhaps the peace of family life, or the least troublesome
order of sexual relationships. One person believes that this end can be
attained only through monogamous marriage, and considers it, therefore, to be morally good; another believes the same of polygamy. One
may be right, the other wrong; they differ, not by their final valuations,
but only by virtue of their insight, capacity of judgement, or experience.)

Whether there is actually among men a multiplicity of moralities
incompatible with one another, or whether the difference in the moral
world are only specious, so that the philosopher would find everywhere,
under the many disguises and masks of morality, one and the same face
of the one Good, we cannot now decide. In any case, there are wide
regions in which the unanimity and security of moral judgements is
substantiated. The modes of behaviour which we group together under
the names reliability, helpfulness, sociability are everywhere judged to
be 'good', while, for example, thievery, murder, quarrelsomeness pass
for 'evil' so unanimously that here the question of the common property
can be answered with practically universal validity. If such characters
are found for a large group of actions, then one can apply himself to
the 'exceptions' and irregularities, that is, to those cases in which the
same behaviour evokes divergent moral judgements in different times,
among different peoples. Here one finds either that there is no different
ground for the judgement from that in all ordinary cases, but that it is
merely more remote, hidden, or applied under altered circumstances; or

one must simply note the fact as indicating a new or ambiguous meaning of the word 'good'. And finally, it happens, of course, that certain individuals hold different opinions regarding good and evil from those held by people of their time and community. In these cases it is quite as important to make out the content and causes of their opinions as in any other more regular cases, if the persons in question are important as prophets, moral writers, or morally creative men; or if their teachings disclose hidden currents or impress their moral judgements on humanity and the future.

7 MORAL NORMS AND MORAL PRINCIPLES

The common characteristics which a group of 'good' acts or dispositions exhibits can be combined in a *rule* of the form: A mode of action must have such and such properties in order to be called 'good' (or 'evil'). Such a rule can also be called a 'norm'. Let it be understood at once, however, that such a 'norm' is nothing but a mere expression of fact; it gives us only the conditions under which an act or disposition or character is actually called 'good', that is, is given a moral value. The setting up of norms is nothing but the determination of the concept of the good, which ethics undertakes to understand.

This determination would proceed by seeking ever new groups of acts that are recognized to be good, and showing for each of them the rule or norm which all of their members satisfy. The different norms, so obtained, would then be compared, and one would order them into new classes such that the individual norms of each class had something in common, and thus would all be subsumed under a higher, that is, a more general, norm. With this higher norm the same procedure would be repeated, and so on, until, in a perfect case, one would at last reach a highest, most general rule that included all others as special cases, and would be applicable to every instance of human conduct. This highest norm would be the definition of 'the good' and would express its universal essence; it would be what the philosopher calls a 'moral principle'.

Of course, one cannot know beforehand whether one will actually arrive at a single moral principle. It might well be that the highest series of rules to which the described way leads simply shows no common character, that one has, therefore, to stop with several norms as highest rules, because despite all attempts none higher can be found to which these could be reduced. There would then be several mutually independent meanings of the expression 'moral good', several mutually independent moral principles which only in their totality would determine the concept of morality, or perhaps several different concepts of the moral, depending upon the time and the people. It is significant how little these possibilities have, in general, been considered by philosophers; almost all have at once sought a single moral principle. Quite the contrary is true of the practical moral systems, which ordinarily do not attempt to establish an all-inclusive principle; as in the case of the catechism, which stops at the ten commandments.

For those who believe that the sole task of ethics consists in the determination of the concept of the good, that is, in the establishment of one or several moral principles, the completion of the described procedure would exhaust the theme of ethics. It would be a pure 'normative science'; for its end would lie in the discovery of a hierarchy of norms or rules which culminated in one or several points, the moral principles, and in which the lower levels would be explained or 'justified' by the higher. To the question, 'Why is this act moral?' the explanation can be given, 'Because it falls under these definite rules'; and if one asks further, 'Why are all the acts falling under this rule moral?' this would be explained by saying, 'Because they all fall under that next higher rule'. And only with the highest norm – with the moral principle or moral principles – is the knowledge of the validating grounds, a justification, no longer possible in this way. There ethics is at an end for him who sees it as a mere normative science.

8 ETHICS AS A 'NORMATIVE SCIENCE'

We now see clearly what meaning the phrase 'normative science' can have, and in what sense alone ethics can 'justify' an act or its valuation. In modern philosophy since Kant, the idea repeatedly appears that ethics as a normative science is something completely different from the 'factual sciences'. It does not ask, 'When is a person judged to be good?' or, 'Why is he judged to be good?' These questions concern mere facts and their explanation. But it does ask, 'With *what right* is that person judged to be good?' It does not trouble itself with what is actually valued, but asks: 'What is valuable? What should be valued?' And here obviously the question is quite different.

But *this* manner of opposing normative and factual sciences is fundamentally false. For if ethics furnishes a justification it does so only in the sense just explained, namely, in a relative-hypothetical way, not absolutely. It 'justifies' a certain judgement only to the extent that it shows that the judgement corresponds to a certain norm; that this norm itself is 'right', or justified, it can neither show nor, by itself, determine. Ethics must simply recognize this as a fact of human nature. Even as a normative science, a science can do no more than *explain;* it can never set up or establish a norm (which alone would be equivalent to an absolute justification). It is never able to do more than to discover the rules of the judgement, to read them from the facts before it; the origin of norms always lies outside and before science and knowledge. This means that their origin can only be apprehended by the science, and does not lie within it. In other words: if, or in so far as, the philosopher answers the question 'What is good?' by an exhibition of norms, this means only that he tells us what 'good' *actually* means; he can never tell us what 'good' *must* or *should* mean. The question regarding the validity of a valuation amounts to asking for a higher acknowledged norm under which the value falls, and this is a question of *fact.* The question of the justification of the highest norms or the ultimate values is senseless, because there is nothing higher to which these could be referred. Since modern ethics, as we remarked, often speaks of this absolute justification as *the* fundamental problem of ethics, it must be said, unfortunately, that the formulation of the question from which it proceeds is simply meaningless.

The perversity of such a formulation of the question will be exhibited by a famous example. John Stuart Mill has often been justly criticized because he thought himself able to deduce from the fact that a thing was desired that it was in itself *desirable.* The double meaning of the word desirable ('capable of being desired' and 'worth desiring') misled him. But his critics were also wrong, for they rested their criticism upon the same false presupposition (expressly formulated by neither), namely, that the phrase 'in itself desirable' had a definite meaning (by 'in itself' I mean 'for its own sake', not merely as a means to an end); but in fact they could give it no meaning. If I say of a thing that it is desirable, and mean that one must desire it as a means if one desires a certain end, then everything is perfectly clear. If, however, I assert that a thing is desirable simply in itself, I cannot say what I mean by this statement; it is not verifiable and is therefore meaningless. A thing can be desirable only with respect to something else, not in itself. Mill believed himself able to deduce what is in itself desirable from what actually is desired; his opponents held that these had nothing to do with one another. But ultimately neither side knew what it said, for both failed to give an absolute meaning to the word 'desirable'. The question whether something is desirable for its own sake is no question at all, but mere empty words. On the other hand, the question of what actually is desired for its own sake is of course quite sensible, and ethics is actually concerned only with answering this question. Mill succeeded in arriving at this real question, in the passage criticized, and thus freed himself of the senseless form of the question, to be sure, less by his false argument than by his healthy instinct, while his opponents remained tied to it and continued to search for an absolute justification of desire.

9 ETHICS AS FACTUAL SCIENCE

Such norms as are recognized as the ultimate norms, or highest values, must be derived from human nature and life as facts. Therefore, no result of ethics can stand in contradiction to life; ethics cannot declare as evil or false those values which lie at the foundation of life; its norms cannot demand or command anything that is in a real opposition to those final norms recognized by life. Where such opposition occurs it is a sure sign that the philosopher has misunderstood his problem, and has failed to solve it; that he has unwittingly become a moralist, that he feels uncomfortable in the role of a knower and would prefer to be a creator of moral values. The demands and claims of a morally creative person are merely subjects for investigation for the philosopher, mere objects for cognitive consideration; and this holds also if he should by chance, at other times, be this creative man himself.

We just said that there could be no real opposition between the meaning of the word 'good' that is actually accepted in life, and the meaning found by the philosopher. An *apparent* difference can of course occur, for language and thought are very imperfect in daily life. Often the speaker and valuer is himself not clear as to what he expresses, and often his valuations rest on a false interpretation of the facts, and would at once change with a correction of the mistake. The philosopher would have the task of discovering such errors and faulty expressions, and would have to recognize the true norms that lie at the root of moral judgements, and place them in opposition to the apparent ones which the agent, or valuer, believes himself to follow. And in so doing he would, perhaps, find it necessary to delve deep into the human soul. Always, however, it would be an actual, already fundamental norm that he would find there.

The ultimate valuations are facts existing in human consciousness, and even if ethics were a normative science it would not cease because of this to be a science of *facts.* Ethics has to do entirely with the *actual;* this seems to me to be the most important of the propositions which determine its task. Foreign to us is the pride of those philosophers who hold the questions of ethics to be the most noble and elevated of questions just because they do not refer to the common *is* but concern the pure *ought.*

Of course, after one is in the possession of such a system of norms, of a system of applications of the concepts good and evil, one can consider the connections of the members of the hierarchy, the order of the individual rules, quite independently of any relation to actuality; one can investigate merely the inner structure of the system. And this holds even if the norms are not the really valid ones, but are falsely considered such, or are freely imagined and arbitrarily established. The last case would indeed possess only the interest of a game and would make no claim to the name of 'ethics'. Ethics as a normative science would, however, furnish a hierarchical order of rules, in which all acts and attitudes and characters would possess a definite place with respect to their moral value. And of course this would be true not only of existing acts and attitudes, but also of all possible ones; for if the system is to be of any value it must beforehand supply a place for every possibility of human behaviour. After becoming acquainted with the highest norms, one can consider the whole system without any reference to actual behaviour, by merely considering the possible. Thus Kant emphasized that for his moral philosophy it was indifferent whether or not any moral will actually existed. Hence ethics conceived as a theory of norms would exhibit the characteristics of an 'ideal science'; it would have to do with a system of ideal rules, which could, of course, be applied to actuality, and would only thereby possess any interest, but the rules would have meaning quite independently of this application, and could be investigated in their relations to one another. Thus someone might have invented the rules of chess, and might have considered their application to the individual matches even if the game had never been played, except in his mind, between imaginary opponents.

10 ETHICS SEEKS CAUSAL EXPLANATION

To recapitulate: We began with the position that the task of ethics is to 'explain the moral good', and we asked, first, what sort of thing this 'good' is which we want to explain. We found that this subject-matter of ethics is not given to us as simply as, say, the subject-matter of optics, light, that is, by a mere sensation; but that for its determination the discovery of a 'moral principle' or a whole system of principles or rules is necessary. If we call a discipline that concerns itself with such a system a 'normative science', we see that this theory of norms affords nothing more than the discovery of the meaning of the concept 'good'. In this it exhausts itself. There is no question in it of a real explanation of the good. It offers ethics only the object which is to be explained. Therefore we have from the outset rejected the view of those philosophers who consider ethics to be merely a normative science. No, only where the theory of norms ends does ethical explanation begin. The former fails completely to see the important, exciting questions of ethics, or, worse, turns them aside as foreign in essence to ethics; in truth it fails, except through mistakes, to get beyond the mere linguistic result of determining the meanings of the words 'good' and 'evil'.

It does of course also give us a kind of pseudo-explanation, namely, that which we call justification. Explanation always consists of the reduction of what is to be explained to something else, to something more general; and actually the norms are thus referred back to one another, until the highest are reached. These, the moral principles (or *the* moral principle), according to definition, cannot be referred to other ethical *norms,* and cannot therefore be morally justified.

But this does not mean that all further reduction must be impossible. It might be that the *moral* good could be shown to be a special case of a more general kind of good. Actually the word 'good' is used in an extra-moral sense (one speaks not only of good men, but also of good riders, good mathematicians, of a good catch, a good machine, and so forth); it is therefore probable that the ethical and the extra-ethical meanings of the word are somehow connected. If the moral good can in this manner be subsumed under a wider concept of the good, then the question, 'Why is moral behaviour good?' could be answered by, 'Because it is good in a more general sense of the word'. The highest moral norm would be justified by means of an extra-moral norm; the moral principle would be referred back to a higher principle of life.

Possibly the reduction could go on a few more steps, but the final norm, the highest principle, can in no way be justified, for the very reason that it is the last. It would be senseless to ask for a further justification, a further explanation. It is not the norms, principles, or values themselves that stand in need of and are capable of explanation, but rather the actual facts from which they are abstracted. These facts are the acts of giving rules, of valuation, of approbation in human consciousness; they are thus real events in the life of the soul. 'Value', 'the good', are mere abstractions, but valuation, approbation, are actual psychic occurrences, and separate acts of this sort are quite capable of explanation, that is, can be reduced to one another.

And here lies the proper task of ethics. Here are the remarkable facts which excite philosophic wonder, and whose explanation has always been the final goal of ethical inquiry. That man actually approves of certain actions, declares certain dispositions to be 'good', appears not at all self-explanatory to the philosopher, but often very astonishing, and he therefore asks his 'Why?' Now, in all of the natural sciences every explanation can be conceived as a *causal* explanation, a truth which we need not prove here; therefore the 'why' has the sense of a question concerning the *cause* of that psychical process in which man makes a valuation, establishes a moral claim. (We must make clear that when we speak of the discovery of the 'cause', we mean by the term 'cause' only a popular abbreviation for the statement of the complete laws governing the event to be known.)

In other words, the *determination* of the contents of the concepts of good and evil is made by the use of moral principles and a system of norms, and affords a relative justification of the lower moral rules by the higher; scientific *knowledge* of the good, on the other hand, does not concern norms, but refers to the cause, concerns not the justification but the explanation of moral judgements. The theory of norms asks, '*What* does actually serve as the standard of conduct?' Explanatory ethics, however, asks '*Why* does it serve as the standard of conduct?'

11 FORMULATION OF THE FUNDAMENTAL QUESTION

It is clear that in essence the first question is a dry, formal matter that could win little interest from man did it not have such importance for practice, and if the path to its answer did not offer so many opportunities for profound insight into human nature. The second question, however, leads directly to these profundities. It concerns the real grounds, the actual causes and motives that drive one to distinguish between good and evil, and call forth the acts of moral judgement. Not only judgements, but also *conduct,* for this follows upon judgement. The explanation of moral judgement cannot be separated from the explanation of conduct. To be sure, one should not believe, without further reason, that everyone arranges his conduct according to his moral judgements. Obviously, that would be a false assumption. The connection, although indissoluble, is more complicated. What a man values, approves, and desires is finally inferred from his actions — better from these than from his assertions, though these, too, are kinds of action. What kind of demands one makes of himself and others can only be known from one's conduct. A man's valuations must somehow appear among the motives of his acts; they cannot, in any case, be discovered anywhere else. He who traces the causes of conduct far enough must come upon the causes of all approbation. The question of the causes of conduct is, therefore, more general than that of the grounds of moral judgements; its answer would give more comprehensive knowledge, and it would be methodologically profitable to start with it even if it were not necessary to begin with the study of conduct as the only thing observable.

Therefore, we may and should replace the question raised above, 'What motives cause us to establish moral norms?' by the othe question, 'What are the motives of conduct in general?' (We formulate the question in this general way and do not at once restrict it to *moral* actions because, according to what has been said, it might be possible to deduce valuations and their motives just as well, if not better, from immoral or neutral acts.) We are the more warranted in relating our question at once to *conduct*, since man interests himself in valuations only because conduct depends upon them. If moral approbation were something that remained enclosed in the depths of the heart, if it could never appear in any way and could not exert the least influence on the life, happiness and unhappiness of man, no one would bother himself with it, and the philosopher would become acquainted with this unimportant phenomenon only by an act of introspection. That wonder concerning the moral judgements of man, which we have described as the earliest impulse leading to the formulation of ethical questions, is above all wonder at his own actual moral behaviour.

Therefore, we inquire into the causes, that is, the regularity and order, of all human actions, with the aim of discovering the motives of moral actions. And we profit in so doing because we can postpone the question regarding the essence of morality, the moral principle, until we solve the problem of the natural law governing behaviour in general. When, however, we come to know about action in general, it will certainly be much easier to learn what is peculiar to moral actions and to define the content of the concept 'good' without difficulty. Perhaps it will turn out that we no longer feel the necessity of determining a sharp boundary for it (just as, after the physical explanation of light, the question of how and whether the concept of 'light' is to be distinguished from that of heat radiation or ultra-violet radiation loses all interest).

12 THE METHOD OF ETHICS IS PSYCHOLOGICAL

Thus the central problem of ethics concerns the causal explanation of moral behaviour; all others in relation to it sink to the level of preliminary or subordinate questions. The moral problem was most clearly formulated in this way by Schopenhauer, whose sound sense of reality led him to the correct path here (if not in the solution) and guarded him from the Kantian formulation of the problem and from the post-Kantian philosophy of value.

The problem which we must put at the centre of ethics is a purely psychological one. For, without doubt, the discovery of the motives or laws of any kind of behaviour, and therefore of moral behaviour, is a purely psychological affair. Only the empirical science of the laws which describe the life of the soul can solve this problem. One might wish to derive from this a supposedly profound and destructive objection to our formulation of the problem. For, one might say, 'In such case there would be no ethics at all; what is called ethics would be nothing but a part of psychology!' I answer, 'Why shouldn't ethics be a part of psychology?' Perhaps in order that the philosopher have his science for himself and govern autonomously in this sphere? He would, indeed, thereby be freed of many burdensome protests of psychology. If he laid down a command, '*Thus* shall man act', he would not have to pay attention to the psychologist who said to him, 'But man *cannot* act so, because it contradicts psychological laws!' I fear greatly that here and there this motive, though hidden, is at work. However, if one says candidly that 'there is no ethics', because it is not necessary to label a part of psychology by a special name, then the question is merely terminological.

It is a poor recommendation of the philosophical spirit of our age that we so often attempt to draw strict lines of division between the sciences, to separate ever new disciplines, and to prove their autonomy. The true philosopher goes in the opposite direction; he does not wish to make the single sciences self-sufficient and independent, but, on the contrary, to unify and bring them together; he wishes to show that what is common to them is what is most essential, and that what is different is accidental and to be viewed as belonging to practical methodology. *Sub specie aeternitatis* there is for him only *one* reality and *one* science.

Therefore, if we decide that the fundamental question of ethics, 'Why does man act morally?' can be answered only by psychology, we see in this no degradation of, nor injury to, science, but a happy simplification of the world-picture. In ethics we do not seek independence, but only the truth.

3 The Nature of Ethics

Hans Reichenbach

... One conclusion can be immediately drawn from the analysis of modern science. If ethics were a form of knowledge it would not be what moral philosophers want it to be; that is, it would not supply moral directives. Knowledge divides into synthetic and analytic statements; the synthetic statements inform us about matters of facts, the analytic statements are empty. What kind of knowledge should ethics be? If it were synthetic, it would inform us about matters of fact. Of this kind is a descriptive ethics which informs us about the ethical habits of various peoples and social classes; such an ethics is a part of sociology, but it is not of a normative nature. If ethics were analytic knowledge, however, it would be empty and could not tell us what to do, either. For instance, if we define a virtuous man as a man who always chooses the maxim of his actions in such a way that it could be made the principle of a general legislation, we would know what we mean by the term 'virtuous man', but we could not prove that we should aspire to be virtuous men. The phrase a 'virtuous man', when so defined, is merely an abbreviation for the long-winded Kantian formulation about the maxim of actions, and could be replaced by any other name, for instance, by the term 'Kantian'; but why should we try to be Kantians? If ethical statements are analytic, they are not moral directives.

Source: Hans Reichenbach, *The Rise of Scientific Philosophy,* University of California Press, 1951, chapter 17 (minus first paragraph). Copyright 1951 by The Regents of the University of California; reprinted by permission of the University of California Press.

The modern analysis of knowledge makes a cognitive ethics impossible: knowledge does not include any normative parts and therefore does not lend itself to an interpretation of ethics. The ethico-cognitive parallelism renders ethics a bad service: if it could be carried through, if virtue were knowledge, ethical rules would be deprived of their imperative character. The two-thousand-year-old plan to establish ethics on a cognitive basis results from a misunderstanding of knowledge, from the eroneous conception that knowledge contains a normative part. It is chiefly the misinterpretation of mathematics that is responsible for this error. We saw that from the time of Plato to that of Kant mathematics was conceived as a system of laws of reason that control the physical world; from such a synthetic a priori there was only a short step to the conception that reason can dictate to us moral directives which have an objective validity, such as was assumed for the laws of mathematics. If it turns out that mathematics is not of this kind, that it does not supply laws of the physical world but merely formulates empty relations that hold for all possible worlds, there is no longer any space left for a cognitive ethics. Knowledge cannot provide the form of ethics because it cannot provide directives.

I explained above (chap. 4*) that the source of the cognitive interpretation of ethics is presumably to be found in the use of logic and knowledge for the derivation of ethical implications. If you want this aim you must also want this and that — implications of this kind are accessible to cognitive proof. By cognitive proof I mean a proof employing the laws of logic in combination with the laws of physics, or sociology, or other sciences. Thus if you wish to reap you have to sow; this implication is proved with the help of the laws of botany. A great many ethical controversies are concerned with such implications; that may be the reason for the erroneous conception that all ethical considerations are of the cognitive type. It seems as though during an ethical discussion we sharpen and deepen our ethical insight, in the same way that, in the opinion of Plato and Kant, we sharpen and deepen our insight into the nature of space through geometrical analysis. But the development of geometry has shown us that the latter conception is mistaken, that there is no insight into the nature of space, that different forms of space are possible and that a geometrical demonstration merely derives *if-then* statements, or relations between axioms and theorems. There is no geometrical necessity, only a logical

---

*Not reprinted here. —*Ed.*

necessity concerning the consequences that follow from a given set of axioms; the mathematician cannot prove the axioms to be true.

Had Spinoza foreseen this result of the modern philosophy of mathematics, he would not have attempted to construct his ethics after the pattern of geometry. He would have been horrified at the idea that non-Spinozistic ethics could be constructed which would possess the same kind of cogency that his own system possessed, and that if his axioms were of the nature of geometrical axioms, they could not be given a demonstrative proof. It would not have helped him to turn them into results of experience, like the axioms of geometry, for empirical truth is not what he wanted. He wanted to establish ethical axioms that are unquestionable. He wanted axioms that are *necessary*.

But if the word 'necessary' is to mean anything comparable to logical necessity, then there can be no moral necessity. When we feel that during an ethical discussion our insight is sharpened and deepened, such achievement must not be regarded as proving the existence of an ethical insight. What we see better after an analysis of ethical problems is the relation between ends and means; we discover that if we want to satisfy certain fundamental aims we must be willing to pursue certain other aims, which are subordinate to the first in the sense of the means to an end. Such a clarification is of a logical nature; it shows that, in view of physical and psychological laws, the end logically requires the means. This argument is not merely parallel to logical proof — it *is* logical proof. Philosophers who speak of ethical insight confuse the logical evidence of the implication between ends and means with a supposed self-evidence of the axioms.

And yet, when decisions are to be made, implications between ends and means are not sufficient to determine our choice. We must first decide for the end. For instance, we may be able to prove the implication: if stealing were permitted, there would be no prosperous human society. In order to derive the conclusion that stealing should be forbidden, we must first decide that we want a prosperous human society. For this reason, ethics needs moral premises, or moral axioms, which state primary goals, whereas means represent secondary goals. When we call them axioms, we think of ethics as an ordered system which is derivable from these axioms, whereas the axioms themselves are not derivable in the system. When we restrict the consideration to a specific argument, we use the more modest term 'premise'. There must be at least one moral premise for an ethical argument, that is, one ethical rule which is not derived by this argument. This premise may be the conclusion of another argument; but going farther up this way, we remain at every step with a certain set of moral premises. If we succeed in ordering the totality of ethical rules in one consistent system, we thus arrive at the axioms of our ethics. This analysis can be summed up in the thesis: logical necessity controls merely the implications between moral axioms and secondary moral rules; but it cannot validate the moral axioms.

But if the axioms of ethics are not necessary or self-evident truths — what then are they?

The ethical axioms are not necessary truths because they are not truths of any kind. Truth is a predicate of statements; but the linguistic expressions of ethics are not statements. They are directives. A directive cannot be classified as true or false; these predicates do not apply because directive sentences are of a logical nature different from that of indicative sentences, or statements.

An important kind of directive is given by imperatives, which we use for the direction of persons other than ourselves. Consider the command 'shut the door'. Is this imperative true or false? We need only pronounce the question in order to see that it is nonsensical. The utterance 'shut the door' does not inform us about matters of fact; nor does it represent a tautology, that is, a statement of logic. We could not say what would be the case if the utterance 'shut the door' were true. An imperative is a linguistic utterance to which the classification true-false does not apply.

What then is an imperative? An imperative is a linguistic utterance which we use with the intention of influencing another person, of making the other person do something we want to be done, or not to do something we want not to be done. It is a matter of fact that this aim can be reached by the use of words, though that is not the only way to reach it. Instead of saying 'shut the door' we could seize the man's hands and guide them in such a way that the door would be shut. However, that would not only be impolite but it would also be inconvenient for us, since it would be easier to do the thing ourselves. We therefore prefer to make use of the fact that our fellow men are conditioned to respond to words as instruments of our will. The imperative mood of the command makes it clear that even grammatically speaking the command is not a statement. Not all commands, however, are articulated in the imperative mood. The statement in the indicative mood 'I should be glad if the door were shut' may be uttered by me in the sense of a command and, in fact, may represent a better instrument of achieving my aim than would the sentence in the imperative mood; politeness is not only a policy of diplomats but is also recommended for the little diplomacies of everyday life. Our utterance is a command disguised as a statement.

But is not the utterance 'I should be glad if the door were shut' a statement concerning my wishes? It is; only in this case it is employed as a command. However, it is true that whenever an imperative is uttered there exists a *correlated statement* which informs us about the will of a person. Thus to the imperative 'shut the door' corresponds the indicative statement: 'Mr. X wishes the door to be shut'. This statement is true or false and can be verified like other psychological statements. Sometimes the correlated statement is used in place of the command. For the purpose of logical analysis it is convenient always to express imperatives in the imperative mood and thus to distinguish them grammatically from statements.

Although imperatives are neither true nor false, they are understood by other persons and therefore have a meaning, which may be called an *instrumental meaning.* It is to be distinguished from the *cognitive meaning* of statements, defined in the verifiability theory of meaning (chap. 16*). Moreover, every imperative possesses a *cognitive correlate,* given by the correlated statement.

Like imperatives, directives concerning our own actions are expressions of volition, which as such are not true or false and therefore belong among volitional utterances. Acts of volition may concern various objects; we want food, shelter, friends, pleasure, and so forth. That we find in ourselves acts of volition, is a matter of fact; they are distinguished from perceptions or logical laws in that they appear as products of our own in a situation leaving us choice. I may go to the theatre or I may not; it is my will to go. I may help another man or I may not; it is my will to help him. Whether it is true that we have a freedom of choice is a different question; for the definition of an act of volition it is sufficient that we at least believe that we have the possibility of choice. For this definition it is therefore irrelevant where volitions come from, and we do not ask, at the moment, whether we are conditioned to our volitions by the milieu in which we grow up, or whether our volitions flow from certain fundamental urges, like the sexual urge or the urge for self-preservation. Let us simply acknowledge the psychological fact that we make volitional decisions which direct our behaviour.

---

*Not reprinted here.—*Ed.*

Only if the volitional decision concerns actions to be done by other persons does it assume the form of an imperative. Sometimes the imperative is uttered with the threat of enforcement through power; for instance, the power of the governmental authorities, or of the authority of the officer; it then is called a command. Other imperatives are wishes, which are also expressed in the imperative mood. Thus we say, 'Please give me a cigarette'.

If a command is directed or a wish addressed to us, in other words, if we are on the receiving side of the imperative, we may respond positively or negatively. A positive response consists in an act of volition on our side directed toward carrying out the imperative and may even include a readiness to give corresponding imperatives to other persons. A negative response consists in an act of volition directed against carrying out the imperative. This alternative is expressed through the words 'right' and 'wrong'. Thus if I am told 'you should go and see Paul', I may answer 'that is right', and then start with preparations for a visit to Paul. The positive response to an act of volition expressed through an imperative thus consists in a secondary act of volition of a similar kind generated in the receiver. If the response is negative, the secondary act of volition is opposed to the first. Linguistic usage does not always draw this clear distinction between the alternatives yes-no and right-wrong, but employs them interchangeably. It may appear justifiable, however, to regard the distinction explained as a proper interpretation of the terms.

Whereas we have for directives referring to other persons the grammatical form of the imperative, we have no such linguistic form for the directive addressed to ourselves. For this reason we express such directives in the form of an indicative sentence reporting about the setting up of the directive, as in the sentence 'I will go to the theatre.' Sometimes we address ourselves as though we were talking to a different person, applying the imperative mood; thus we say to ourselves, 'Old fellow, do write that letter'. By means of this rather schizoid method it is possible to transfer to ourselves the notation applying to the receiving side of an imperative, and to speak of secondary acts of volition raised in ourselves through an imperative which we give to ourselves.

These considerations will clarify the difference between cognitive sentences and directives. If I am given a cognitive sentence, or statement, and I agree with it, I say 'yes', meaning that I regard the statement as true. For instance, if you tell me that it is a long way to Tipperary, I say 'yes', meaning I, too, regard it as true that it is a long way to

Tipperary. If you tell me, however, that stinginess is bad, I express my agreement by saying 'that is right'. What you mean is a directive and thus an expression of your will, namely, you say: I wish that there were no stinginess. My answer is a corresponding directive; it means I, too, wish that there were no stinginess. The positive answer to a directive is not an affirmation of the cognitive kind; it consists in a secondary act of volition, expressed in an utterance indicating that the listener shares the will of the speaker.

The considerations so far given refer to directives of all kinds. Let us now study those directives which are called *moral directives,* or moral imperatives.

It is a characteristic mark of a moral directive that we regard it as an imperative and feel ourselves to be on the receiving side of it. We thus regard our act of volition as a secondary one, as a response to an imperative given by some higher authority. What the higher authority is, is not always clearly known. Some persons claim it is God, others contend it is their conscience, or their daemon, or the moral law within them. These are, obviously, interpretations in picture language. Psychologically speaking, the moral imperative is characterized as an act of volition accompanied by the feeling of an obligation, which we regard as applying to ourselves as well as to other persons. Thus we regard it as our obligation, and as the obligation of everybody, to support the needy where that is possible. Volitional aims other than moral are not accompanied by the feeling of obligation. If a man wants to become an engineer, he will usually not feel obliged to decide for this aim, nor does he wish that all others have the same aim as he. It is the feeling of general obligation which distinguishes moral imperatives from others.

How can we explain the fact that moral volitions appear to us as secondary volitions, as the expression of an obligation? I think the explanation is that these volitions are imposed upon us by the social group to which we belong, in other words, that they are originally group volitions. This origin accounts for their superpersonal dignity and for the feeling of subordination with which we make the moral decision. Psychologically, this origin is understandable. The rules not to steal, not to kill, and so forth, were rules the enforcement of which was necessary for group preservation. As generations passed, individuals were conditioned to these rules; and in our own education we were subject to a conditioning process of the same kind. No wonder, then, that we feel ourselves on the receiving side of the moral imperatives; in fact, we are. If a feeling of duty is regarded as characteristic for moral aims, such a conception mirrors the fact that moral aims were instilled into us forcibly, whether through the authority of the father or of the teacher or by the pressure of the group in which we lived.

If ethics is social in its origin, how is it possible that there are anti-social ethics?

An ethics which we regard as antisocial can still be a group ethics. Thus criminals have an ethics of their own class; within their class they do not steal or kill, but they oppose their class to the larger class of what we call a civilized society and disregard all moral obligations with respect to this wider class. Students of a high-school class may regard their class as a group opposed to the teacher and find it their moral right to deceive and harass him. Conversely, there are teachers who are highly esteemed by the students and are seldom deceived; such a teacher has succeeded in making the students incorporate him into their group. The working class has an ethics of its own; so has the class of big capitalists, or the aristocracy of countries that have not yet eliminated the remnants of feudalism. Even the Nazi ethics was a group ethics, tailored to the needs of the so-called master race. The completely individualistic ethics of Nietzsche's superman or of Machiavelli's prince is an extreme case in which all moral rights are reserved for one man. Such ethical systems have never been carried through except on paper. they represent a strange mixture in which the authority psychologically derived from group will is transferred to one man, who is regarded as the only individual whose will is to be respected.

The ethics of our social and political life is a conglomeration of group ethics of various strata. Nations have grown through fusion of states and merging of social groups; they have taken over the ethical rules of older times, especially through the codified law, which per-petuates the moral systems of the Romans, of feudalism, and of the Church. No wonder that the result is no consistent system. The obedient citizen who attempts to satisfy all moral rules of a nationwide society soon finds himself confronted by ethical conflicts. Should he support the needy or attempt to get hold of their pennies by the methods of good business? Should he work for the welfare of the nation by con-tributing to the suppression of strikes, or by supporting labour in its fight for better economic conditions? Should he stand for freedom of speech or support the government of a state that does not tolerate the teaching of Darwin's theory of evolution in its universities? Should he honour the teachings of the Bible or demand that the offspring of the people that wrote the Bible be excluded from public offices? Should he advocate equal rights for all races or uphold regulations which provide for segregation of streetcar passengers who have abundant pigmentation in their skin? It is not an easy matter to work one's way through the muddle of moral rules of present-day society.

Where, then, is the ethics that answer all our questions? Can philosophy provide such a system?

It cannot. That is the answer we should frankly give. The attempts of philosophers to fashion ethics as a system of knowledge have broken down. The moral systems thus constructed were nothing but reproductions of the ethics of certain sociological groups; of Greek bourgeois society, of the Catholic Church, of the Middle Class of the preindustrial age, of the age of industry and the proletarian. We know why these systems had to fail: because knowledge cannot supply directives. Who looks for ethical rules must not imitate the method of science. Science tells us what is, but not what should be.

Does that mean resignation? Does it mean that there are no moral directives, that everybody may do what he wants?

I do not think so. I think it is a misunderstanding of the nature of moral directives to conclude that if ethics is not objectively demonstrable everybody may do what he wants.

To inquire into this problem let us go into a detailed study of the volitional nature of moral directives by a grammatical analysis of the phrase 'he should', which can be regarded as the grammatical form of a moral directive. (For our purposes, the phrase may be regarded as synonymous with 'he shall' and with 'he ought to'.) We saw that the phrase cannot mean there is an objective moral law from which the imperative is derivable. What, then, does it mean? There remain two different possible meanings of the phrase.

The first is an *implicational meaning:* we know that the person referred to has adopted a certain aim, and we wish to say that this aim implies the action under consideration. For instance, we say 'Peter should not smoke', meaning that from the aim of being healthy it is derivable, because of Peter's physiological constitution and by the use of the laws of physiology, that he should not smoke. In other words, the decision not to smoke is entailed by the decision to live in good health; it therefore is called an *entailed decision.* The obligation of the entailed decision is of the implicational type and represents not a moral, but a logical obligation.

The second is the meaning of a *subjective imperative* on the part of the speaker: I, the speaker, wish that he do this or that. According to this interpretation, moral directives include an indispensable reference to the speaker; they are expressions of a volitional decision by the speaker. If this conception is assumed, it is impossible to eliminate the speaker from the meaning of a moral directive; the phrase 'he should' includes, in a hidden form, the phrase 'I will', and we thus arrive at a *volitional ethics*.

The logical nature of this conception can be analysed as follows. The use of such expressions as 'he should not lie', or 'lying is morally bad', represents a pseudo-objective mode of speech; what is expressed is actually an attitude of the speaker. The phrase 'he should' is comparable to terms such as 'I' and 'now', which refer to the speaker, or the act of speech, and convey different meanings in the mouths of different persons. Such terms are called *token-reflexive*. The word 'token' denotes an individual instance of a sign; if two persons utter the same word, each of them utters a different token, or instance of the word. Usually, the different tokens have the same meaning. However, if the terms are token-reflexive, each of the tokens has a different meaning. If each of two persons says 'President Franklin D. Roosevelt', the two tokens denote the same person. But if each of them says 'I', the two tokens denote different persons. The word 'reflexive' indicates this reference of the meaning to the token.[1]

Both the implicational and the token-reflexive meaning are employed. But the implicational meaning of the phrase 'he should' cannot be used for moral premises, or moral axioms, since these premises do not express implications, but are directives. They thus contain the phrase 'he should', in a token-reflexive meaning. This meaning of the phrase is transferred from the premises through the derivation to every ethical rule. To understand this transfer, we may think of derivations in the cognitive field, which transfer the truth of the premises to the conclusion. If the premises were not asserted, neither could the conclusion be asserted. Likewise, if the ethical premises were not advanced as directives, that is, in the meaning of a nonimplicational and thus token-reflexive 'he should', neither could the ethical conclusion have the character of a directive.

It may happen that the two meanings of the phrase 'he should' are combined; then an implicational 'should' is asserted which refers to a premise advanced with the token-reflexive 'should'. This double mean-

---

[1] For a further discussion of token-reflexive terms see the author's *Elements of symbolic logic* (New York, 1947), p. 284. Since imperatives are token-reflexive, they are not equivalent to their cognitive correlates; two identical imperatives, uttered by different persons, have different cognitive correlates.

ing must be clearly recognized. The implicational 'should' then assumes a moral connotation; but it does so only because the directive assumed as the premise of the person referred to is a moral imperative supported by the speaker. Thus we say 'the President should open this country to displaced persons', meaning that from the aim of helping the displaced persons, which we know the President adheres to and which we support, it is derivable that immigation to this country is the only available means of reaching this aim. A moral connotation of 'should' in the implicational meaning is therefore reducible to the use of 'should' in the volitional meaning. If the directive is not shared by the speaker, the 'he should' loses its moral character. Thus we say 'instead of conquering Paris, Hitler should have invaded England'. We mean that it would have been in the interest of Hitler to invade England, and thus mean an implicational obligation; but since we do not share Hitler's aims, the word 'should' is not used as a moral imperative. This illustration makes it clear that the reference to the speaker is inseparable from the moral meaning of the phrase 'he should'. The recognition that the phrase 'he should' in its moral meaning is a token-reflexive term is the indispensable bases of a scientific analysis of ethics.

With the intention of escaping the subjective reference of ethical terms, a third interpretation of the phrase 'he should' is sometimes attempted. According to this interpretation, the phrase means as much as 'the group wishes that he do this or that'. This meaning seems to eliminate the subjectivity from moral obligations. However, this interpretation is not tenable. When group will is concerned, we use the phrase 'he should' only if its meaning is reducible to one of the first two interpretations. First, we use it when the action follows from the will of the person concerned, in whose interest it is to honour the group will; then the phrase has the implicational meaning of the first interpretation. Second, we use the phrase when we share the group will; and only in this case is the phrase meant to express a moral obligation. For instance, if a criminal betrays his accomplices, we know that his group condemns such a behaviour; a member of the group, therefore, would say 'he should not have talked'. When *we* utter this sentence, we might use the implicational 'should' and express the opinion that being silent would have been in the interest of the criminal, who perhaps is exposed to acts of vengeance by the group. However, if we utter the sentence in the sense of a moral judgement, we wish to say that we regard it as a moral obligation of the man to protect his group; then the phrase is token-reflexive and includes an expression of the will of the speaker.

We arrive at the result that moral directives are of a volitional nature, that they express volitional decisions on the part of the speaker. This result may at first sight appear disappointing; it looks as though we have no longer any solid ground on which to establish our volitions. Is it necessary, however, that we be on the receiving side of an imperative in order to feel entitled to follow it, and in order to demand that others follow the same imperative? It was the feeling of obligation resulting on the receiving side of a group will that was misconstrued by philosophers as an analogue of cognitive necessity, as the compulsion of a law of reason or of an insight into a world of ideas. As we have discovered that the analogy breaks down, that the feeling of obligation cannot be transformed into a source of the validity of ethics, let us forget about the appeal to obligation. Let us throw away the crutches we needed for walking, let us stand on our own feet and trust our volitions, not because they are secondary ones, but because they are our own volitions. Only a distorted morality can argue that our will is bad if it is not the response to a command from another source.

You answer: 'If moral directives are volitional decisions, it appears justified that everyone set up his own moral directives. But how can someone demand that others follow his directives? You appeal to us to trust our own volitions and not to feel ourselves on the receiving side of an imperative; at the same time, you demand the right for everyone to set up imperatives for others. Is not that a contradiction? The volitional interpretation of imperatives seems to lead to the conclusion that everybody may do what he wants, that is, to anarchism'.

Let us first study the inference expressed in your last statement. Assume that I set up the imperative that a certain person behave in a certain way. You answer: 'No, he may do what he wants'. Obviously, the phrase 'may do' in your answer is the opposition to my imperative; you wish to say that although I am entitled to set up my own imperatives, I am not entitled to set up universal obligations, that is, imperatives for others. The clause 'Mr. X is not entitled' is not a cognitive sentence; it is an imperative, meaning 'Mr. X should not do this or that'. So you have answered me by an imperative; you command that I should not set up imperatives for others. What is the title on which you base your imperative? You set your will against my will; and I do not see why I should recognize your will and renounce setting up directives for others.

The problem represented by your inference is important enough to be given a closer examination. Let us first consider the clause 'everybody has a right'. It can mean, first, that the legal authorities do not restrict the activities of any person. That is a cognitive statement, but it is not what you mean by your conclusion. To make my point clear, let us insert the assumed meaning of the clause into the total statement. The statement 'if a moral directive is a matter of a volitional decision, the legal authorities will not restrict the activities of any person' is of questionable truth and is not what you wish to say. Second, the clause 'everybody has a right' can mean that no one's activities should be restricted. The word 'should' indicates an imperative; according to the previous analysis, it can have two meanings. The first is that of an imperative given by the speaker, which is you; your sentence then means: 'If a moral directive is a matter of a volitional decision, I insist that there be no restrictions upon the activities of any person'. If that is what you want to say, you do not establish a logical relation, but merely pronounce a volition of your own and thus do not arrive at an inference. The second meaning of 'should' is that of a logical implication leading to a derivable imperative for the person referred to. So what you mean is: 'If a man adheres to the principle that a moral directive is a matter of a volitional decision, it follows that he adheres to the imperative that there be no restrictions upon the activities of any person'. But is that a valid inference? I do not see how such a conclusion can be derived logically, because it is perfectly consistent for a man to want certain aims and also want other persons to be restricted in those activities which would oppose these aims.

Let me state the last argument somewhat differently. You wish to show that I am logically committed to the entailed decision: 'No person should be restricted in his activities'. If this is to be a derivable imperative, it must be derived from other imperatives. But thus far I have not uttered any imperatives. I merely made the cognitive statement that moral directives are matters of volitional decision. From this cognitive statement you can not derive any imperative. You can derive imperatives from other imperatives, or from imperatives in combination with cognitive sentences, but never from cognitive sentences alone. So your inference is invalid.

You see that the volitional interpretation of moral directives does not lead to the consequence that the speaker should allow everybody the right to follow his own decision; that is, it does not lead to anarchism. If I set up certain volitional aims and demand that they be followed by all persons, you can counter my argument only by setting up another imperative, for instance, the anarchist imperative 'everybody has the right to do what he wants'. You cannot prove, however, that my system of a volitional ethics is inconsistent, that logic compels me to allow everybody the right to do what he wants. Logic does not compel me to do anything. The directives I set up are not consequences of my conception of ethics, either; nor does logic tell me what imperatives I should regard as obligatory for all persons. I set up my imperatives as my volitions, and the distinction between personal and moral directives is also a matter of my volition. Directives of the latter kind, you remember, are those which I regard as necessary for the group and which I demand everybody to comply with.

Now you are in complete despair. You retort: 'Maybe what you say is true, logically speaking; but do you really think — you, the author of a book on scientific philosophy — that you are the man to give you moral directives, which by their nature cannot be true. I have my moral directives, that is true. But I shall not write them down here. I do not wish to discuss moral issues, but to discuss the nature of morality. I even have some fundamental moral directives, which, I think, are not so very different from yours. We are products of the same society, you and I. So we were imbued with the essence of democracy from the day of our birth. We may differ in many respects, perhaps about the question of whether the state should own the means of production, or whether the divorce laws should be made easier, or whether a world government should be set up that controls the atom bomb. But we can discuss such problems if we both agree about a democratic principle which I oppose to your anarchist principle:

Everybody is entitled to set up his own moral imperatives and to demand that everyone follow these imperatives.

This democratic principle supplies the precise formulation of my appeal to everybody to trust his own volitions, which you regarded as contradictory to my claim that everybody may set up imperatives for other persons. Let me show now that the principle is not self-contradictory. Assume, for instance, I set up the imperative that if there is more than one room to each person in a house, the surplus rooms should be opened to persons who have no rooms of their own. You set up the imperative that no one should be compelled to open his house to other persons. You have a surplus room in your house and I demand that it be opened to a victim of the housing shortage; if I have the power to enforce my demand through the authority of the government, say by making my regulation a law through a referendum, I shall even do that. However, I leave you the right to demand that such law be repealed. It is therefore the difference between the right to act and the right to demand a certain action which saves my principle from being a contradiction. I demand that you act in a certain way, but I do not demand that you renounce you demand to the contrary. That is good democracy; and in fact, it corresponds to the actual procedure in which differences of volition are fought out in a democracy.

I do not derive my principle from pure reason. I do not present it as the result of a philosophy. I merely formulate a principle which is at the basis of all political life in democratic countries, knowing that in adhering to it I reveal myself as a product of my time. But I have found that this principle offers me the opportunity to propagate and, in large measure, to follow my volitions; therefore I make it my moral imperative. I do not claim that it applies to all forms of society; if I, the product of a democratic society, were placed in a different society I might be willing to modify my principle. But let us examine this principle which for our society appears to be the most suitable one.

The principle is not an ethical doctrine, answering all questions of what we should do. It is merely an invitation to take active part in the struggle of opinions. Volitional differences cannot be settled by the appeal to a system of ethics constructed by some learned man; they can be overcome only through the clash of opinions, through the friction between the individual and his environment, through controversy and the compulsion of the situation. Moral valuations are formed in the pursuit of activities; we act, we reflect about what we have done, we talk to others about it, and act again, this time in what we regard as a better way. Our actions are trials to find out what we want; we learn through error, and often we know only after our action is done whether we wanted to do it. Volitional aims usually do not come to us with the clarity of a vision, but more often constitute the subconscious or semi-conscious background of our attitudes; and those which do appear clear and bright, like stars showing our paths, often lose all their attractiveness as soon as they are reached.

Whoever wants to study ethics, therefore, should not go to the philosopher; he should go where moral issues are fought out. He should live in the community of a group where life is made vivid by competing volitions, be it the group of a political party, or of a trade union, or of a professional organization, or of a ski club, or a group formed by common study in a classroom. There he will experience what it means to set his volition against that of other persons and what it means to adjust oneself to group will. If ethics is the pursuit of volitions, it is also the conditioning of volitions through a group environment. The exponent of individualism is shortsighted when he overlooks the volitional satisfaction which accrues from belonging to a group. Whether we regard the conditioning of volitions through the group as a useful or a dangerous process depends on whether we support or oppose the group; but we must admit that there exists such group influence.

How, then, is it possible that volitions are modified and harmonized in a group? What is the process that conditions volitions?

There can be no doubt that this process, to a great extent, is the learning of cognitive relations. I said above that implications between imperatives are accessible to logical proof. The part played by such implications is much greater than is usually assumed. We are often mistaken about the relations between our aims. If some fundamental aims are the same, quite a few moral issues are transformed into logical issues. For instance, the question whether private property is sacred is no longer a moral question, once we recognize the aim that a minimum of adequate living conditions should be guaranteed to all citizens. It then is a matter of sociological analysis whether this aim is better reached through private enterprise or through state ownership of the means of production. The difficulties in this case result from the imperfect state of the science of sociology, which cannot give us unambiguous answers, comparable to the answers given by physics. Among the adherents of a democracy, most political issues are reducible to cognitive controversies. It is our hope, therefore, that such issues will be settled through public discussion and peaceful experiments rather than by resort to war.

Most volitional decisions we are confronted with are entailed decisions entailed by more fundamental aims which we set for ourselves. It is for this reason that cognitive clarification is of so great an import for moral questions. Apart from political questions, we may mention questions of education, health, sex life, the civil law, the criminal code, and the punishment of criminals. Thus the question whether a sentenced criminal should be put into a penitentiary is not a moral, but a psychological question for all those who are agreed that the jurisdiction of the state should attempt to produce as many socially adjusted citizens as possible. That person released from penitentiaries are usually conditioned to the contrary of this aim is borne out by too many experiences.

It is a psychological fact, however, that even when a cognitive clarification is reached it is difficult to change volitional attitudes. We may know that since we want a certain fundamental aim we must also accept a certain other decision, and yet we hesitate to do so. Thus we may be convinced that a criminal should not be punished, but should be put into an environment that offers him possibilities of a readjustment. Nevertheless, it may be difficult for us to overcome the call for punishment, the desire for revenge, that has dictated so many of our regulations for criminals. Again, the ethics of sex relations is filled with so many taboos that it is extremely difficult to overcome habitual prejudices even when psychological considerations have made it clear that we must change some of our traditional valuations if we want happier and healthier men and women. In all such cases, the cognitive result has to be supported by a readjustment of our volitional attitudes. It is in this respect that education through the group plays an indispensable part. Only through living in an environment in which the new valuations are carried through do we learn that we can accept them; do we acquire the force to will what logical derivation has shown to be a consequence of our fundamental aims. The psychology of volitional attitudes is not settled by logical argument; it is logic in combination with group influence that helps us to organize our volitional setup.

Are all moral questions answerable through a reduction to common fundamental aims? The fact that we are all human speaks for such an assumption, since it appears plausible that the physiological similarities between men include a similarity of volitional aims. Other facts speak against the assumption, since certain groups, such as the nobility in feudal states, or the capitalists in the capitalist state, or the members of the party in control of a oneparty totalitarian state, enjoy a definite advantage from maintaining the privileges of their class.

I think the answer to the question is not so very important. We saw that knowledge of an implication between aims does not *eo ipso* change volitional attitudes; that is to say, if such knowledge is to lead to a revision of decisions, it must be accompanied by a conditioning of volitions. If such conditioning is necessary and possible, it does not matter so much whether it concerns fundamental or entailed decisions. Even fundamental volitions are accessible to group influence, and will change under the suggestive power of an environment that exemplifies other volitions and their consequences.

Such adjustment to the necessities of the group is often made difficult by adherence to an absolute ethics. If a person has been indoctrinated in the theory that moral rules constitute absolute truth, he will be greatly inhibited from abandoning such rules and may remain unamenable to the conditioning by the group. Conversely, if a person knows that moral rules are of a volitional nature, he will be ready to change his goals to some extent if he sees that otherwise he cannot get along with other persons. Adaptation of goals to those of orher persons is the essence of social education. Naive egoism encounters resistance if it is set against the egoism of others, and the egoist will soon discover that he fares better when he cooperates with the group. The give and take of social cooperation offers much deeper satisfaction than does obstinate refusal to abandon one's goals. Thus the person educated in an empiricist approach to ethics is better prepared than the absolutist to become an adjusted member of society.

This is not meant to imply that the empiricist is a man of easy compromise. Much as he is willing to learn from the group, he is also prepared to steer the group in the direction of his own volitions. He knows that social progress is often due to the persistence of individuals who were stronger than the group; and he will try, and try again, to modify the group as much as he can. The interplay of group and individual has effects both on the individual and on the group.

Thus the ethical orientation of human society is a product of mutual adjustment. The recognition of relations between various goals plays only a limited part in this process. The greater part is played by psychological influences of a noncognitive kind, emanating from individuals to other individuals, from individuals to the group, and from the group to individuals. The friction between volitions is the propelling force of all ethical development. It may therefore be admitted that power plays a leading part in the change of moral valuations — if power is measured by any form of success in asserting one's volitions against those of other persons. The widest meaning of the word is not restricted to the power of arms. Other forms of power can be equally or even more efficient: the power of social organization, the power of a social class that has discovered its common interests, the power of cooperative groups, the power of speech and writing, the power of the individual that shapes the pattern of a group through exhibiting outstanding behaviour. Yes, it is power that controls social relationships.

We should not commit the fallacy of believing that the struggle for power is controlled by a superhuman authority that leads it to an ultimately good end; nor should we commit the complementary fallacy of believing that the good is to be defined as that which is the most powerful. We have seen too many victories of what we regard as immorality, too much success of mediocrity and class egoism. We try to pursue our own volitional ends, not with the fanaticism of the prophet of an absolute truth, but with the firmness of the man who trusts in his own will. We do not know whether we shall reach our aim. Like the problem of a prediction of the future, the problem of moral action cannot be solved by the construction of rules that guarantee success. There are no such rules.

And there are no rules by means of which we could discover a purpose, or a meaning, of the universe. There is some hope that the history of mankind will be progressive and lead to a better-adjusted human society, although there are strong tendencies to the contrary. To believe that the physical universe is progressive in the human sense, is absurd. The universe follows the laws of physics, not moral commands. We have been able to a certain extent to comply the laws of physics to our own advantage. That some day we shall control larger parts of the universe is not impossible, though none too probable. It is more likely that finally the human race will die with the planet on which its life began.

Whenever there comes a philosopher who tells you that he has found the ultimate truth, do not trust him. If he tells you that he knows the ultimate good, or has a proof that the good must become reality, do not trust him, either. The man merely repeats the errors which his predecessors have committed for two thousand years. It is time to put an end to this brand of philosophy. Ask the philosopher to be as modest as the scientist; then he may become as successful as the man of science. But do not ask him what you should do. Open your ears to your own will, and try to unite your will with that of others. There is no more purpose or meaning in the world than you put into it.

FURTHER READING

1 RELEVANT WRITINGS BY LOGICAL POSITIVISTS AND SYMPATHIZERS

Ayer, A. J. *Language, Truth and Logic,* London, 1936; second edition, 1946.
'Verification and Experience', *Proceedings of Aristotelian Society,* Vol. 37 (1936–37). Reprinted in A. J. Ayer (ed.), *Logical Positivism,* London, 1959.
The Foundations of Empirical Knowledge, London, 1940.
'Logical Positivism – A Debate' (with F. C. Copleston), in Paul Edwards and Arthur Pap (eds.), *A Modern Introduction to Philosophy,* New York, 1965.
Philosophical Essays, London, 1965.
Part of my Life, Oxford, 1978.
Ayer, A. J. (ed.) *Logical Positivism,* London, 1959.
Bridgman, P. W. *The Logic of Modern Physics,* London, 1927.
Brown, R. and Watling, J. 'Amending the Verification Principle', *Analysis,* Vol. II (1950–51).
Carnap, Rudolf *Der Logische Aufbau der Welt,* Berlin, 1928; translated by R. George as *The Logical Structure of the World,* London, 1965.
Logische Syntax der Sprache, Vienna, 1934; translated by Amethe Smeaton as *The Logical Syntax of Language,* London and New York, 1937.
The Unity of Science, translated M. Black, London, 1934.
Philosophy and Logical Syntax, London, 1935.
'Testability and Meaning', *Philosophy of Science,* vols. 3 (1936) and 4 (1937). Reprinted in Herbert Feigl and May Brodbeck (eds.), *Readings in the Philosophy of Science,* New York, 1953.
Meaning and Necessity, Chicago, 1947.
'Empiricism, Semantics and Ontology', in *Revue internationale de philosophie,* vol. 4, No II (1950). Reprinted in Leonard Linsky (ed.), *Semantics and the Philosophy of Language,* Urbana, Ill., 1952.
The Philosophy of Rudolf Carnap, ed., P. A. Schilpp, La Salle, Ill., 1963.
Rudolf Carnap: Logical Empiricist, ed. J. Hintikka, Dordrecht, 1976.
Feigl, Herbert and Brodbeck, May (eds.) *Readings in the Philosophy of Science,* New York, 1953.
Feigl, Herbert and Sellars, Wilfrid (eds.) *Readings in Philosophical Analysis,* New York, 1949.

Hempel, C. G. 'Problems and Changes in the Empiricist Criterion of Meaning', *Revenue internationale de philosophie,* vol. 4 (1950). Reprinted in Leonard Linksy (ed.), *Semantics and the Philosophy of Language,* Urbana, Ill., 1952. Also reprinted in Ayer (ed.), *Logical Positivism* (see above).

'The Concept of Cognitive Significance: A Reconsideration', *Proceedings of the American Academy of Arts and Sciences,* vol. 80 (1951).

Aspects of Scientific Explanation, Collier, 1965.

Kraft, Victor *The Vienna Circle,* New York, 1953.

Mises, Richard von *Positivism: A study in Human Understanding* Cambridge, Mass., 1951.

Neurath, O. *Otto Neurath: Empiricism and Sociology,* ed. M. Neurath and R. S. Cohen, Dordrecht, 1973.

Neurath, O., Carnap, R. and Morris, C. (eds.) *Foundations of the Unity of Science,* Chicago, 1969. Originally published as *International Encyclopedia of Unified Science,* ed. O. Neurath et al., Chicago, 1938.

Reichenbach, Hans *The Rise of Scientific Philosophy,* University of California Press 1951.

'The Verifiability Theory of Meaning', *Proceedings of the American Academy of Arts and Sciences,* vol. 80 (1951). Reprinted in Feigl and Brodbeck (eds.), *Readings in the Philosophy of Science* (see above).

Schleichert, H. (ed.) *Logischer Empirismus – der Wiener Kreis,* Munich, 1975.

Schlick, Moritz *Fragen der Ethik,* Vienna, 1930; translated by D. Rynin as *Problems of Ethics,* New York, 1961.

Gesammelte Aufsätze, Vienna, 1938.

Philosophical Papers, vol. II (1925-1936), ed. H. L. Mulder and B. van de Velde-Schlick, Dordrecht, 1979.

2 CRITICAL DISCUSSIONS

Berghel, H (ed.) *Wittgenstein, The Vienna Circle and Critical Rationalism,* Dordrecht, 1979.

Berlin, Isaiah 'Verification', *Proceedings of Aristotelian Society,* vol. 39 (1938–39). Reprinted in G. H. R. Parkinson (ed.), *The Theory of Meaning,* Oxford, 1968.

Brody, B. A. (ed.) *Readings in the Philosophy of Science,* Englewood Cliffs, 1970.

Church, Alonzo, Review of Ayer's *Language, Truth and Knowledge,* in *Journal of Symbolic Logic,* vol. 14 (1949).

Evans, J. L. 'On Meaning and Verification', *Mind,* vol. 62 (1953).

Ewing, A. C. 'Meaninglessness', Mind, vol. 46 (1937).
Lazerowitz, Morris 'The Principle of Verifiability', *Mind*, vol. 46 (1937).
  'Strong and Weak Verification', *Mind*, vols. 48 (1939) and 59 (1950).
  Reprinted in M. Lazerowitz, *The Structure of Metaphysics,*
  London, 1955.
  'The Positivistic Use of "Nonsense"' ', *Mind*, vol. 57 (1946). Reprinted
  in *The Structure of Metaphysics.*
Malcolm, Norman 'The Verification Argument', *Knowledge and Certainty,* Cornell, 1975.
Passmore, John 'Logical Positivism', *Australasian Journal of Psychology and Philosophy,* vols. 21 (1943), 22 (1944), and 26 (1948).
  A Hundred Years of Philosophy, London, 1957.
Popper, Karl R. *The Logic of Scientific Discovery,* London, 1959.
Quine, W. V. 'Two Dogmas of Empiricism', *From a Logical Point of View,* Harvard, 1953.
Russell, Bertrand *An Inquiry into Meaning and Truth.* London and New York, 1940.
Russell, L. J. 'Communication and Verification', *Proceedings of Aristotelian Society,* supp. vol. 13 (1934).
Stace, W. T. 'Metaphysics and Meaning', *Mind,* vol. 44 (1935). Reprinted in Edwards and Pap (eds.), *A Modern Introduction to Philosophy* (see above).
Urmson, O. *Philosophical Analysis,* Oxford, 1956.
Waismann, Friedrich 'Verifiability', *Proceedings of Aristotelian Society,* supp. vol. 19 (1945). Reprinted in G. H. R. Parkinson (ed.), *The Theory of Meaning,* Oxford, 1968.
  'Language strata', in A. G. N. Flew (ed.), *Logic and Language,* Second Series. Oxford, 1953.
Warnock, G. J. 'Verification and the Use of Language', *Revue internationale de philosophie,* vol. 5 (1951). Reprinted in Edwards and Pap (eds.), *A Modern Introduction to Philosophy* (see above).
Wisdom, John 'Metaphysics and Verification', *Mind,* vol. 47 (1938). Reprinted in *Philosophy and Psycho-analysis,* Oxford, 1953.
Wisdom, J. O. 'Metamorphoses of the Verifiability Theory of Meaning', *Mind,* 1963.

3 RELEVANT WORKS BY WITTGENSTEIN AND WAISMANN
(See remarks in Introduction, pages 3–4.)

Waismann, F. *The Principles of Linguistic Philosophy,* London, 1965.
  Ludwig Wittgenstein und der Wiener Kreis, Oxford, 1967; translated as *Ludwig Wittgenstein and the Vienna Circle,* Oxford, 1979.

How I see Philosophy, London, 1968.

Philosophical Papers, Dordrecht, 1977.

Wittgenstein, L. *Tractatus Logico-Philosophicus,* 1921; translated
    C. K. Ogden, London, 1922; and D. F. Pears and B. F. McGuinness,
    London, 1961.

Philosophical Investigations, Oxford, 1958.

The Blue and Brown Books, Oxford, 1964.

Zettel, Oxford, 1967.

Philosophical Grammar, Oxford, 1974.

Philosophical Remarks, Oxford, 1975.

Wittgenstein: Sources and Perspectives, ed. C. G. Luckhardt, Cornell,
    1979.

INDEX

Page numbers in italics refer to sections.